Chronicle of a Generation

Chronicle
of a Generation

An Autobiography

by

Raymond B. Fosdick

HARPER & BROTHERS PUBLISHERS

NEW YORK

Library of Congress catalog card number 58–11047

To

My Brother

Harry Emerson Fosdick

With a lifetime of affection

Contents

*

Chronicle of a Generation

I

*

The Family Background

SOME years ago, while browsing through the library of the
County Historical Society in New London, Connecticut, I came
across the diary of a man named Joshua Hempstead who had
lived in that town in the first half of the eighteenth century.
Like most of our colonial forebears he had many skills: he was
a farmer, a carpenter, a surveyor, a shipwright, a sailor and
trader, an attorney, a justice of the peace and a judge of pro-
bate. But more than anything else he was an interpreter of his
generation, and his four volumes of closely written manuscript,
covering nearly fifty years, throw a vivid light on the life and
customs of his day.

Those days seem far away. "Mr. Adams preached al Day,"
Hempstead records on nearly every Sunday—often shortened
to "mr. adams pr. al D." Or he describes his trip to Maryland
and the five hard days in getting to New York City: "We Rid
to Rye and New Rochel, a dreadfull Rocky Country." There is a
sense in which his generation had more in common with the civilization of the Caesars than it had with ours. Transportation and
communication were no more rapid than they had been two or
three thousand years before. Nothing swifter than a horse was
known to Alexander the Great or to Joshua Hempstead, and the
Anglo-Saxons would have understood both the agricultural
methods and the carpentry of the eighteenth century.

And yet to those of us who are no longer young the diary has a familiar overtone. We can reach back through the years and touch with our fingertips the life it describes. My great-grandfather whose home was in Western New York never saw a railroad train. My grandfather, whom I remember well, did not live to talk over a telephone. My father died before airplanes were commercially in wide use.

The generation I represent is in a sense a bridge or a corridor between a past that is now long outmoded and a future of continual, revolutionary change. We have lived through an almost unique period of transformation, unique because it represented the first sudden acceleration of pace, the first swift turnings of the wheel—a wheel soon to be driven by nuclear power. Our early roots go back to the Victorian period, but we were projected, without preparation or time for adjustment, from a comfortable gradualism into the kaleidoscopic alterations of the twentieth century.

A record of the effect upon one mind of the events of this generation may conceivably serve a purpose, and this chronicle speaks for itself. Just as Joshua Hempstead wrote down his varied experiences, I have tried to tell the story of mine. He draws back the curtain on his life and times with no preliminary explanation. The record begins: "1711, September 8th Saturday. I workt at ye Ship about ye Stern . . . a making 15 foot Rails." Unfortunately I cannot introduce my narrative with so practical an accomplishment.

*

Few grandsons can ever understand their grandfathers. To me as a small boy my Grandfather Fosdick with his ragged white beard seemed stern and forbidding, and his black eyes bored through me in a frightening way. And yet as I read the yellowing newspaper clippings about him, the tributes of his

associates, the letters of his friends and students, the resolutions adopted at his death, I come across words like "genial"
and "companionable," strange words when applied to him. That
he was a man of moral power, I have no doubt; that phrase is
used again and again in describing him. Perhaps back of the
formidable exterior and behind the black piercing eyes there
was another personality whom a small boy could not know.

He was two years old when his parents, just after the War of
1812, brought him across New York State in a covered wagon,
and settled in a log cabin south of Buffalo. Behind him stretched
six generations of the Fosdick family that had lived in America
—carpenters, blacksmiths, shipwrights and farmers. Sometimes they were soldiers, too, and they fought in the early In-
dian wars, in the French wars, and in the Revolution. Occasionally their names broke through the pages of local history, as
when the wife of one of them was arrested and imprisoned for
witchcraft in the Salem hysteria, or when another became an
important leader in the General Court of Connecticut, or when
still another—a stubborn and perhaps fractious fellow—was
momentarily highlighted by this scanty record from Joshua
Hempstead's diary: "Samuel Fosdick stood in ye pillory for
ye third time." This Samuel was my great-great-great grandfather.

They were a doughty lot—those Puritan ancestors—and they
followed the sturdy traditions of independence which they had
brought with them from England.

My grandfather grew up in the wilderness. He knew well
the stern realities of frontier life. As a boy, he helped to cut
down the woods and tear out the stumps so that there could
be space for crops. The fields around the house where he lived
are still outlined by the stone fences he helped to build. He
carried to the mill the meager supply of grist, slung in a bag
over his shoulder. He was barefoot most of the year, and even

in the winters of his early youth he had no shoes. But he was strong and robust, with a roughhewn exterior which in his maturity made him a formidable personality.

What the pioneer did in conquering and taming the wilderness has been celebrated in song and story. Less well celebrated has been what the wilderness did to the pioneer. Its molding power on American character, the impact of necessity in shaping social habits and political thinking—this is not so clearly understood. Out of the frontier came our egalitarian democracy, our dislike of dictation, our belief in individual initiative. It produced a race of self-reliant, resourceful, confident men, capable of brilliant improvisation, ready to take quick advantage of the industrial revolution which was riding at their heels.

Perhaps the greatest gift of the frontier was a sense of freedom, born of the knowledge that no barriers denied a man's right to move ahead. Out of this freedom came hope and ambition and energy and faith in ever widening horizons. My grandfather rode forward on this wave of freedom, sharing with the underprivileged of his generation a passionate belief in Jeffersonian democracy and in the rugged creed of Andrew Jackson. Grandfather's schooling was sketchy, limited to two or three winter months out of the year; but once he learned to read he read whatever he could get his hands on. The covered wagon that had brought the family across New York State carried just two books: the Bible and Shakespeare. To the end of their lives the children in the family knew Shakespeare. He molded their speech; their adult letters to each other, of which many survive, are lighted with his phrases.

Early in his life my grandfather determined to be a teacher, and he began his career at the age of sixteen—in a log school where the children's fees were paid in cords of wood. Apprenticed as a carpenter, he taught himself Latin, with the Latin grammar propped up on the carpenter's bench as he worked. But teaching was the ambition and love of his life, and he moved to Buffalo where he could give it full rein. His career as a teacher lasted for nearly half a century, and he became Buffalo's Superintendent of Education in the years following the Civil War, bringing to his task such a fighting resolve to reorganize a demoralized public school system that his name was remembered long after his death.

At the end of his life, as he looked back on his early days, he wrote: "As a family we struggled against ignorance and poverty." I have always been proud of that sentence—proud that he put ignorance ahead of poverty as an enemy to be fought. And he never completely succeeded in his struggle with poverty. Few teachers ever do. All his life he lived close to the margin, and in his old age I remember the anxious contrivances of my parents to provide for him. One of the favorite verses he used to recite was "Over the Hill to the Poorhouse."

In trying to picture my grandfather I have to remember that in his young manhood he had been swept away by the great Baptist revival of the early nineteenth century, and had deserted the church of his fathers. In a sense it was a return to the earlier Puritanism, a reaffirmation of the virtues of self-denial, rigor and earnestness, accompanied, perhaps, by an unconscious fear of ease and grace and light-heartedness. My grandfather's less inhibited younger brother, writing years afterward, said:

I remember seeing the old Baptist Elders herding candidates into the Jordan—or rather, the 18-mile Creek. Brother Samuel and his wife received eternal salvation by being plunged beneath the flood, with many others, back of the burying ground. Brother John [my grandfather] had his sins washed away in the muddy Conowango, and I remain unwashed for the reason that I do not take much stock in the "Water Cure." But if I could be assured that when I leave this earth I should meet the loved and lost ones,

I would try and swim Lake Erie if it were necessary to accomplish the end. I do not know what we shall meet or be after death. As I live on I am doubting, doubting, and shall continue to doubt . . . The great stumbling block with me is the imperfection of Christians.

I am sure my grandfather never doubted. He was sustained by the literal faith of his Puritan forefathers. His was the cosmology of his time, with its crude anthropomorphism and its material penalties and rewards. I remember one of his favorite hymns:

> My Father is rich in houses and lands;
> He holdeth the wealth of the world in His hands.
> With rubies and diamonds and silver and gold,
> My Father is rich: He has treasures untold.

For a man who came out of grinding poverty perhaps there was real appeal in such a vision. And yet to my grandfather, religion was not only a set of rigid beliefs; it was a dynamic force. In retrospect I am confident it was the central core that gave purpose and meaning to his life. Out of his often unlovely but always sturdy orthodoxy came the propulsion which not only made him a great teacher but which fired him in the discharge of what he conceived to be his civic responsibilities. He lectured for temperance reform; he was a lay-preacher for prisoners in the jails and prisons of Buffalo. Believing with Seward that "there is a law higher than the Constitution," he served as a conductor on the Underground Railroad, where he was assigned to spirit the runaway slaves on the last leg of their journey across the Niagara River into Canada. In his house one night on Ellicott Street, a slave, hidden in a closet, died of fright, thinking, mistakenly, that he heard the footsteps of the federal officers. Quite apart from the risk of detection and arrest, my grandfather was embarked on dangerous business—particularly in a rowboat at night on a treacherous stream—and it was business that required muscular arms and a stout heart.

What my grandfather would have been like without my grandmother I cannot even imagine. She was the daughter of the Baptist minister of the church my grandfather attended, but she had dancing, mischievous eyes. Her father had been stationed in various pastorates in New Jersey and New York, and she had a cultural sophistication which my grandfather lacked. The girls of her generation—and of later generations as well—kept "memory albums," in which relatives, friends and admirers inscribed appropriate sentiments. I have the album which belonged to my grandmother, and while its contents are rather lugubrious, with their primary accents on death and the necessity of early piety, I notice that an occasional gay but restrained note is introduced by students from Brown University and Princeton. However a student from Syracuse, where she was living at the time, followed the usual doleful line in a poem to her called "To Syracuse: Written immediately after the explosion by which 30 lives were lost, August 20, 1841." Just what exploded, the poem does not declare; probably it was one of those newfangled steam engines that were pulling stage coaches on rails at the reckless and breath-taking speed of fifteen miles per hour. A few lines from the poem will suffice to indicate its general tenor.

> Oh! dreadful moment, when Jehovah spoke
> In thundering accents 'mid the fire and smoke;
> When, at His beck, the dark-winged Angel's breath
> Blew to His feet thy citizens in death!
> And what dread objects, blacked and blooded o'er,
> Rose with the flash and fell amid the roar!
>
> Oh! Syracusans! look above to God,
> And own His goodness in this dreadful rod.

Oh! not in vain doth He in judgment come
And strike His terrors to your pleasant home.
Let Him not then unheeded speak today,
But turn, Oh! turn from all your sins away.

This was doubtless the atmosphere in which my grandmother was brought up, and it was an atmosphere which survived into the years of my childhood. In spite of her theology—perhaps because of it—my grandmother, as I remember her, was a serene and gracious person, with an active mind, avidly interested in newspapers and what was happening in the world, discussing with my father the new books and ideas that were current, particularly in the field of politics. I remember her especially in her long, black widow's veil, sitting in the pew of the little Baptist Church in Westfield, New York, and driving back in the old buggy through the cemetery to pause for a moment in silence beside the grave of her husband. An old daguerreotype shows the two of them sitting side by side, in what must have been their best clothes—he with his black unruly hair and grim dour face, and she with her dancing eyes looking into the camera as if she were saying:

Time's glory is to calm contending kings . . .
To tame the unicorn and lion wild.

Perhaps she said this to him. He knew his Shakespeare and I am sure he would have appreciated it.

*

When my grandfather finished his career as Superintendent of Education in Buffalo, he accepted the position of principal of the Westfield Academy in Westfield, New York, where on the edge of the small village he bought a farm that looked out on the Chautauqua hills separating Lake Erie from Lake Chautauqua. It was in Westfield that my father first met my mother. He was walking up from the depot, returning from his sophomore year in college—the first college-trained man in our family line—and tradition has it that he saw her standing under a syringa bush in her mother's yard. She was seventeen years old.

They waited to be married until he had graduated from Rochester University. Following in his father's footsteps he had obtained a position in the Buffalo school system—at a salary of $1200 a year. They were married in Westfield and as a wedding trip they drove with a horse and buggy to Buffalo, sixty miles away. He was twenty-two years old and she was nineteen. Mother once told me, with tears in her eyes, how her mother with self-denying sacrifice had saved up five dollars as a wedding present for her—a dime or a nickel at a time, kept in a pickle jar. Grandmother said she didn't want her daughter to be married without having a little money of her own. So father with his $1200 job ahead of him, and mother hugging her tiny dowry, drove confidently down the Lake Erie road into the future.

I do not need my father's assurance that mother was a pretty girl; even the old tintypes, taken at the time, bring out her radiance. My father had inherited his father's curly black hair, but the black eyes which had come down for three generations were at last muted, and father's brown eyes danced like his mother's. He had a light-heartedness, a capacity for gaiety, a love of fun and laughter, which were not in keeping with the Puritanism of his father's family. And that buggy ride to Buffalo must have been a joyful trip, with father in high spirits, singing aloud as he always did when he was happy, and quoting to mother from his favorite author—Artemus Ward.

Mother's family—the Weavers—came from a long line of

farmers and coopers that had drifted from Rhode Island west across New England and New York State. My Grandfather Weaver was a shy and gentle person, who was never very effective in what he undertook, but we children adored him. My grandmother, on the other hand, was an extraordinary character—a woman of force and conviction. What her education had been I do not know, but she was a natural leader, whether in the Baptist church or in the temperance movement or in the crusade for woman's rights. I remember meetings which she addressed, at her house, where all the women wore little bows of white ribbon as badges of the temperance cause. She could write as well as speak, and I have always believed that if her talents had not been circumscribed by poverty and the limiting environment of a small village she would have made a definite mark on her generation.

My mother had her father's gentleness and her mother's force of character. She was an amazing combination of both. She was fun-loving, too, like my father, but with less of his vivacity. Her education was more than adequate. In spite of the fact that Westfield was a small village, its school facilities were unusual, and mother graduated from the Westfield Academy of which my Grandfather Fosdick had just become the principal. She was a student under him long enough to take his course in moral philosophy which she always said meant little to her. Her primary interest in her early days was in music, and somewhere she acquired the ability to express herself on paper in effective prose. Years later, she and father were active participants in the Chautauqua Literary Circle—that amazing outburst of adult education which swept through the last two decades of the nineteenth century and into the twentieth—and mother's papers which she prepared and presented to the local group show genuine gifts of condensation, arrangement and happy phrasing. I have her papers now, written in her beautifully shaded,

Spencerian handwriting, and I wonder how, in the midst of her household cares, with no help and often in precarious health, she found time to prepare them—papers on Charlemagne, for example, and Madame de Staël and the early leaders in the crusade for woman's rights.

But there was an indomitable streak in mother. Duty for her was indeed the stern daughter of the voice of God. Beneath her quiet gentleness and instinctive sympathy she had a granite-like quality. Duty and honor and truth were her standards, and with these standards there could be no compromise. She was deeply devout, and outside of her family and children the church was perhaps her major interest. But her concern was personal rather than institutional. The Golden Rule was something to be lived; the Sermon on the Mount was an intimate daily experience. The ideals that she cherished for her children had to do not with fortune or success but with character and service.

There was a simplicity about mother's religion that was more in keeping with the Beatitudes than with the theological controversies and moral legalisms of the Baptist Church of her generation. She had little interest in the philosophical or speculative approach to religion. Her emphasis was invariably on conduct—not what people professed to believe but what they did. But her judgments of conduct were kindly and tolerant, mellowed by an understanding of human weakness. I remember that a neighbor of ours—a young man—married the girl of his choice rather suddenly, and the baby came three months later. My Grandfather Fosdick's house echoed the moral judgments of the Puritans; but mother, in a flash of flame quite unlike her usual self, ardently defended the young couple. "They love each other, don't they?" she demanded. "What more do you want and what else is there to say?"

I recall mother particularly in her role as confidante; we

children told her everything—our secret hopes and thoughts, our ambitions and disappointments. Although she was objective in her judgment of her children, nevertheless she was one with us; never did she fail us in sympathetic understanding. To us she was the court of final resort and ultimate wisdom. She had been born and brought up on a farm and there was a delightful earthy tang about her, and a hard, practical core of common sense which underlay what father playfully used to call "her incorrigible idealism."

*

Father's shrewd judgment in picking the seventeen-year-old girl standing under the syringa bush was matched by mother's intuition in recognizing behind the handsome eyes the sturdy purpose and nobility of character of Frank Fosdick. It is easy to idealize one's parents, particularly when they have been long in their graves, but I have before me the countless letters and testimonials of father's teachers and pupils, and I know personally of so many people whose lives he shaped and inspired, that I am confident my recollection of him is not exaggerated. For fifty-four years he was connected with the public school system of Buffalo, part of the time as head of a public school, part of the time as professor of Latin and Greek in the high school, but most of the time as principal of Masten Park, "the new high school on the hill." To generations of school children he was known as "Pop," a term that symbolized not only the affection in which he was held but the character of his relationship with young people. To walk with him down Main Street in Buffalo, especially in his later years, was a revealing experience. He knew everybody and everybody knew him; and he had an extraordinary gift for remembering the names and faces of hundreds of his former pupils.

The fascination of his life was children. To his own children he was a source of endless delight, entering into their games, wrestling with his sons and even with his daughter, fishing with them on the Niagara River or in the deep pools of the Chautauqua Gulf. Anything that children did seemed to interest him. He never could pass a vacant lot where boys were playing ball without stopping to watch them. He kept himself young by sharing the interests of youth. And he had sheer genius in handling young people. He not only understood them but he loved them, and he wanted to be with them. He enjoyed their society, whether they were babies or teen-age youngsters or grown-up young men and women coming back to his school from their college work to call on him.

And yet no children ever took advantage of him. He expected obedience and obtained it without difficulty. Punishments he abhorred. There was something about him—a dignity, a presence, a sudden steely look in his eyes—which instantly froze any tendency to impertinence. We children were pupils at his school, and I remember when a class under a new teacher would get out of hand, father's tall form unexpectedly appearing in the doorway would bring a trance-like silence, and the disorder would evaporate under the look in his eyes.

As I recall him now, after all these years, I think of him as one who was given the golden talent of bringing encouragement and inspiration to others. His great gift was his ability to build pride and ambition in a boy or girl. He could create in young people the desire to succeed, to be of use in the world. Even today, long after his death, he lives in the memory and affection of the generations of children, most of them now grown old, whose lives were shaped by the warmth and magnetism of his personality.

In his old age many honors came—awards, degrees, and the recognition that is given to a man who has become almost an institution in his community. I doubt if these things meant a great deal to him; but among his papers I found this letter which evidently had brought him satisfaction and which throws a light on the kind of man he was.

Dear Dr. Fosdick:

The other night, during the commencement exercises at the Masten Park High School, a little incident occurred for which I wish personally to thank you. As you will remember, the hall was packed, so that many of the people were standing. There was one elderly person who attracted you, not only because she was standing but because she was a very old lady. You stepped down from the platform, went to the back of the room, and assisted her to a chair on the stage. That old lady happened to be my mother. She had come from Silver Creek to Buffalo to see her niece graduate, and she tells me it was one of the greatest events of her life. She could not thank you because she speaks no English, but I want you to know how deeply she appreciated your courtesy, and what it meant to her.

Mother's religious interests were warmly shared by my father who, because of his position in the school community, was a conspicuous figure in the church. From our earliest days, religion was for us children a vital part of the air we breathed. Church attendance was required; indeed it was so natural a part of our lives that we never questioned it. On Sunday mornings we went to church services and to Sunday school; on Sunday evenings we went to the young people's meeting and again to church services. Wednesday evenings we attended prayer meeting. Moreover our social life was largely bound up with the church—the suppers, the picnics, the fairs, the sleigh-rides, the Thanksgiving and Christmas plays and celebrations.

At home there were morning prayers in which the whole family participated, and, of course, no meal was eaten without the preliminary grace, or "blessing," as we called it. I do not remember that in our early days we ever rebelled against this strict regime; it was part of the life of the whole community; it was what everybody did. Your friends might go to a different church—the Methodist or the Presbyterian, perhaps—but the regime was the same in the small, predominantly Protestant villages of Lancaster and Westfield where we lived in our early years.

I do recall that to me it seemed a little unfair when my Grandmother Fosdick used to ask her visiting brother-in-law, who was an evangelist, to conduct special family prayers during our summer holidays in Westfield. His prayers seemed endless, and embarrassingly personal, because he prayed for every member of the family by name, telling God in an intimate way just what our individual difficulties were. I always associated these occasions with black horsehair furniture, because we gathered in the parlor where we never ordinarily sat and kneeled down with our faces pressed against the prickly upholstery. This Uncle John of ours advertised himself as "the Quaker evangelist," and I felt better about the matter when I overheard my father, who evidently had some misgivings about him, say to his sister, my Aunt Dora: "Uncle John is no more of a Quaker than I am a Chinaman."

There were three of us children, my brother Harry, my twin-sister Edith and myself, the twins being younger than Harry by five years; and we were brought up on the crude theology which characterized my grandfather's era. Yet I cannot remember either my father or my mother talking to us about damnation or hell-fire or any of the rest of the horrendous doctrine which was the bulwark of the church. If they believed in it they kept it to themselves. But of course we were exposed to it in other ways—through the church, the Sunday school, and the books we read. There were two children's books in particular, called

Line Upon Line and *Precept Upon Precept,* which retold
the stories of the Old Testament, and which my twin-sister
Edith and I read with absorbed interest and a kind of shudder-
ing fascination. Or rather Edith read them to me, because she
was quicker than I, and learned to read long before I mastered
the art. Those two books are still in the possession of the family,
and an excerpt or two will illustrate their tone and content:

> God cut off Absalom in the midst of his wickedness. God is very
> angry with children who behave wickedly to their parents, and he
> often punishes them by letting them die while they are young,
> and sending their souls to hell.

> You see, dear children, how angry God is with liars, and what
> dreadful punishments he sends them. Never try to get things by
> telling lies, for if no one should find you out, God sees you, and
> will send you to hell.

> Now count how many plagues God had sent to Pharaoh and the
> people of Egypt . . . What dreadful plagues these were! But
> there will be much worse plagues in hell. I hope, dear children,
> that you will obey God and not make him angry with you.

> If you are sick, my little darling, pray to God . . . Are you afraid
> lest God should send you to hell and let you burn forever and
> ever? Then you must pray to God to spare you.

And yet I am sure this kind of literature did us no particular
harm. At the same time we were reading it, we were reading
Hans Christian Andersen's fairy tales, and "Jack and the Bean-
stalk," and a book called *The Princess and the Goblin;* and
we lived in a world of make-believe, in which Jack and his
giant had the same credibility as David and Goliath, and
Karen's dancing red shoes vied with Elijah's chariot of fire; and
life was an exciting medley of Satan and Jehovah and goblins
and fairy princesses and dragons and heroes and Santa Claus
and Sin.

My brother Harry took his religion far more seriously than Edith and I did. In spite of mother's attempts to reassure him, he went through a period of anxiety over the idea that somehow he had blasphemed against the Holy Ghost, which, according to the Gospel of St. Matthew "shall not be forgiven . . . neither in this world, neither in the world to come." Edith and I, on the other hand, were enchanted with the idea of the Holy Ghost. In the fairyland we lived in, it took on an adventurous significance that had something to do with an unusual kind of haunted house. We probably discussed this concept with mother. I can picture her gentle patience, although how she explained the mystery and the abstraction to our vaulting imaginations I do not know.

Such a religious environment as surrounded us in our early youth could have led either to morbidity or to a rebellious cynicism. That it led to neither was due, in large part, to our parents. Father's background of Latin and Greek, particularly his contact with Greek thought, led him—so it seems to me— to a healthy kind of skepticism which developed during the days of our childhood. His voluminous papers and addresses indicate a steady growth in his own thinking from an unquestioning acceptance of the theology of his father to a final affirmation of the Greek principle that the unexamined life is no life for man, and that there are no areas of thought and experience around which magic circles can be drawn to protect them from obsolescence.

At what period my own emancipation began I do not know. On the flyleaf of my first Bible, in my sprawling childish handwriting, I find this query: "Cain took a wife. Where did he get it?" However, this heresy did not prevent me from joining the Baptist church at the age of eleven with Edith, both of us being admitted to membership after total immersion—an archaic and dismal initiatory rite.

I vividly recall an experience which began when I was about

thirteen or fourteen. To supplement the family income, father, who had an excellent baritone voice, led the congregational singing in the First Baptist Church of Buffalo, while the rest of the family went to a church nearer our home. We developed the habit of discussing at the Sunday dinner table the ideas of the two sermons. One of the ministers was a liberal; the other was orthodox. Out of this conflict we children began to realize that even in the field of religion, ideas and concepts have no final and conclusive form. All systems of theology "have their day and cease to be"; they are as transient as the cultures they are patterned on. I do not mean to imply that we came to this conclusion all at once, or expressed it in these words. But it was the beginning of a process of emancipation; it was a new approach to the old absolutes into which we had been born.

Father was the leader in these Sunday dinner discussions, but it was Darwin who really precipitated the issue. Through the influence of Huxley and Herbert Spencer, Darwinism was becoming a powerful explosive to break the log-jam of the old traditionalism, and we children heard the new doctrine with amazement and delight. But if Darwin was true, what became of the first chapter of Genesis?

The discussions around the dinner table developed such a pitch of excitement, that we could scarcely wait until the following Sunday to continue them. Father and Harry did most of the talking, Harry with his mature and eager mind ranging far ahead of his younger brother and sister. Mother took little part in the discussions, except to say from time to time, as all mothers do: "Don't let your dinner get cold." I think she was a little uneasy, and felt we were straying rather far from the familiar landmarks which had guided her to the good life. But she sensed the significance of the occasion to us, and symbolized it in her understanding way by allowing Edith and me for the first time to have real coffee at these Sunday dinners, thus indicat-

ing in tangible form that we had been admitted to the fellowship of maturity and could share with our elders their intellectual and aesthetic satisfactions.

These Sunday dinner discussions stand out in my mind as a
definite turning point. They were the beginning of a new freedom, the planting of a new kind of seed. Out of them grew the
developing conviction that the life of the spirit is not dependent
upon the obscurantisms of orthodoxy, and that moral values
and ideals do not require the abdication of intelligence and
critical judgment. A fourteen-year-old boy does not express his
thoughts in these large words, but I caught the spirit of the
new approach; and sixty years ago, in the provincial areas of
Western New York, it was an amazing discovery.

II

*

Growing Up in Western New York

O URS was a close-knit family, bound together by affection
and loyalty. In spite of what seems, in the perspective of more
than half a century, to have been our preoccupation with the
solemn issues of theology, we were a gay and hilarious group.
Nobody could be associated with father and escape the contagion of his high spirits. His gaiety was woven into our lives.
He played the flute and mother played the piano, and their
duets together, performed in the privacy of the family, were a
delight to their uncritical children. As a family we generally
sang as we worked—and there was plenty of work to do.

It was not only affection and loyalty that held us together; it
was a common sharing of family problems. My father, for example, believed that all of us should be currently informed as
to the condition of the family finances; and from our early days
we children were brought into these sober conferences. I use
the word sober, for the condition of the family exchequer was
always precarious and frequently disastrous. When father and
mother were married, his salary as a teacher was $1,200 a year;
twenty years later, with three children to educate, it was $1,400.
During most of his long life as a teacher and as head of a great
school his salary did not exceed $2,500; only at the end when he

was approaching his seventies was it increased.

It has been a tradition in America to underpay its teachers, and the tradition is still maintained. All my life I have heard the arguments that a teacher has a secure job and long vacations, that he works only ten months out of the year, that he is a dedicated person and his chief compensations are not of the material sort. But as a child brought up in a teacher's family I know how hollow and unconvincing these arguments can be. In these family conferences on finances, father's meticulously kept account-book focused the discussions, and I still remember its headings: "Meat and Milk," "Groceries," "Clothing," "Rent," "Donations," "Miscellaneous." Always the question before us was how we could keep expenses down. The rent of our house in Lancaster was fifteen dollars a month. By modern standards the house was primitive, with no inside toilet and with no running water except the pump in the kitchen sink. Heating was by stoves, but there were only three of them, and the bedroom which Harry and I shared had no stove at all. In my earlier days my clothes were hand-me-downs from Harry, and Harry's clothes were from father; and I remember vividly my first "boughten" overcoat, which came direct from a store and which to my infinite surprise nobody had worn before me.

And yet with all these limitations, I cannot recall that we children ever felt that we were "poor." That word to us represented a frightening category in which we did not belong. Perhaps the main reason for this was that all our friends lived just the way we did. There were bigger houses than ours in Lancaster, but nobody had running water or an inside bathroom. Even when we moved from the suburbs into the city of Buffalo, the new contrast between wealth and the lack of it did not oppress us. The magnificent houses on Delaware Avenue merely represented a kind of life in which we did not participate. Our friends lived as simply and meagerly as we did; father's close associates were teachers, faced with the same financial problems as himself. We children were conscious of the problems—indeed we lived with them on intimate terms—but the burden of the anxiety was of course carried by our parents.

How deep that anxiety was I did not appreciate until years later, for a child does not really understand, in terms of gnawing fear, what a note at the bank means to those whose income is close to the line of subsistence, or how a mortgage on a house can become a hideous nightmare; nor does he comprehend to what lengths devoted parents will go in the way of personal sacrifice and desperate expedients to give their children a fair start in the world. To my father and mother a fair start meant education and all that the word implies, and with the scanty means at their command they were determined that their children should have the best education available. To attain that ambition they denied themselves everything—travel, music, amusement, new clothes, and father gave up his cigars and frequently walked instead of taking streetcars. Even now I am amazed at their gallant courage in attempting to put three children through college. It is a feeling that goes deeper than amazement, for in a situation like this we are in the presence of something age-old—the immortality of sacrifice. Shakespeare understood it: "Upon such sacrifices . . . the gods themselves throw incense."

*

My grandfather's indispensable hired man, Sam Raynor, had a number of objections to our family which he expressed in vivid Anglo-Saxon prose. Among them—and perhaps the least serious—was the charge that we were "the readingest dern family" he had ever seen. Around the green-shaded "student lamp" we gathered every evening, each person with his book. I do not remember our parents reading aloud to us, or even determining what we should read. Ours was a home in which personal independence was cherished and encouraged, and this extended to our choice of books. The only limitation was the narrow supply. We had no money with which to buy books, and in Lancaster and Westfield in our day there were no public libraries. But somebody had had the good sense to supply the Sunday school library with a few titles in addition to the regular devotional reading, and from this source Edith and I were introduced into the world of *Alice in Wonderland* and *Hans Brinker or the Silver Skates*—to mention two that I specifically recall.

When Edith and I were about ten years old an event occurred which to us seemed providential. Father had a cousin living in Chicago who died leaving his books to our family. The news of the bequest reached us long before the books themselves, and the period of waiting seemed interminable. There must have been about three or four hundred of them in the box that was finally delivered to our barn in Lancaster, and in retrospect it was one of the most exciting days of my life. Out of the box came such treasures as *Robinson Crusoe* and *Swiss Family Robinson* and *Tom Sawyer* and *Tom Brown's School Days*. There was a sprinkling of Alger and Oliver Optic, and Edith drew two books which she wept over for years: *The Wide, Wide World* and *Queechy*. They were too lachrymose for my taste, but Edith's reading generally was wider than mine; at the age of ten and eleven she was ranging through Thackeray, while I was absorbed with Dickens's *Child's History of England*. Indeed it was history that always fascinated me—any kind of history— and it was to history that I instinctively turned in my college work.

One of the important influences that shaped our reading as children was the fact that father's only brother, Charles Fosdick,

was himself a writer of boys' books under the nom de plume of
Harry Castlemon. Harry Castlemon is largely unknown to this
new generation, but in my boyhood he ranked with Horatio
Alger, Jr., Oliver Optic and Edward S. Ellis—all three of
them now nearly forgotten—and his books sold by the thousands. He wrote sixty during his lifetime, but like many authors
of that period, he sold his manuscripts to the publishers for a
fixed price, and received no royalties from extensive sales. His
*Gunboat Series, Frank Nelson Series, The Sportsman's Club
Series* brought him wide acclaim among boys, and he lives today in the hearts of those who, like myself, grew up in the last
two decades of the nineteenth century. First editions of his
books are now collectors' items, and a descriptive bibliography
of his work has recently been published by a member of the
staff of the Library of Congress.

Uncle Charlie lived in Westfield, just down the road from my
grandfather's farm. I think Grandfather was torn between pride
in having an author for a son and a sort of guilty shame that the
author in question wrote boys' adventure books. In those days
there was a strong disrepute, at least in conservative church
circles, that attached to all books for boys, even when they were
as innocuous and well written as Harry Castlemon's. And some
years later, when a public library was opened in Westfield, my
uncle's publications were banned from its shelves, although he
was more widely known than any other citizen of the village. If
Harry Castlemon could have written some volumes of pedagogy
or of Baptist exegesis, my grandfather and his sober contemporaries would have been supremely content—that is, if the
theology had been orthodox. I think it was to meet my grandfather's objections that my uncle used a nom de plume instead
of his own name. As it was, Castlemon's books were not allowed
in my grandfather's house, but we children got them from my
uncle's library—with father's knowledge and consent. They

were worth going for, and they colored my whole childhood with high adventure.

There was an air of mystery about my uncle which as a child I never quite understood. As a boy he had run away from home and joined the Union Navy on the Mississippi River during the Civil War. He came back with a bullet in his leg, a sabre cut across his head and a broken nose. Then for a while, before settling in Westfield, he knocked around the new West. He was a striking figure with black eyes and long black hair curling on his shoulders. Moreover he had a flair for living and perhaps one or two rather conspicuous human frailties which shocked the pious pretensions of his contemporaries. And he refused to go to church. This in itself would have made him a man of mystery in the small village of Westfield. As I recall him after all these years—and we children were fond of him, although a little awed by him—I think perhaps he was the most colorful specimen our family has produced.

But our reading was not confined to the adventurous tales of my uncle. We ranged far and wide through whatever books we could get. More and more my interests were absorbed in history—particularly, at this early stage, in the local history of the Niagara frontier. Across the river from us, in Canada, were the ruins of old Fort Erie, and down the river within easy reach of my bicycle lay the battlefields of the War of 1812: Lundy's Lane, Chippewa and Queenstown Heights. Haunted by the memory of "old, unhappy, far-off things," their ancient gravestones and grass-covered earthworks had a bewitching beauty. When I was fifteen I spent the summer writing a history of the siege of Fort Erie, based on such documents as I could get at the Buffalo Historical Society and on extensive examinations of the old ruins and the outlying trenches which in those days were plainly visible. At that time no such history had been written, and my ambition to fill the gap was cruelly shattered when the editor of the Buffalo *Express*, to whom I submitted my manuscript as a possible contribution to his Sunday edition, returned it promptly. There is no sorrow so poignant as the first rejection slip.

In time, other intellectual interests began to find a place in my life, although my introduction to them was occasionally accidental. One Saturday morning when I was sixteen years old I met Arthur Detmers walking down Main Street in Buffalo. He was a contemporary and close friend of my father's, himself a high school teacher, although in a different school.

"Raymond, have you a few minutes to spare?" he asked me.

"Certainly, sir," I said. We always said "sir" to our elders.

Taking my arm he led the way to Otto Ulbrich's bookstore, where in a small, back room there were two comfortable chairs. He went to the bookshelves and took down Wordsworth's poems, and seating me in one chair while he took the other, he read me "Tintern Abbey." I had never heard it before; indeed I had never read any of Wordsworth, and I scarcely knew the name. The impact of the poem and of the occasion and of Arthur Detmers' voice is with me yet. If the text of the poem were lost, I think I could restore it from memory.

> . . . . How oft,
> In darkness, and amid the many shapes
> Of joyless daylight; when the fretful stir
> Unprofitable, and the fever of the world,
> Have hung upon the beatings of my heart,
> How oft, in spirit, have I turned to thee,
> O sylvan Wye! Thou wanderer thro' the woods,
> How often has my spirit turned to thee!

Years later, with the memory of this occasion still vivid in my mind, I took a train from London to Monmouth near the Welsh border, and the next morning hired a boatman to row me down the Wye to Tintern Abbey, past "the steep and lofty cliffs," the hedgerows, and "the wild green landscape," where the slowly moving stream seems to say with Wordsworth:

> If solitude, or fear, or pain, or grief,
> Should be thy portion . . .

*

Our home life was so intimately bound up with the life of father's school that it was difficult to tell where one left off and the other began. As freshmen, Edith and I entered father's new school, the Masten Park High School, the year it was opened, in 1897. Although it burned down afterward, and was apparently flimsily built, for its day it was considered a magnificent structure, housing 1200 pupils. It was, of course, co-educational; father had nothing but scorn for segregated education in secondary schools. "Boys without girls are barbarians," he used to say, "and girls without boys are prigs."

Father had chosen the faculty for his new school with something almost akin to prayer. He wanted the best, and in those days school principals had wide discretion in the choice of their associates. Consequently we came under the instruction of a really extraordinary group of dedicated teachers who shared with father his devotion to the profession. I remember well my introduction to the world of Latin and Greek—not only the language but the history. It was a new world of values and ideas, a humane world somehow untouched by corrosion and decay; and to a boy who had run with his gang on the streets of Lancaster and Buffalo in the rough, normal process of growing up, it was a civilizing experience. I remember, too, the course in geology under an inspiring teacher, and our field trips to the Eighteen-Mile Creek and the lower Niagara gorge, where

the pre-human past lay exposed to our view, and we hunted for
specimens of the trilobites and crinoids of the Cambrian Age.

Vivid in recollection, also, is the debating society which we
called the "Senate," where every Friday afternoon those of us
who were interested learned that an amendment *of* an amendment *to* an amendment is out of order, and that a motion to ad-
journ is not debatable. We learned, too, to some extent at least,
the knack of expressing ourselves on our feet; and our debates,
doubtless rather crude, covered the whole range of contemporary topics: woman suffrage, the Boer War, free silver, the direct election of United States Senators, and, of course, the
tariff. It was a broadening experience in the discipline of ordered discussion—an introduction to the techniques by which,
in the democratic process of individual compromise and adjustment, decisions can be reached which bind us all.

But my chief recollections of that period center around
father's informal talks to the entire school in the assembly hall.
We met every day, marching into the room to music the first
thing in the morning. He spoke easily and simply in words that
young people could understand—about our work and the ideals
of the school and fair play and sportsmanship and our responsibility to live up to the hopes and sacrifices of our parents and
the significance of our democratic heritage. Apparently he spoke
about anything that happened to come into his mind. He never
preached to us, and there was always a vein of quiet humor that
ran through his comments. On these occasions, without any
pretense at oratory or any trick of speaking, he held his student
audiences in a magnetic grip. Once when the school took the
law into its own hands and ran away to greet a returning
athletic team at the railroad station, father's castigation the
next morning left us silent and breathless. I remember to this
day his last two sentences, delivered in a tone that he must have
inherited from my grandfather: "Never before have I been

ashamed of this school. Now go!" He nodded sternly to the pianist, and the twelve hundred of us marched out of the assembly as noiselessly as we could, feeling that the day of doom had come.

It was in this school and under these influences that we left our childhood finally behind us, and began to reach toward maturity. I sometimes think that adolescence is of all ages the best. Certainly for us it was a happy age. We had many friends and there was a healthy relationship between boys and girls. "You'll dance anyway and you might as well be good dancers," father had said to Edith and me. So he sent us to a small dancing school, which shocked the Baptist traditions of his mother. But father had long since begun to break with those traditions. As small children he had taught us to play cards at a time when card-playing was one of the scarlet sins of the church. So now he encouraged our going to the school dances. He and mother believed that quite apart from its delights, which they fully approved, dancing was a therapeutic measure in moderating the awkwardness of adolescence. On their part this was a long step from the drab rigidities of Puritanism and the unconscious fear of ease and grace which had beset the generation of their parents.

Thus our intellectual awakening was also a social awakening. As I look back on this period of nearly sixty years ago, it seems to me, although my perspective may be cloudy, that we lived in an atmosphere of greater social tolerance than surrounds the children of today. For one thing there was no distinguishable line between rich and poor; I do not recall that wealth or the lack of it had anything to do with our social relationships. Certainly there were no religious prejudices. In my boyhood I never heard of such a thing as anti-Semitism. The only difference between Baptists and Catholics and Jews and Presbyterians was that they went to different churches. I am equally certain, too,

that there were no racial prejudices. Buffalo, in my time, as today, contained large German and Polish populations, but they
attended the public schools not only with no social discrimination but with little awareness on our part that they were "different." We had but few colored boys and girls at Masten Park
in my day, but they were absorbed into the life of the school
without question. However, there may have been some problem here of which I was not conscious, because at our "senior
ball" I remember father suggested to me that as president of the
class it might be a happy idea if I took the first dance with one
of the colored girls, Cynthia by name. She was a beautiful
dancer and I was glad to do it, although I doubt if at the time I
understood the full significance of his proposal. I think he was
remembering the fright of the runaway slave who had died
hidden in the home on Ellicott Street when he himself was a
boy; and he wanted to underscore, for me and for my classmates, his father's passionate faith and his own deeply held
belief in the dignity and potential worth of all the sons and
daughters of men, regardless of the color of their skins. That
faith had come out of the bitter years of the anti-slavery movement, and for him and his father it had been consecrated by
the bloodshed of a civil war and hallowed by the life and death
of Abraham Lincoln. For father it was one of the chief principles of his creed, and it was upon this principle that he ran his
school.

*

I suppose that father's school would have been called progressive by the standards of those days. Certainly in our part
of the country it was regarded as one of the outstanding institutions in secondary education, and its certificate admitted its
graduates to the colleges of the East. But progressive or otherwise, we were nevertheless the children of the Victorian era.

The great storms of insecurity and violence which burst upon the twentieth century were already in the making, but we were not aware of them; they were being built up in a Sargasso Sea far beyond our horizons, and there were no hurricane warnings to alert us. Our lives were untouched by any influences from abroad; indeed, as far as we knew or cared, they were untouched by influences outside of Buffalo. We had never traveled. New York City, the center of Tammany and sin, was a far-away place that we read about, but no member of the family had ever seen it. Erie, Pennsylvania, a hundred miles from Buffalo, was as far from home as I had ever been, and I went there on my bicycle because it was only forty miles up the lake shore road from Westfield. We lived a contented, provincial existence that was anchored to three centers: the home, the school and the church. Our faith was in work, and we held strongly to the Puritan belief that success was the result of character, and that the man who failed was the man who had not tried sufficiently hard.

Of course the Spanish-American War stirred us a bit, and we stood on the curb and cheered madly as the 65th New York National Guard regiment marched down the street to the depot to entrain for the front. There were patriotic speeches at school, and the national colors appeared permanently on the platform in the assembly room. We cheered even more madly over the news of Dewey's victory at Manila and the destruction of the Spanish fleet at Santiago; and I remember appearing in a school tableau called "Cuba Libre." Finally we cheered again when two or three companies of regular troops, stationed at Fort Porter, came swinging up Delaware Avenue on their way back from Cuba, their faces bronzed and full-bearded.

But the excitement died down, and apparently the consequences did not concern us, for I have no recollection of hearing them discussed. In any event, whatever the Republican

Party did would have been right, for father's republicanism
went back to Lincoln and he never wavered in his loyalty. He
gave an almost fanatical devotion to James G. Blaine, "the
plumed knight," and while my middle name, Blaine, was bestowed on me in honor of my great-grandfather, the Reverend
Jacob Blain, my father insisted on adding the final "e" out of
his loyalty to James G. We were Republicans in the same sense
that we were Baptists—we were born to it. Our conscious allegiance to the party began on that memorable night in 1888
when Edith and I, five years old, were allowed to sit up to see
father march in a torchlight procession in the triumphant campaign of Harrison and Morton. Four years later, when the news
reached us that Cleveland and Stevenson had beaten Harrison
and Reid, it seemed like a denial of God; and I presume my
father used the occasion to recite his favorite quotation from
Lowell:

> Right forever on the scaffold,
> Wrong forever on the throne!

Bryan, to us, was anathema. When he drove down the lake
shore road into Westfield in his first campaign in 1896, and
spoke from an open carriage, the children of the village, including the Fosdick children, waved goldenrod at him to show him
how we felt about his silver heresy. McKinley we regarded as
the great Christian statesman—the friend of labor, the apostle
of the full dinner pail. The sinister figure of Mark Hanna in the
background we dismissed as a figment of the diseased imagination of the Bryanites. We lived a sheltered life in a sort of back-
water between the East with its face toward Europe and the
Middle West where the tides of Populism were strongly flowing.
We read of the death of Queen Victoria without emotion and
with little interest. Of the growing pains of labor in our own
country, and the slow rise of the dispossessed to a new dignity

and a new power, we were utterly unaware. The daily tasks and satisfactions of our lives absorbed us. We washed the dishes and made the beds and cut the grass. We ran errands for the corner druggist, delivered telegrams, and collected, on a commission basis, the annual dues of the Society for the Prevention of Cruelty to Animals. We often danced or sat in hammocks with the girls we liked, reading aloud from Matthew Arnold's "Sohrab and Rustum" or Tennyson's "Idylls of the King" or—in more daring moments—from Stephen Phillips' "Marpessa." It was a serene and happy time, and a sunlit future seemed to beckon us.

Two days before I left home to enter Colgate University as a freshman, President McKinley was assassinated in Buffalo. I had seen him that morning with Vice-President Theodore Roosevelt driving up Delaware Avenue in an open victoria to visit the Pan-American Exposition. The grim news spread through the city with incredible rapidity; and I left for college in a depressed mood, feeling suddenly that the long shadows of ominous things to come were falling across what had promised to be the bright pattern of the twentieth century.

III

*

College Years

W HEN I entered Colgate in 1901, I had never seen an
automobile or an airplane or a moving picture, nor had I ever
listened to a radio or heard a phonograph record. If by some
telescoping of time those of us in Buffalo who walked down
Main Street to the depot on our way to college could have been
projected as unseen spectators into the Main Street of today, we
would have found it a bewildering chaos. Not only would its
pace have startled and perhaps frightened us, but its mechanical gadgets and even the meaning of its advertising signs would
have been beyond comprehension.

I went to Colgate for two reasons: first, because Harry had
gone there and had had a richly rewarding college life; and
second, because of all the colleges within reasonable distance
from home it seemed the one that was best adapted to the
limited finances of the family.

Colgate, when I matriculated, was primitive. Magnificently
situated on a hill in a small village in the Chenango Valley
south of Utica, it consisted of a run-down recitation building
whose classrooms were heated by stoves, a tiny chemical laboratory, a library whose book collection was meager and a small
gymnasium. In addition there were two dormitories, East and
West College, so dilapidated that they were not used. The
students lived in fraternity houses down in the village or

boarded in private homes. The student body consisted of 150 pupils, and my class, with 53, was the largest entering class in the history of the institution up to that time.

But what Colgate lacked in size and physical facilities, it made up in the extraordinary quality of its teaching in the freshman and sophomore years. The courses were rigidly prescribed—largely Latin, Greek, mathematics and rhetoric— but they were given by able and devoted professors: "Kai gar" Andrews in Greek, "Prof Jim" Taylor in mathematics, "Johnnie" Green in Latin, Ralph Thomas in rhetoric and public speaking. Even today I am conscious of the debt I owe these men now long in their graves. Taylor's courses in analytical geometry and the calculus were far more than mathematics; they embraced ethics and philosophy and the immeasurable destinies of men. And when Andrews took us through the plays of Euripides and Sophocles, we stood on the edge of the great questions about the meaning of life and the significance of tragedy. In the presence of such teaching, a run-down building and a classroom heated by a stove were unimportant and irrelevant.

I remember in clear detail Thomas's courses in public speaking — oratory, it was called, and oratory in those days was apt to be on the rotund side. We practiced voice control—"speak from the diaphragm," Thomas used to exclaim— and we recited "declamations" before the entire student body in which every gesture and the emphasis of every word were carefully drilled. By modern standards the performances must have been highly artificial and stilted, but we learned at least that there were effective and ineffective ways of expressing ourselves in public, and we sought for perfection in such practice sentences as these:

The Duke of Wellington was not a man of an excitable temperament; his mind was of too martial a cast to be easily moved. And yet notwithstanding his habitual inflexibility, I cannot help thinking that when he heard his Roman Catholic countrymen—for we are his countrymen—designated by a phrase as offensive as the abundant vocabulary of his eloquent confederate could supply, I cannot help thinking that he ought to have remembered the many fields of fight in which we have been the contributors to his renown.

I haven't the slightest idea where those sentences came from, but I can recite them glibly, with appropriate gestures, even to this day. In this type of exercise, Harry had made an outstanding mark for himself, and had taken all the prizes available in oratory and public speaking; and I sought with qualified success to emulate his record.

One of the advantages of our relatively simple life at Colgate was the intimate social contacts between students and professors. It was not considered *infra dig*, nor was there any charge or even suspicion of "boot-licking" if a student dropped into the home of a professor for a social call. Indeed, on Sunday afternoons, the entire student body went "calling," and the faculty held open house, where ideas and opinions, academic or otherwise, were freely discussed in the hospitable intimacy of the professors' families. It was a community of scholars in an almost medieval sense, made possible by the limited size of the student body, housed in a small country village. Later, when I went to Princeton, it came to me as a shock to discover that this kind of relationship was not only uncustomary but was considered in questionable form.

*

It is a wonder that college boys who are intellectually sensitive keep their balance and reason. The horizons open up so rapidly and the new ideas come flooding in from such divergent

directions that stimulation is often accompanied by bewilderment, and exhilaration and bafflement go hand in hand. My
sophomore year I moved from the fraternity house to a room
in a private home where I could have more time to read, and
there under a green-shaded kerosene lamp, and often with
little sleep, I spent the nights in the extra-curricular pursuit of
ideas that beckoned from books. It was a one-sided interest
that absorbed me. I had little conception of the natural sciences
and none at all of the social sciences. Nor did I have much
concern for the world of contemporary events. The great
anthracite coal strike of 1902, under the leadership of the gallant
John Mitchell, was headline news in my freshman year. And
I remember the long discussions of the problem I had with a
miner's son who was a member of our fraternity; but in spite
of his vivid and passionate argument, the episode seemed
somehow remote—an echo from a world in which I did not
live.

It was the humanistic studies that engrossed me, and it was,
of course, typical Victorian humanism—Browning and Tennyson and the selections included in the four volumes of Ward's
English poets; the *Rubaiyat* of Omar Khayyam, which became
a kind of Bible for me, as it did for so many of my generation;
John Fiske's treatises in the field of evolution; the short stories
of de Maupassant; every kind of history I could lay my hands
on, particularly Macaulay and Gibbon; but above all else,
Emerson's essays. My introduction to Emerson was somewhat
accidental. The hundredth anniversary of his birth was celebrated at the college, and I was asked by the committee in
charge of the arrangements to speak for the student body at
the meeting. It required considerable preparation and plunged
me into the hypnotic fascination of his writings.

It was out of this discursive reading that I ran headlong into
a philosophical cul-de-sac where I floundered for over two

years. It was the age-old problem of evil—the impossible recon-
ciliation of a benign providence with injustices that are never
corrected and suffering that is never atoned. If this is a morally
ordered cosmos, based upon meaning and purpose, if the God
of the New Testament has any validity, why do we live in a
world of hideous brutalities and irrational inequalities which
have to wait for rectification and redress in a problematical
world to come? Why is the course of natural phenomena replete
with every kind of cruelty which if committed by human beings
would be met with abhorrence? Why is the God of our imagination a monster, so that even Tennyson in his "In Memoriam"
lashes out at Him?

I suppose it was Tennyson and Emerson who led me to this
impasse—Emerson with his grim comment on providence: "It
is of no use to whitewash its huge, mixed instrumentalities or
to dress up that terrific benefactor in a clean shirt." But the
Rubaiyat posed the same problem, too, in words that seemed
to me at the time to be inspired:

> Oh, Thou, who man of Baser Earth didst make,
> And e'en with Paradise devise the Snake
> For all the Sin wherewith the Face of Man
> Is blackened—Man's forgiveness give—and take.

It is difficult for me to recapture today the mood of depression
and the savage moral bitterness and revolt with which I wres-
tled with this unanswerable question that has tortured the
minds of men from the days of Job. It underlay my thinking
day and night. In an attempt to illustrate the dilemma as I saw
it, I wrote short stories, modeled after de Maupassant, which
were published in the Colgate student paper, and others later
at Princeton in the *Nassau Literary Magazine*. One of them, I
remember, was called "The Hand of God," and its theme was
the idea that men with all their imperfections are better than

the gods they create. I found the theme in the familiar lines of
King Lear:

> As flies to wanton boys, are we to the gods;
> They kill us for their sport.

Of course an experience of this kind was not at all uncommon
to the young people of my generation, particularly if they came
from homes like mine where a belief in the moral basis of the
universe had been part of the air we breathed. Youth is suddenly confronted with the existence of pain and injustice, and
the question springs to its lips: If God is not to blame for evil,
then who?

It takes time to work one's way out of the pessimistic fatalism
that is the concomitant of such a spiritual struggle. And it
requires some degree of maturity to realize that there are
questions in life—even insistent questions—that cannot be
answered. We resign ourselves to the inexorable necessity of
by-passing the problems we cannot solve. We learn that we
have to go on without the answers. I think it was Woodrow
Wilson who gave me the greatest help on this, although I never
spoke to him about it and never heard him discuss it. As I came
to know him, I had a feeling that with his intense devotion to
the things of the spirit, he probably had lived with the same
knotty problem; and if he could find a way forward, then I
could, too.

Out of this mood, in time, came a positive stimulus difficult to
define. It was based initially on an emotional reaction: men
have a responsibility to carry on in this world, even if the gods
desert them. There is a job to be done; there are injustices to
be corrected, evils that need not occur. Within the framework
of human possibility, we can make this world an inviting home
to live in instead of a place to freeze and fight and starve in.
If there is a divinity that shapes our ends, so much the better;

but even without it, we are not robbed of hope nor is our responsibility in any way lessened.

This position, of course, dodges as many philosophical questions as it attempts to solve; but it was the position I took with me when I left college, and even in later and darker years it served as an armed redoubt to retreat to, when the front positions had been driven in.

*

My life at Colgate was by no means an unrelieved stretch of melancholy. No son of my high-spirited father could be a recluse. I enjoyed to the full the social life of my fraternity, and entered with enthusiasm into its gaiety, particularly its dances with the professors' daughters and the village girls. With a gun I tramped for endless miles over the autumn hills, hunting rabbits and partridge. I played basketball two or three times a week and was a substitute on the class football team, by general consent its least promising player. For I was no athlete. When with the other members of the freshman class I first came out on the playing field, the physical director, our beloved Doc Huntington, thinking that in my long and rangy figure he might have the makings of a distance runner, asked me to sprint around the quarter-mile track. As I came panting in over the finish line, he shook his head sadly and said: "You're just as rotten as your brother."

With all its advantages—and they were many—Colgate, for me, had its drawbacks. The intellectual shelves of a small college cannot be as completely stocked as in a large university, and I began to hear of the new president of Princeton, Woodrow Wilson, and his challenging courses in jurisprudence and constitutional law. I heard of the lectures in English literature that Henry van Dyke was giving at the same institution, and particularly of the courses and seminars in medieval and modern history. The upper class courses in Colgate in my time were limited. Nothing was offered in history, economics or any of the social sciences. One could go on with Latin, Greek and mathematics, and there were a few scattered but excellent courses in such subjects as English, geology and pedagogy. But I was not much interested in this kind of diet, and as I came to the end of my sophomore year, although I spoke of it to no one, I was thinking earnestly of the possibility of transferring to Princeton.

The difficulties, however, seemed insuperable. How could it be financed? And what prospect was there at Princeton of working one's way through? At this juncture, my mother, to my great delight, came to college to visit me. In those pre-automobile days one could hire from the livery stable for a dollar a horse and buggy for a whole afternoon and evening; and in beautiful sunshiny May weather she and I drove through the shaded roads of the Chenango Valley. As always, I told her of my hopes and dreams. She listened in her quiet way, asking a few questions, and then she said suddenly:

"My boy, you are going to Princeton."

"But how, mother?" I demanded.

"I don't know," she said, "but I'm sure it can be done. In any event the decision has been made." With her confidence and firmness to support me, I questioned it no further, and we drove back through a golden sunset, talking gaily of the future. "Dear girl," I wrote her after she returned home to Buffalo—and she preserved the letter—"you have helped me in so many decisions. Whatever would we do without you?" It was the last decision in which her help was available. She died suddenly a few months later, leaving behind a family paralyzed with grief and a memory of gentleness and strength and wisdom that is still vivid and persuasive after all these years.

*

Three days after I entered Princeton, the following September, I met Woodrow Wilson. It was entirely by accident. I saw him approaching me on the walk across the front campus, and I recognized him from his pictures. At Colgate it was an iron-clad custom for undergraduates to take their hats off to the president, and I assumed, erroneously, that the same tradition held at Princeton. I therefore doffed my hat to him. He smiled and took off his hat to me. Then he stopped and said:

"You're new here, aren't you?"

"Yes, sir," I replied.

"And I see you are not a freshman," he continued, because I was not wearing the prescribed freshman cap.

I told him I was entering as a junior, and I answered two or three of his questions about Colgate. He chatted in a friendly manner for a minute or two, and then, as we parted, he said:

"I wish you would drop in to see me."

This was my introduction to Princeton, and I am sure that no welcome was ever so stimulating to a lonely and somewhat bewildered student coming to an institution in which he did not know a soul. I assumed that Mr. Wilson meant what he said, and a week or two later I called on him at his house, just as we were accustomed to do at Colgate. It was the beginning of a long and occasionally intimate association which lasted until his death over twenty years later.

Wilson on first appearance was not what would be called a handsome man. Indeed he was curiously homely. He had what he himself described as a "horse face"—a long, thin and generally unsmiling visage with strong jaws. He had also an extraordinarily keen gaze, which could sometimes be disconcerting. But his eyes were nevertheless his best feature; they could light up with humor and kindliness, and his whole face would soften as it reflected his thoughts. His figure was tall and lithe, and he held himself erect and walked with a brisk pace. When I first met him he was forty-seven years old, and the mark of leadership was on his face and in his whole bearing.

What I remember initially about him at Princeton was the way he conducted chapel. Attendance at college chapel in my time was compulsory—five days a week and once on Sunday—and the whole business, rooted in Calvinistic traditions, was heartily disliked by the students. Once when a group of undergraduates approached Wilson on the question of making chapel attendance optional, he replied with mock gravity: "Why, gentlemen, it *is* optional. If you wish to go to chapel you may." But when Wilson himself conducted the chapel exercises, as he did once or twice a week, he brought an atmosphere of reverence and sincerity which subdued even the students of Nassau Hall of my boisterous generation. He had a magnificent, resonant voice, and I can still recall his incomparable reading of the scriptures—his favorite nineteenth Psalm, for example: "The heavens declare the glory of God; and the firmament showeth his handiwork"; or the thirteenth chapter of I Corinthians: "And now abideth faith, hope, charity, these three." When these old words came ringing through the chapel, carried by the magnetism of Wilson's voice, I do not say that the students were spellbound, but they were significantly silent.

His prayers were even more compelling. They generally had to do with the hope that we young men might be worthy and effective tools in the hands of an omnipotent will. They were always extemporaneous, but no matter what the occasion, he invariably concluded them with the section from the Episcopalian prayer book which begins: "Almighty and most merciful Father, we have erred and strayed from thy ways like lost sheep," and which ends with the sentence: "And grant O most merciful Father, that we may hereafter live a godly, righteous and sober life, to the glory of thy holy Name."

In trying to understand the personality of Woodrow Wilson

we have to remember that first and foremost he was a deeply religious man. With the exception of Gladstone, probably no man in supreme power in the life of any nation was so profoundly imbued by the Christian faith. He came from a Calvinistic background, and he was sturdily and mystically Christian. He believed that God was working out His purposes in this world, and once he made up his mind that a particular course of action represented the will of God, nothing could shake him loose from it. "God save us from compromise," he used to say; or again: "Let's stop being merely practical and find out what's right." I remember when I last saw him, in his house on S Street in Washington, a few weeks before he died, we discussed the recent progress that the League of Nations had been making. With tears rolling down his face he said: "You can't fight God!" To him the underlying principle of the League of Nations represented the fulfillment of a preordained purpose, and if he took any pride in the situation at all, it was that he had been an instrument—however faulty—in carrying out the will of God.

That this aspect of his character frequently made him appear unyielding and stubborn cannot be denied. That it was one of the great sources of his strength is equally true. He was a man to whom the realities of the life of the spirit were very real, and those of us who heard his occasional lay sermons before the Philadelphian Society in Princeton will never forget the subdued but intense tones of his voice in those evening hours, as with quiet eloquence he upheld the priority of spiritual values in the lives of men.

Of course he was one of the great public speakers of his generation. I would be inclined to say that he was the greatest orator I have ever heard, although the word orator in our day has taken on a somewhat invidious meaning—sound and fury, signifying nothing. But there was no trace of the rotund or of bombast in Wilson's method of speaking, no forensic attitudes, no histrionic gestures. Indeed he employed few gestures, the only one I can recall being the use of the forefinger of his right hand pointed at his audience. His power lay in the precision of his mind, in the matchless lucidity of his argument, and in his passionate sincerity. His influence on his listeners was almost hypnotic, and he could fairly bring them to their feet with a stirring phrase. I remember one night after his election to the White House, but before he had taken office, he spoke at a dinner in New York City. I do not recall what the occasion was, but in referring to some evil influences or threatening figures in public life he electrified his audience by the grim comment in measured accents: "We'll hang them on a gibbet higher than Haman's."

His addresses were almost invariably extemporaneous, although he prepared his outlines with care. Once when he was asked by some undergraduates to make a speech he inquired how long it should be. "It doesn't matter," he was told. "It matters to me," he replied. "If you want me to talk for ten minutes, I need two weeks to prepare. If you want me to speak for half an hour I need a day. If you have no time limit I am ready right now." And yet he never memorized an address, and he seldom used notes. The words seemed to flow naturally and logically with uninterrupted cadence.

I heard Lloyd George at the top of his form in the budget debates in the House of Commons in 1909. I heard Asquith and Lord Balfour on several occasions, and William J. Bryan as well, particularly in his later days. I heard Senator Beveridge and other great speakers of their time. In sheer ability and power it seems to me that Wilson towered above them all. He was a scholar in action, a prophet touched by fire, with unmatched strength to persuade and move the hearts of his listeners.

This ability to express himself in cogent, vivid phrase was one of the reasons, I suspect, why he was so outstanding as a teacher. I have never seen his equal in a classroom, whether the room was a lecture hall, crowded with four or five hundred students, or a curtained-off cubicle for a hastily improvised seminar, or, best of all, his study in Prospect, the President's home at Princeton, with three or four of us asking him questions. More than any other man I have ever met he seemed to personify the dignity and power of ideas. He made the life of the intellect attractive. It was through him that we became aware of our inheritance of the rational tradition that was born in ancient Greece—a tradition of candid and fearless thinking about the great questions of liberty and government, of freedom and control.

Wilson's regular courses were in jurisprudence and in constitutional government, given on the top floor of old Dickinson Hall to a class of perhaps five hundred students. He always started his lectures with the salutation: "Good morning, gentlemen." He generally had a page of notes on the lectern in front of him—notes written in shorthand, for he was a master of shorthand—but he seldom appeared to refer to them. Occasionally he would interrupt his lecture with the remark: "Now gentlemen, I suggest you take this down," and he would dictate slowly and succinctly some idea he had been developing. I still have my old notebooks which I kept in his classes, and I find they contain such sentences as these:

The associated life out of which law springs produces many things: natural ties, ties of habit or affection, ties of interest, a developed set of rules of social morality. Law takes up whatever is in this way completed—whatever has been made ready and reduced to a uniform rule of conduct—and provides it with a compulsive sanction.

Is it any wonder that a man who taught this kind of doctrine should, sixteen years later, describe the proposed prohibition law as unworkable and send it back to the Congress with a stern veto?

Or take this from my notebook, obviously the outline of an idea far more extensively treated:

> Morality is a great deal bigger than law. The individual morality is the sense of right or wrong of one man. The social morality must strike an average. This is where reformers make their tragic mistake. There can be no compromise in individual morality; but there *has* to be a compromise, an average, in social morality. There is indeed an element of morality in the very fact of compromise on *social* undertakings.

Here Wilson was posing a difficult question: how to draw a rational line between the individual conscience and social action. The question has plagued the minds of thoughtful men from the days of Plato; and with Wilson's own passionate convictions and fighting spirit, it proved to be the major problem which he had to face again and again.

I can still see his strong, long-jawed, animated face and hear the cadences of his amazing extemporary eloquence. No matter how he began them, his sentences always came out in perfect form. Occasionally when he plunged headlong into an involved sentence structure, I would think to myself: "There's a sentence he can't extricate himself from"; but I was always wrong. Not only were his sentences works of art, but his argument was presented with a convincing skill and an intellectual brilliance which held his students spellbound, so that frequently they broke into applause and stamped their feet at the end of his lectures—an almost unheard of occurrence in the conservative traditions of Princeton.

It was not in his regular lectures, however, but in his informal and sometimes casual contacts with the students that he made his deepest impressions—his occasional talks at Whig Hall, one of the two debating societies on the campus; the more or less informal seminars at which his attendance, because of his adminstrative duties, was necessarily irregular; and particularly the occasional meetings with small groups in his own home. On some of these evenings his brother-in-law, Stockton Axson, read Browning or Wordsworth to us. Wilson was fond of poetry and read it himself with great effect.

I recall on one occasion—just what it was I don't remember —the dramatic earnestness with which he described the Covenanter movement in Scotland in 1638—the forbidding Sunday morning in Greyfriars churchyard, under the shadow of Edinburgh Castle, when the grim and determined citizens signed their names to the Covenant on a flat tombstone just outside the door. Years later, because I had never forgotten his description of it, I went to the churchyard to see for myself the setting and background of the incident. To Wilson it was one of the outstanding events in the long struggle for liberty. It was here that freedom of conscience took root; this was a stepping stone by which the past made its way into a future of wider justice. We who had the privilege of listening to him when he was in this kind of mood always came away feeling that we had been in the presence of someone upon whom had fallen the mantle of the old prophets of liberty.

In Wilson's system of social philosophy, Locke and Bagehot seemed to be the high priests, and in his lectures he quoted them constantly. To some he may have given the impression that he was interested in theory to the exclusion of everything else. But he had a way of illustrating his theory by graphic references to the present; and by indirection he introduced us to a new world of reality in which ideas were put to practical ends. It was through him that many of us received our first impressions of the color and significance of contemporary events. Our academic work largely centered on Latin, Greek and mathematics. It was the wisdom of the past that preoccupied us. We now entered a realm in which the current Russian-Japanese war was a matter of deep concern, and the question of efficient government on both the local and national level was of intriguing interest.

Of course Wilson had a lighter and gayer side which we students seldom saw, and it was not until later, when I got to know him better, that I realized how significant a part of his personality it was. He was a superb raconteur, with an amazing fund of anecdotes and stories. Indeed his dialect stories, told in Scotch, Irish or Negro accents, were often side-splitting, and a few of them I recall even today. Any kind of foolish verse or limerick had a strong appeal to him, and he could recite scores of them. He had, too, a lively wit, and some of his retorts are still cherished in the memory of his friends. For example, the mother of one of his students urged him to make Princeton a coeducational institution.

"Why?" he asked.

"To remove the false glamor with which the two sexes see each other," she replied.

"My dear madam," Wilson shot back, "that is the very thing we want to preserve at all costs!"

In his later years, certainly, he did not hesitate, on informal occasions, to employ a picturesque kind of slang if it suited his purpose; and he could come out with a good healthy "damn" if the occasion required it. But I never heard him go beyond this in the way of expletives, and I doubt if he did. Always he was restrained by a natural fastidiousness, an innate temperance of taste.

I have frequently been asked whether during my student days

Wilson was a liberal in his political and social thinking. The word liberal, of course, is capable of wide definition, but I cannot say that at that time he was in any sense a militant progressive. He seemed to be more of a Federalist than a Democrat, more of a Hamiltonian than a Jeffersonian, and I suspect that at this point in his career he had a kind of intellectual impatience with the practical processes of democracy. For example, he was opposed at that time, and even later, to woman suffrage. "I do not believe in it," he used to say, "but I never argue against it, for there *are* no logical arguments against it." Wilson's awakening to a new social and political awareness came, I am sure, after I graduated. But to the students of my time the word "liberal" or "conservative" had no particular significance. It was enough for us that Wilson challenged our ability to think and led us to some appreciation of the place and power of ideas in the life of men.

I speak only as a single student at Princeton of over fifty years ago. For me Wilson lit a lamp which has never been put out. All my life I have remembered him as the inspiring teacher who introduced us to the kingdom of the mind, and held up before our eyes what Whitehead later called "an habitual vision of greatness."

*

There were other teachers, too, at Princeton, although they seemed to me of lesser magnitude. Garfield, who later went to Williams, gave a course in politics which opened up a whole new field of practical application. Henry van Dyke's popular lectures in English literature were stimulating and enjoyable, and he took us through a wide range of reading from Dryden and Pope through the Victorian era. In this area of what was then called "belles lettres," Professor George M. Harper's course in Shakespeare seemed to me far superior, giving us an understanding of this matchless source of wisdom, insight and solace which has always remained with me. And then of course there was history—for me an endless delight—and we sat at the feet of men like McElroy and Paul van Dyke, and traced the puzzled and occasionally gallant lives of the generations which had gone before us.

But there was more to Princeton than the faculty—excellent as it was. To a student entering from another college, perhaps the most startling and inspiriting phenomenon was the operation of the honor system. The statement which we signed at the end of our examination papers—"I pledge my honor as a gentleman that during this examination I have neither given nor received assistance"—was as solemn and binding an undertaking as I had ever participated in. Never during my time as a student at Princeton did I see or hear of anyone cheating in an examination. There were no professors or monitors to watch us; and in the middle of our tests, we habitually went out on the campus to smoke. Three or four hundred men might be taking the examination in the same room, and the only official present would be a graduate student who was there merely to receive the papers at the end of the period.

Behind this system was the unanimous moral judgment of the student body, backed by a fierce kind of loyalty. Cheating was the ultimate and unforgivable sin, and anyone who violated the oath would have been run off the campus.

Coming from Colgate where, as in many other colleges at the time, we were watched during examination periods by sharp-eyed professors and their assistants, this new atmosphere was a tonic, and I was not surprised to learn—although the point is now questioned—that the system had been introduced at the urging of Woodrow Wilson before he had been promoted from a professorship to the presidency. To be sure, cheating at Colgate had been held in contempt by the majority of students, but there were some who resorted to the practice, particularly, in our opinion at the time, the theological students who came over from their seminary to join our classes. But the Princeton system was a new way of life, a refreshing conception of honor, enforced not by rules but by opinion; and its unqualified success was undoubtedly one of the many contributing factors which led some of us, years later, to subscribe to Wilson's high faith that public opinion and the conscience of mankind could be definitely harnessed to enforce a reign of law far wider than any of us had imagined.

The record of my life at Princeton would not be complete without reference to my classmate Norman Thomas, whose broad humanitarianism and distinguished career as head of the Socialist Party in the United States have endeared him to thousands. When I first knew him he was a tall, lanky youngster with expressive blue eyes and dark hair. He was an effective debater and perhaps the most brilliant student in the class, for he was our valedictorian on commencement day. It was our love of debating which drew the two of us together, for we were both members of Whig Hall, and both of us were on the varsity debating team in our senior year. Norman was planning to enter the ministry and we had many long discussions on the subject. Theologically I was far more radical than he; and it never occurred to me in those days that a time might come when his position on anything would be further to the left than mine. I remember trying, without too much success, to get him interested in Frank Norris's two novels, *The Octopus* and *The Pit*, which I had just read with such absorption that they seemed to me infinitely superior to anything that Henry van Dyke was having us read in his course in nineteenth century English literature. I recall, too, that when the Wright brothers made their first airplane flight at Kittyhawk in December, 1903, Norman and I both used the topic for our prescribed extempore five minute talks in Whig Hall, and both of us agreed that while the feat was an interesting stunt, it had no practical significance.

As I look back on our college life together I am amazed at the limited interest which Norman and I had in economic questions. In this respect, of course, we reflected the predilections of our generation. The consciousness of aroused social forces, of new conceptions of justice that were struggling to be born, had not penetrated the academic seclusion in which we lived. The impact of these fresh ideas on the eager mind of Norman Thomas had to wait for a later period and for a more hospitable climate than the Princeton of our day.

*

My undergraduate years at Princeton were intellectually provocative and fruitful, but I cannot say that they were entirely happy. Anyone who enters a college in his junior year has a handicap to overcome, because the alliances and friendships which make college life a rich and memorable experience have already largely been formed. In my case the difficulty was heightened—at least so it seemed to me—by the fact that my classmates were socially so much more developed and mature than I. Many of them had come from private schools like Lawrenceville and Exeter and Mercersberg, where they had had advantages and contacts beyond anything a high school boy in Buffalo could obtain. Many of them, too, had traveled and knew their way about the world, or at least about the country, whereas I had seen New York City for the first time when I came through it on my way to Princeton, and central New York State was as far away from home as I had ever been.

Moreover, there was a definitely developed caste system in the life of Princeton in my day, centering around the upper

class clubs, whose colorful hatbands, flashing along Nassau
Street and across the campus, proclaimed the exclusive privileges of their wearers. About three-fifths of the upper class-
men belonged to the clubs, the remaining two-fifths bearing
a kind of stigma based upon a scale of social values enforced
by custom. There had been fraternities at Colgate, but they
included practically the entire student body. In fact, I cannot
now recall any classmate there who was not a member; and
the social cleavages which I encountered at Princeton were
new in my experience.

But perhaps the chief difficulty was the forlorn state of my
finances. Mother's death found the family fortunes at their
lowest ebb, with father heavily in debt trying to make ends
meet. Edith was in Vassar, and Harry was just recovering
from a long illness; and I felt I could not call on father for
much if any help. It is true I had a scholarship which covered
my tuition; the difficulty was the somewhat important one of
getting enough to eat and paying for my room in Edwards
Hall, the lowest priced dormitory on the campus—the home
of the "untouchables." In those days there was no organized
bureau of student self-help such as is now a feature of our
educational institutions. In my anxiety and bewilderment I
called at the Dean's office to seek advice, for that was the custom at Colgate when a student was in trouble; but the reception I received from a clever, sarcastic young assistant sent me
embarrassed and with flaming cheeks to the street, under the
impression, heightened undoubtedly by my own sensitiveness,
that a penniless student was not welcomed at Princeton. I never
talked with Wilson about my problem, because even at Colgate one did not take one's troubles to the president.

But by dint of many expedients I managed to survive. I
peddled books on a commission basis through the college dormitories; I found some tutoring to do; with a few of my equally

impecunious classmates I discovered a place where we could get board for two dollars and a half a week; and finally I edited and published a book called *Princeton Verse*—a selection of college poetry from the beginning of the institution—which was of some help during my senior year. And there was always "prize money"—for essays, orations or debates. I tried for everything available along this line, and was occasionally successful.

I remember with particular clarity a disastrous incident which occurred during my senior year. A gold medal, "valued at $150.00," according to the announcement, was offered annually to a member of Whig Hall who proved his superiority in a debate on a subject related to French politics. The medal was known as the "Baron de Coubertin award," and had been founded a number of years before. It was limited to seniors, and in our year only two members of Whig Hall signed up for the contest—Norman Thomas and myself. Neither of us cared anything about the medal, but both of us were in desperate need of the one hundred and fifty dollars, and we agreed that the winner would sell it. I had had previous experience in turning in a gold medal for hard cash. Under the stipulations of the award, the subject of the debate was not announced until the day before the event. Neither Norman nor I knew anything about French politics or any other Gallic activity, but as soon as we learned what the debate was about, we rushed to the library to get what material we could. To insure complete spontaneity and extemporaneousness the award provided that sides should be chosen by flipping a coin two or three hours before the debate.

Baron de Coubertin need not have been concerned about the spontaneous character of the contest, certainly in the year Norman and I debated for the prize. It was a kind of spontaneity based on a complete ignorance of facts, language and background. The chairman of the committee of judges was Professor "Jeremy" Ormond, head of the department of philosophy. In his high, squeaking voice and deliberate enunciation he began his announcement of the result of the contest with this devastating sentence which neither Norman nor I have ever forgotten: "Before announcing the name of the gentleman who has won the competition, the judges wish me to say that in their deliberate opinion it was the worst debate they have ever listened to." He then went on to say that the medal had been awarded to me.

In spite of the inauspicious nature of the victory I could hardly wait for the medal to come, for I needed the one hundred and fifty dollars. When it was finally received, through the State Department, it turned out to be a beautiful thing of shining gold, two inches across, handsomely inscribed, and enclosed in a leather case lined with silk. But the romance had departed with Ormond's verdict, and without compunction and with no regrets I took the first train to New York, where I hurried to a goldsmith's on Maiden Lane. He hefted the medal in his hand, looked at it a bit dubiously, I thought, and then retired behind a screen. It seemed as if he was gone a long time and I grew anxious. When he finally appeared he said:

"It isn't worth very much."

"It's worth a hundred and fifty dollars," I exclaimed.

"I beg your pardon," he said, "It's worth just about seventy-five cents."

"But it's gold," I cried.

"No it isn't," he replied. "It's an alloy with a thin gold wash."

I still have the medal. Years ago my wife had it framed. It really is a beautiful thing, although age has been a bit unkind to the gold wash. I have always felt that part of Norman's sparkle and his irrepressible gaiety have been due to the inextinguishable merriment which the memory of this event has always brought him. But to me, at the time, it was a financial disaster of the first magnitude.

*

As commencement approached I found myself with no clearer an idea of what I wanted to do in life than I had had when I entered college. The ministry seemed to be definitely out. Not only did it involve intellectual hurdles which I could not take, but I felt myself emotionally unsuited for its requirements. I probably would have dismissed the idea at once if it had not been for my brother Harry, who, after a promising career at Union Theological Seminary, had taken his first church in Montclair, New Jersey, where his preaching was beginning to attract attention. He and I had come from the same family environment, and we were bound together by close ties. With his convictions stemming so naturally from our common inheritance and with his success so clearly foreshadowed, it was inevitable that the possibility of a career in the ministry should occur to me; but I soon discarded it as alien to anything that I could do.

My father was anxious that I should teach, although he was too wise to press me in the matter. "It is a noble profession," he wrote me, "and of course I am prejudiced in favor of the high school level. The boys and girls of that age are so responsive, and you can mold them into any pattern you like."

But I was not ready for a decision. The echoes of far off things beyond the academic horizons were beginning to find a response in my mind. Wilson's vivid interest in the contemporary scene had aroused me, although I was scarcely aware of it. The world of political action began to loom as a new attraction; and in the fall of my senior year, at the invitation of the local Republican committee, I had spoken at some cam-

paign meetings in the villages around Princeton on behalf of
Theodore Roosevelt who was running against Parker. I doubt
if I was fully aware of the issues involved or had any particular
enthusiasm for Roosevelt, but I enjoyed the speaking and the
excitement. With these new interests coming to life, I did not
want to commit myself to a teaching career or to any other
career until I had explored more fully my own aptitudes and
the possible paths ahead. Consequently when the Boudinot
fellowship in history was offered to me, making possible
another year at Princeton, I gladly accepted it.

It was an event that occurred on Commencement Day, however, that by a curious chain of circumstances really gave
direction to my interests. Commencements in those days were
distinguished—if this is the right word—by "orations" delivered by members of the graduating class, and I was invited to
be one of those performing this customary rite. A month or
two earlier I had been profoundly stirred by a book by Jacob
Riis, called *How the Other Half Lives,* a terrifying analysis of
slum conditions in New York City. It had been published some
years earlier, but I had not seen it nor heard of it until I came
on it by accident while browsing through the college library.
It occurred to me that the conditions which it portrayed, if I
could examine them myself, might afford an interesting basis
for my oration, and I therefore spent two or three long week-
ends in New York City, roaming around the lower East Side.
I remember that I talked, among others, with Lillian Wald,
the distinguished founder of the Henry Street Settlement, and
I may have tried to see Mr. Riis himself, although I have no
recollection of any visit with him. I was shocked and literally
sickened by the conditions I found—the swarming tenements,
the sweatshops, the dirt, the reeking filth, the disease, the un-
imaginable odors. It was my first contact with the contortions
of squalor, ugliness and misery in such threatening and hope-

less forms, and I came back to Princeton in hot anger that life could be so ignoble and cheap, and human dignity so degraded in a city distinguished for its wealth and high professions. I had, of course, no solution to suggest, but I wrote an oration that reflected my indignation and resentment not only of a city government which failed to correct what seemed to me possible of amelioration, but of a social system which tolerated such hideous inequalities. I remember I ended with a stanza from Markham's poem, "The Man with the Hoe," which had recently been published, beginning with the lines:

O masters, lords and rulers in all lands,
How will the Future reckon with this Man?

By a strange oversight which probably had never occurred before at Princeton, and certainly has never occurred since, nobody in charge of the commencement arrangements asked for an advance copy of my proposed remarks. Harry Covington, professor of public speaking, was supposed to be responsible, but he had a delightful habit of procrastination, and I presume he forgot it. As was customary in those days I memorized the oration and spoke without notes. It was a distinguished audience of trustees and guests gathered in Alexander Hall, with Woodrow Wilson presiding and Grover Cleveland sitting on the platform, and my remarks fell on the startled ears of conservatism and respectability. It was undoubtedly a brash performance, redeemed in part, perhaps, by my obvious earnestness. The judgments of youth are harsh judgments, and moderation and sobriety are acquired virtues. As I turned to leave the platform I saw a look of displeasure on Wilson's face. It was too obvious to escape notice. But a few minutes later I became conscious of at least one of the reasons for his annoyance. An honorary degree was conferred on George B. McClellan, Mayor of New York, who had been sitting on the platform during my acerbic comments on the conditions in his city.

As I was leaving Alexander Hall after the ceremonies, I heard someone call my name. It was Mayor McClellan, resplendent in his velvet slashed gown and the new orange and black hood of a doctor of laws. He was a trim, soldierly looking figure, not yet forty years old, built like his father, the Civil War general who had brought so much sorrow to President Lincoln. He came striding across the grass and shook my hand warmly.

"Congratulations, Fosdick," he said. "That was dramatic and interesting. But I really think conditions are not quite so bad as you believe. This situation isn't static. You ought to have seen New York ten years ago."

Out of that conversation grew a relationship which altered the course of my life. And it was the beginning of a friendship which lasted over many years.

While Wilson expressed his pleasure at the award of the fellowship in history and the fact that I was coming back to Princeton for another year, he never spoke to me about my "oration." Such a polemic would not have been in accord with his balanced and disciplined mind, and I suspect he charged it up to the exuberance of youth. Nearly twenty years later, a grim and broken man sitting painfully in a chair in his house on S Street in Washington, he said to me:

"You've been traveling in bad company." He was referring to my friendship with Colonel House.

"I hope it hasn't been too bad," I replied, anxious to keep the conversation on an easy level.

"Well, you're young," he said with a smile. And he added: "The advantage of age is that it brings a better perspective."

Perhaps he was right, although now that I have reached well beyond his years I am not so sure. Maturity and age have their excellences, but youth has its virtues, too.

IV

*

From College Halls
to Tenements

My postgraduate year was the happiest year of my academic life. For the first time since I came to Princeton I was not borne down by gnawing anxieties about finances. To be sure the Boudinot fellowship paid little, but I supplemented it by undergraduate tutoring; and while there was no wide margin between income and necessary outgo, the apprehension of earlier years was temporarily relieved.

Moreover I lived in the comfortable surroundings of the new graduate school—not the massive Gothic structure which now crowns the hill beyond the golf course, but an old-fashioned residence called Merwick on Bayard Lane, an estate of eleven acres with the house attractively renovated to serve the convenience of Princeton's few graduate students. Grover Cleveland lived across the way, and Henry van Dyke's beautiful home adjoined us. There was a dignity about Merwick, a kind of urbane living to which as an undergraduate I had been unaccustomed. "The Master," so called, was a cultured and warmhearted professor of art and archeology, Howard Crosby Butler, and under his charge we gathered for dinner in the evenings in academic gown, with other members of the faculty as our frequent guests. It was a stimulating environment, made even more attractive by my gradual introduction to the informal social life of the village of Princeton. There were dances at the Inn—cotillions we called them in those days—and skating and canoeing with faculty daughters and their friends on Stony Brook or the canal, for Mr. Carnegie had not yet given his lake to the university. My chief recreation, however, was roaming through the woods with a gun, in areas now obliterated by Princeton's urban development.

Wilson said to me at the beginning of the term: "Take this year to read." And I followed his advice with enthusiasm. While I took a few courses—in English history and economics, as I recall it—most of my time was spent with books, particularly books dealing with political science and sociology about which I knew nothing. I still remember a book by John Graham Brooks, *The Social Unrest*, which brought me an uneasy awareness of a strange and disturbing world. And as a background and stimulus there was always the pull of my early interest in the Victorian humanism of my time. Years later Dr. Henry van Dyke sent me a paper I had prepared in one of his postgraduate courses, in which I undertook to trace the theory of evolution in Tennyson's "In Memoriam," a poem that antedated Darwin's *Origin of Species* by more than fifteen years.

Of course every graduate student in my day had to have a "thesis" which was supposed to be the center of his work. My choice of title was determined by a curious circumstance. Woodrow Wilson had only recently published his five volume *History of the American People*, and the brief reference which he made to the Fenian insurrection of Canada in 1866 proved to be inaccurate. Most of the disturbance in that unimportant and relatively bloodless episode had occurred just across the Niagara River from Buffalo, and as a boy I had often tramped over the battlefield of Ridgeway where the chief skirmish was fought. One day while we were talking in Wilson's study about the compulsions of historical research I ventured to point out the fact that he had confused the struggle at Ridgeway with an old fort, a few miles away, which had been the scene of savage fighting in the War of 1812. He took it with his characteristic graciousness.

"Fosdick," he said, "the trouble is there is no material on the Fenian insurrection. I couldn't find anything. Now *there*," he continued, "is an excellent topic for a doctor's thesis. Why don't you undertake it?"

So I found myself embarked on a piece of research over which I labored for a year but which in the end turned out to be something of a blind alley.

During that graduate year I saw Wilson only occasionally. I had taken all his courses as an undergraduate, and his mounting administrative duties as president of the university made it impossible for him to continue his seminars. Once our contact had to do with the subject of debating in which he was much interested. I had had some experience during my undergraduate years in debating on the intercollegiate level, and one day he sent for me during this postgraduate term and asked me if I would lead the team against Yale. I was reluctant to do it because other interests seemed more important, but he was a persuasive man and I yielded. I must tell the whole truth: the Princeton team was beaten, but I had the satisfaction of seeing him jump off his bicycle the next morning on Nassau Street, stride over to the curb where I was standing, and tell me that in his considered opinion the verdict of the judges was unjustifiable. To my lacerated feelings his words were a long-remembered consolation.

Other figures dominated the scene in that happy graduate year. One was Andrew F. West, dean of the graduate school, who because of his formidable opposition to Wilson's policies, was later to be the contributing factor in putting him into the White House. When aroused, West was a ruthless fighter, with a tough tenacity of purpose and a bulldog jaw. Two or three years later, at the height of his struggle with Wilson, I happened to be seated next to him on a train from New York to Boston; and I have never forgotten the vehemence of his language or the unrestraint of his characterizations. But we students in my graduate year saw nothing of this. To us West was a genial spirit, a deeply-read Latin scholar, a dinner companion to whose informed comments we listened with respect. He knew the graduate students personally and the doors of his house across the street were wide open for counsel. I remember when I first talked with him about entering the graduate school he asked me if I had a good warm overcoat. I didn't, but I was too proud to admit it. But this was his approach to his students. He was the father of us all, and we held him in deep affection.

It has always seemed to me an unrelieved pity that two leaders as brilliantly endowed as West and Wilson should have ended their relationship in such a tumult of bitterness. Of course there was fault on both sides. Both men were disinclined to compromise; both had passionate wills. During the struggle my own sympathies lay largely with Wilson, for his ideals, as I saw it, represented a forward-looking policy in educational statesmanship which his opponent did not share. But I never forgot what I owed to West, nor did my affection for him ever falter; and in later years, when partial blindness overtook him, I occasionally visited him in his rose-pleached garden in the new graduate school at Princeton of which he was truly the inspiration and the founder. The last time I saw him old animosities had long been forgotten, and his thoughts ran to his youthful days far back before the Wilson era. When he realized where his memory was taking him, he checked himself. "To live in the past is the habit of age," he said with a smile. "Horace preserved such a man in an immortal hexameter." And he quoted the verse in Latin.

Another figure whom I recall with special vividness during that graduate year was Grover Cleveland. Almost every afternoon his corpulent form with its large head topped by a tall silk hat could be seen, accompanied by Dean West, walking slowly down Bayard Lane across the trolley tracks and up the woodpath on the other side. He had retired from the White House nine years before, and now, nearly 70 years old, he lived quietly in Princeton, the object of universal respect. With strangers he was shy and diffident, and on the few occasions when he came across the street to the graduate school as the guest of the students he seemed singularly ill at ease. But he had a retentive memory and I recall that when I was presented to him as coming from his own city, Buffalo, he said: "Your father had a black beard." Mrs. Cleveland, his wife, whom he had married during his first term in the White House, was a woman of distinguished charm. Considerably younger than her husband, she was at home in any kind of social gathering, and for a few of us students her house was a hospitable center at tea time and occasionally for a card game in the evening. She had been a pupil of my father's in Buffalo, and she used to say laughingly that she was probably the worst Latin scholar he ever had. My father's recollection, however, was quite the contrary. In addition to her attractiveness and warmth she had an amazing gift for remembering names and faces. Once at a reception in the graduate school some twenty-five students were presented to her. Later when she came to go she shook hands with each of us and called every man by his right name. All my life I have wished in vain for such a talent.

Another home where I found a welcome was that of George B. McClellan, mayor of New York City. He had a weekend place at Princeton, not far from the graduate school, to which he could retreat from the political turmoil of the metropolis, and occasionally on Sunday afternoons I would drop in for tea. He had the same attractive personality that apparently characterized his father, and perhaps, too—as I later discovered —some of his father's failings. He had been elected on a Tammany ticket but in his loyalties he was far from being a Tammany man, and the discussions around his hospitable fireplace those Sunday afternoons introduced me to ideas and impressions of the game of practical politics as they played it in New York.

These impressions were heightened by a fortuitous incident during the fall of my graduate year. William Travers Jerome, a picturesque reform leader in New York, was renominated by a citizen's group for the office of district attorney against a strong Tammany ticket. His first term had been a spectacular performance. Arthur Train who served under him called him "a combination of Savonarola, St. George and d'Artagnan"; and his fearlessness and unconventional techniques had made him a popular idol.

As his campaign for re-election developed an appeal was made for speakers, and I was seized with the ambition to enlist. Both Wilson and West whose advice I sought gave strong encouragement to the idea, Wilson remarking that it would be an experience as valuable as anything I could obtain in my graduate course. Some two or three weeks before the campaign ended, therefore, I went to New York and with what must have been considerable presumption offered my services to the speakers' committee. The chairman of the committee, Richard W. G. Welling, a middle-aged lawyer prominent in the reform movement, looked me over from head to toe. Finally he said:

"I don't know that I need any more speakers but I *do* need somebody to help me organize the meetings. Will you do that?"

I agreed at once, and before two days had passed Welling handed me the whole job of detail and I found myself with the entire responsibility for arranging the speakers not only for the district nightly meetings, but for the many horse-drawn trucks, each of which, decorated with pictures and bunting, and equipped with a band and one or two orators, was sent every evening to strategic points about the city. I did not neglect to assign myself to one of these trucks, and after putting in a strenuous day at headquarters I would sally forth in the evening to speak from the tail of a two-horse vehicle. I took my truck to whatever point promised the greatest excitement—to The McManus' district in Hell's Kitchen on the West Side, to Little Tim Sullivan's district on the East Side, and once to 14th Street opposite Tammany Hall, where an exuberant crowd, pouring out of the building, cut my horses loose, burned the bunting, and tipped over the truck.

The last meeting of the campaign was held the night before election at Cooper Union with Jerome himself as the speaker. Like everything that he did he made it a dramatic occasion. One of the strong points of attack of his campaign concerned the houses of prostitution which flourished brazenly under the Tammany regime. In these houses each customer bought from the madam a brass disk or token which he gave to the girl in payment for services, the girl's stipend being later determined by the number of tokens she turned in. That night at the climax of his speech Jerome took a dozen of these tokens from his pocket. "Do you know what these are?" he asked his audience in his rasping voice. Then when he had described their purpose, he thundered: "They are the symbols of a civic and personal betrayal!" And he flung the tokens in a clattering cascade across the platform. I doubt if Cooper Union had ever witnessed a more tumultuous response, and the next day Jerome was triumphantly and overwhelmingly elected.

I returned to Princeton in high spirits and with a feeling that perhaps there were things in life that had greater significance than dusty dissertations on the Fenian insurrection in Canada of 1866.

As my graduate year drew to a close Princeton offered me a

traveling fellowship, the idea being that after getting my master's degree I would spend the second year studying at a German university, probably Heidelberg. In those days a candidate for the doctor's degree—and I had already passed my preliminaries—was scarcely considered educated unless he had studied in Germany. After talking with Wilson I accepted the appointment, although I had an uneasy feeling that I was burning bridges over which I might later want to retreat.

That summer, serving as a counselor at a boys' camp on Lake Champlain, I faced up to the problem of my own future. I had come to the crossroads; what did I want to do? If I went on to Heidelberg it meant that I was headed irrevocably for a teaching career. It meant two years more on the Fenian insurrection, when as far as I was concerned I had already exhausted the subject. I was not especially interested in law, but it seemed like the only alternative, and at least it could become a stepping stone to a more intriguing and serviceable career.

With some misgiving I sent a telegram to Princeton resigning the fellowship. Later when I had an opportunity to talk with Wilson about it, I found he was not pleased with my decision, and when I reminded him that this was precisely what *he* had done, he remarked: "It was one of the less happy periods of my career."

*

I came to New York as so many thousands of other young men have come—in a kind of starry-eyed mood, eager for the new adventure. I had saved enough money from my summer earnings to pay my tuition in advance at the New York Law School and to buy a new overcoat; and I had ten dollars in my pocket. My choice of law school was determined entirely by the state of my finances; actually I had wanted to go to Harvard. In New York, however, the law school had a late afternoon session as well as an evening session, and I could obtain employment by day.

My first contact was with Lillian D. Wald, head of the Henry Street Settlement, whom I had earlier consulted in connection with my senior oration. In those days this institution was widely known as the Nurses' Settlement, and it was the center of Miss Wald's pioneering activities in district nursing. After a discussion of my experience and plans she offered me a residency at the settlement where separate accommodations had recently been completed for two men, whose work, generally speaking, was related to the boys' clubs. The position, of course, paid no salary, but I had my room.

I then went to see Richard Welling who had been chairman of the speakers' committee in the Jerome campaign, and although I had no law he promptly gave me a clerkship in his law office at a nominal salary. Miss Wald and Mr. Welling were the only two people in New York whom I knew.

The year that followed was a liberal education far different from anything I ever got at Princeton. It was due largely to Miss Wald and to the extraordinary environment of the Lower East Side where I lived. This was the time when unchecked immigration was at its height, with often as many as twenty thousand immigrants a day pouring through Ellis Island, and three-quarters of a million every year knocking successfully at our gates. For many of these strangers New York was the compelling attraction, and it was to the Lower East Side that they swarmed in hordes.

The Irish represented the first great flood of immigration; the Germans the second; and now it was the Italians and the Russian and Roumanian Jews who were surging in. The area around Rivington Street represented the densest population of any spot on the globe. The narrow streets, made narrower still by endless lines of pushcarts, were filled day and night with jostling, shoving crowds. Housing conditions were indescribable, and the immigrants took what quarters they could find, paying exorbitant rents for dark and odorous tenements where health and decency were corrupted and betrayed. These newcomers were exploited by steamship companies, by importers of labor, by politicians, by the police, and by their own countrymen. It was the era of the sweatshop in the garment industry and whole families toiled during long-hour working days in disease-ridden tenements.

It was in a desperate challenge to these conditions that Lillian Wald had taken up her work on the Lower East Side. When I first met her she was thirty-eight years old—a striking-looking woman with dark hair, broad forehead, and resolute chin. Already she had established herself not only as a great practical pioneer but as one of the most loved of the notable women of her generation. Among those whose hearts and confidences she had won were mayors, governors, police captains, district leaders, rabbis and priests, revolutionists and pushcart peddlers. Thirteen years before, a trained nurse with little practical experience, she had come to live on the Lower East Side simply because she felt her services were needed there more than anywhere else. "She's either crazy or a great genius," said a friend with whom Miss Wald discussed her plans. And indeed she was a genius, "a social inventor," as Judge Brandeis later called her. Not only did she have great physical vitality and a dynamic personality, but she was endowed with the rarer qualities of social insight and a deep compassion for people. There was a magic about her, compounded of warmth, sympathy, simplicity and common sense.

Her advent was like a clean breeze in the choking atmosphere of the East Side. She gave nursing a new kind of meaning, and she brought it within reach of those who needed it. Her imagination led her swiftly into fresh fields—into the fight against tuberculosis, against infant mortality, against untrained midwifery, against inadequate housing regulations, against unsanitary garment trade conditions. Hers was the insight that led to the development of public school nurses and of school physicians. It was at her suggestion that the Federal Children's Bureau was created; she was one of the driving forces behind the new child labor laws; and it was in the backyard of the Henry Street Settlement that the apparatus was installed in what was one of the first authentic playgrounds of America. More than anything else she served as a mediator between cultural divergencies, an interpreter of one race to another, of one social pattern to another.

She led a crowded, busy life, with days of work beginning early in the morning and lasting far into the night. She was always accessible, and she slept with a telephone beside her, "like a fireman," as she said. Thus she could be available to her "neighbors" if they were in trouble. Whatever she did she did with a complete lack of self-consciousness. There was no pose, no faint atmosphere of sanctity. She would have laughed at the idea that she was a "dedicated" person, and she would not have cared for the adjective, for there was nothing evangelical about her, and she abhorred sentimentality. She was not an institution, but a warm-hearted human being, and she went about her work evenly, courageously and constructively.

"There is no use trying to understand Lillian Wald," said a contemporary, "unless you understand her inordinate capacity for loving people of all sorts and conditions, wicked people, good people—people." One of my vivid recollections is of Miss Wald clad in a dark blue silk kimono, rapping on my bedroom door at two o'clock in the morning, and saying: "Poor Sarah has been picked up again by the police. She's such a dear, and I hate to have her spend the night at the police station. Would you mind going over and getting her out? And if she has no place to sleep bring her back here, and I'll find a bed for her."

On another occasion the noted radical, Emma Goldman, was arrested by the police on a Sunday afternoon just as she was starting a scheduled address at Clinton Hall, only a few blocks from the settlement, and the audience was clubbed into the street. Together with a number of settlement people I was in the audience, and we escaped the clubbing by climbing down a rear fire escape. The subject of Miss Goldman's proposed address was "Philosophic Anarchism," a school of thought which advocated the abolition not only of the armed forces of nations but of the police forces as well, and all forms of authority. While Miss Wald believed this doctrine to be "silly"—to use her word—she was incensed by the flagrant suppression of the right of free speech, and she not only wrote a vigorous letter to the police commissioner but she asked me to see Miss Goldman, if possible, and express her feeling of outrage over the event, inquiring explicitly whether she had a competent lawyer.

That night I called at the police station where Miss Goldman was held without bail, but the police would not allow me to see her. Next morning I went to the magistrate's court where she was arraigned, and managed to give her Miss Wald's message. An enterprising reporter, overhearing part of the conversation, wrote a story for his paper, and that night I read it under the headline: "Princeton man friend of Emma Goldman." It was my first contact with newspapers and I was considerably disturbed. But Miss Wald's simple comment I never forgot, and in later and more stormy years it remained as a constant solace. "You have to take the bad with the good," she said. "The only thing that is important is that you should sleep with a clear conscience."

In spite of the pattern of her life, nothing about Miss Wald suggested the stereotype of the reformer. There was nothing grim or prim about her. She was untouched by puritanical inhibitions. On the contrary, she was endowed with an irrepressible gaiety, a mischievous kind of merriment, and her laughter rang through the rooms and halls of the settlement. She loved amusing anecdotes and told them dramatically; and when we gathered around the long dinner table in the evening—the twenty or more nurses who lived in the settlement, the two male residents, and the inevitable visitors—it was her vividness, brightened by her laughter, that made these occasions memorable.

The visitors whom Miss Wald attracted to the settlement were a source of infinite interest. Jane Addams with her beautiful profile and sad eyes was often with us—a little silent and remote, perhaps, but with an inner glow. And there was Florence Kelley with her blunt speech and fighting crusader spirit. And Julia Lathrop was there, and Mary McDowell, and the Simkhovitches, and a host of other leaders in the wide range of social work. I remember the evenings that Prince Kropotkin, the Russian revolutionist, spent with us. He was a scholar, a gentle, aging man, exiled by the Czarist government and now dreaming in anarchistic terms of a new social order for his country. Another revolutionist, Madame Breshkovsky—"Babushka the Little Grandmother"—who later was exiled by the Czar to Siberia, was also at the settlement, but whether I talked with her I cannot recall. The cause of Russian freedom was one of Miss Wald's deepest interests, and around the dinner table the brutal slaughter of the marching delegation in St. Petersburg the year before, and the Czar's stubborn thwarting of the newly created Duma, were topics of constant discussion.

Altogether that period on the Lower East Side was for me a kind of education I could nowhere else have obtained. I was responsible for two boys' clubs, made up exclusively of Russian Jews. They were an engaging group, averaging, perhaps, sixteen years. I never could entice them into the gymnasium because their whole interest was in discussion and debate, and their talk ranged over a wide field of contemporary social and economic topics. My only difficulty with them was in persuading them to go home at a reasonable hour, for in their eagerness they would have carried on their discussions all night long. In later years, when as successful lawyers, businessmen and rabbis they came to see me, it was a great satisfaction to hear their testimony on what they owed to the settlement.

During that year, too, I joined the district Republican club, for at that time I thought of myself as a Republican, and certainly an affiliation with the Tammany organization of that era would have been abhorrent. The leader of the club was Joe Levenson and I spent many evenings with him and his district captains. They were a tough but likeable lot, and I must have seemed to them like a caricature of academic ignorance. I am sure my association with these doughty fighters was far more valuable to me than it was to them. The only thing we shared in common was a hatred of Tammany Hall.

With all its odor and dirt I came to have a great affection for the Lower East Side, and a profound interest in its people. There was many a flash of color to offset the grimness—the religious holidays with ceremonial candles burning in dark rooms, the bespangled celebrations for the patron saints of far away cities, the gay festivals in the streets, the thousands of pushcarts, the Chinese theatre in a Chinatown that had not yet become a tourist attraction, the brass and copper shops on Allen Street under the elevated. Each ethnic group brought its own usages and traditions, and the fabric of living was intricately and brightly woven.

It was the poverty of the area that upset me; it looked so hopeless. Henry George and his doctrine of Single Tax were much in vogue in those days, and I avidly read his book, *Progress and Poverty*, trying to find some clue to a more promising future. His analysis of the problem seemed lucid and com-

pelling—a breakdown in the means of distribution, a poverty
that remained constant in spite of increasing production and
wealth. But although I knew little of economics, his proposed
remedy appeared far too simple to meet all the complex factors.
I also read Friedrich Engels, the collaborator of Karl Marx,
particularly his book, *Socialism, Utopian and Scientific*, and I
still have the notebook in which I jotted down my impressions
of it. In those Czarist days there was no identification of Marx-
ism with Russia. Like Single Tax it was an untested social theory
floating in the air. But I had no liking for it. I doubt if I understood all its implications, but to my Victorian mind its doctrine
of class-warfare and its crass and openly-proclaimed material-
ism were repulsive, nor have I had occasion to change my
opinion in the years since.

If Henry George and Marx were writing today they would
find a new factor in the situation—a distribution of wealth on a
scale they did not dream of. Poverty in a country like the
United States has by no means been eliminated, but the situation is far brighter than it was when I lived on the Lower East
Side. We cannot, however, be too complacent. Twenty-five
years after I was a resident on Henry Street, in the depth of the
depression of the early thirties, Miss Wald wrote this comment:
"I am torn by the literal starvation I see around me. . . . Yesterday a man who was told that his rent would be paid for two
months and that he would have a quart of milk a day for his
children fell from his chair in a dead faint. The shock was too
much for him because he hadn't been having enough to eat. . . .
I can't endure the loss of dignity to the people who are beggars
for a job. It seems disgraceful that a country so large and resourceful as ours could fail."

*

That first year in New York was for me perhaps the most

unique experience of my life, but it was not without difficulties. Once again the chief factor was the desolate state of my finances. While I had my room free at the Henry Street Settlement, the residents paid for their board at the rate of five dollars a week. And the salary from my clerkship in Mr. Welling's office equalled the amount of the board—five dollars a week. At first I thought I could surmount this discrepancy by getting some tutoring to do, but I failed in the attempt for I had no connections in New York. The immediate difficulty was related to my lunches, for I was unable to get back to the settlement from the office at 2 Wall Street. For a time I tried to go without them, just as I eschewed all trolley cars, but I soon found that dizziness and inertia made this course impracticable. In the end I solved the immediate problem by resorting to an old New York custom —the free lunches which characterized the saloons of those halcyon days. For five cents one could buy a glass of beer, and if there was no great display of greediness one could help himself to an assortment of crackers and cheese, pickles and pretzels, and sometimes, if one were lucky, a real sandwich.

But there remained the problem of obtaining the five cents, for I was literally down to nothing at all; and I resorted to some desperate expedients. I pawned my overcoat, my evening clothes, and some books, but that took me only a little way. Finally I told my sister, Edith, of my predicament. Graduating from Vassar that June she had taken a position as a social worker at the Lenox Hill Settlement House in New York, where she had her board and room and twenty-five dollars a month. She responded to my difficulty with all her characteristic generosity and warmth, and more than once in those difficult months I walked from Henry Street on the Lower East Side all the way up to 72nd Street to borrow five dollars from her scanty resources.

Meanwhile I was attending the New York Law School—

sometimes in its late afternoon sessions, and sometimes in the evening sessions, dependent upon my engagements at the Settlement. I couldn't afford to buy any law books, and I used those I could borrow from my fellow students, or which I could read at the law school library when I had time to go there. My days were crowded. I was at the law office from nine to five o'clock six days a week, for there was no Saturday afternoon half-holiday in those days. I would then rush over to the lectures at the law school, and then home to the settlement where, after dinner, I had my boys' clubs. Such studying as I did was on law office time, and the opportunity was always unpredictable. Sundays were given to studying and reading.

During this period, due in part, I presume, to the fact that I was living under such difficult conditions, I had occasional morbid misgivings about the wisdom of my decision to abandon the academic life. One such moment I recall with peculiar poignancy. Mr. Welling was retained as counsel in a case involving a pump company, and he asked me to prepare a detailed brief on pumps—how they worked, the different principles involved, and the varying methods of manufacture. Before I got through with it, of all the things in the world the one I cared for least was pumps. I had had no technical training whatever, and to me the subject was not only incomprehensible but unutterably dull. One noon during the preparation of the brief I stepped for a few minutes into Trinity Church across the street from the office. It was one of my lunch-less days. I sat down in a pew and looked at the great arched window over the altar. At the moment it seemed to symbolize all the humanistic interests which had so filled my life at Princeton—the books, the poetry, Emerson, Gibbon, even the Fenian insurrection in Canada. And I had exchanged all this for a starving life that centered around pumps!

Youth is fortunately resilient and low moments are never

permanent. However, after about six months I found the strain too great. I was undernourished and overworked, and I came to the conclusion that while the law office experience was undoubtedly valuable, I could no longer afford it. So I obtained a position to teach arithmetic during the mornings to twelve-year-old boys at a private school in Harrison, New York, within easy commuting distance from the city. The salary was twenty-five dollars a week, when I could collect it, and while it took some rapid maneuvering to get back to the law school in the afternoon, it represented a welcome break in the financial stringency.

In later years I often thought of the sympathy and understanding with which Miss Wald would have responded to my difficult situation if I had had the courage to take it to her. But there was a pride, a reticence, a lack of frankness, about the youth of my day which made such confidences difficult. Certainly that was true of me. Indeed it never occurred to me to discuss my plight with Miss Wald, or with anybody else except my sister. However, the experience did me no harm; it left no scars. Thousands of young men and women coming to New York before and since have lived through just such trying days. As veterans who survived the battle we can afford to laugh about it now; and the experience no doubt had value. It is conceivable that it gave a sympathy lighted by insight, a compassionate awareness of the shifting pattern of fortune and mischance in human life.

*

Lord Haldane in his autobiography wrote a sentence which could well be contained in this narrative. "We are apt greatly to underrate," he said, "the parts which accident and good luck have really played in the shaping of our careers and in giving us such success as we have had."

Certainly accident and good luck were responsible for the dramatic turn in my affairs. One day in June at the end of that first year in New York I happened to meet Mayor McClellan on a ferryboat crossing the Hudson River.

"Fosdick," he said, "what are you planning to do this summer?"

"I have made no plans, sir," I replied.

"How would you like to take a job in the city government just as a trial?" he asked. And then he continued: "I have just appointed a young man named John Purroy Mitchel as Commissioner of Accounts. He seems like a promising young fellow and there is a vacancy in his office. Would you like to have it?"

I had never heard of John Purroy Mitchel, but I accepted the offer on the spot.

V

*

Introduction to Politics

MY first interview with Mitchel was anything but auspicious. I appeared at his office by appointment, and was introduced to his associate, John C. Hertle, for in those days there were, by law, two Commissioners of Accounts. Hertle, a somewhat obsequious man, seemed impressed by the fact that I was being appointed at the suggestion of the mayor. After a minute or two of casual conversation, Mitchel strode into the room. He was tall, slender, handsome, and well-dressed, with dark brown hair, gray eyes, firm jaws and a strong face. A political commentator described him as "a gosling with the fuzz on him—lean, lank and long-necked." But to me at that interview he seemed more like a slim, spare greyhound, agile, active, aggressive and determined. Certainly he gave the impression of nervous energy and youthful vigor. He was twenty-eight years old and I was twenty-four.

After shaking hands he said to me abruptly:

"What do you know about accounting?"

"Accounting?" I replied, "I don't know anything about it."

"Well, damn it to hell," he said, with more than a touch of exasperation, "don't you know that you are being appointed as an Examiner of Accounts?"

"No," I replied. "I hadn't the slightest idea what the title was, nor the nature of the job."

Mitchel paced the floor for a minute in undisguised anger; then turning to Hertle he said: "Another one of the mayor's damn hirelings," and he slammed out of the room.

"Oh Commissioner, Commissioner," Hertle called after him in a deprecatory tone, but Mitchel did not hear him.

"He's slightly high pitched," said Hertle to me, although I was almost too overcome by astonishment to hear him. Then before I had recovered my equanimity he took me into a large room where perhaps twenty men were working at desks or tables; and finding me a table he gave me the city charter to read.

Three days later I was still reading the city charter, and I had just come to the conclusion that I would not waste any more time on so empty and footless a job when Mitchel came into the room. Seeing me he walked over and sat down on my table.

"What education have you had?" he asked me.

"Well," I began tentatively, "I have a bachelor's and a master's degree from Princeton."

He stared at me in amazement.

"Well, why in the name of God didn't you tell me so?" he exclaimed. "Don't you know that you and I are the only college graduates in this whole damned office? Let's get out of here."

And he took me to an office adjoining his own, where ultimately I became his first assistant with the title Chief Examiner of Accounts. We seemed to take to each other at once and within a few days we were close friends, lunching together and canoeing in the evenings on the Harlem River; and that summer I spent many of my week-ends at his home on West 162nd Street where as an eligible bachelor he was living with his parents.

Mitchel, who at the age of thirty-four was to become the youngest mayor New York City ever had, was a unique combination of traits and talents. He came of fighting Irish stock.

His grandfather was one of the heroes of the Irish Revolution, and his father, a delightful gray-bearded old gentleman whom I remember well, served on the staff of Stonewell Jackson in the Confederate army. His mother, Mary Purroy, who mingled Spanish blood with her Irish ancestry, was a woman of great force and character, deeply devout and equally determined; and while the young Mitchel during my visits at his home occasionally overrode his father, he never cared or dared to cross swords with his mother. From her he inherited the fire and zest of his personality.

No one could be associated with Mitchel without becoming fond of him. There was a flair of youth about him which he wore like a plume. He had an infectious kind of gaiety and an unusual capacity for friendship. At the same time he was forthright and downright, capable of indignation and passionate anger, and frequently his language was on the purple side. He was not a scholar or a student, and books had no great attraction for him. What distinguished him was the keenness of his mind, his tireless energy, his undeviating integrity, his hatred of expediency, his fairmindedness, and above all, his dauntless fighting spirit. Of the men with whom I have been associated, none except Woodrow Wilson and Newton Baker had his precision in getting to the heart of knotty problems. He could take an involved and complex tangle of facts and almost immediately reduce them to a comprehensible basis. And he had the same quick way of reaching decisions. As an investigator of the crooked ramifications of Tammany Hall he was without parallel; and he strode into the affray with the same quick, youthful, vigorous step with which he always strode into a room.

The office of the Commissioners of Accounts was uniquely fitted for the kind of task which Mitchel undertook. It had been created by the legislature in 1873 as a direct result of the Tweed scandals, and its original purpose was to check the receipts and disbursements of the comptroller's and chamberlain's offices. But somewhere along the line it had been given the right of subpoena and broad powers to investigate the city and county governments of New York. Today it exists under the title of Department of Investigation, a more exact and appropriate name.

Until Mitchel's advent the office had never distinguished itself. In fact, it was more or less a moribund affair, and its wide possibilities had scarcely been employed. But Mayor McClellan had seen its potential uses, and when John F. Ahearn, the Tammany president of the borough of Manhattan, was drastically criticized by a reform organization, he chose Mitchel as Commissioner of Accounts to investigate the charges. A graduate of Columbia University and the Columbia Law School, and the junior partner of a small law firm, Mitchel had been recommended to the mayor by Henry Purroy, a family connection, who was at the time a strong anti-Tammany man.

When I came into the office the Ahearn investigation had been practically completed, but a broad study of the borough president of the Bronx, Louis F. Haffen, was just about to begin. It was on this study that my work was launched, and it was in unraveling the intricacies of the Haffen regime that I got an intimate picture of the evils of municipal corruption: the subtle forms of graft, the nepotism, the tie-in of contractors with city officials, the conception of government as the private preserve of Tammany Hall. It was a lingering echo of Richard Croker's brazenly proclaimed maxim: "I work for my pocket all the time."

The staff of the Commissioners of Accounts office consisted of about ninety people: accountants, detectives, inspectors, process servers, a few chemists and engineers, and the clerical group. I began with the preliminary examination of witnesses in preparation for the case against Haffen, and I served as

Mitchel's junior in the long public hearings in the City Hall, and later in the hearings before the referee appointed by Governor Hughes. Mitchel soon discovered that I had some ability to transfer testimony and evidence into an intelligible written story; and thereafter much of my time was spent in writing the reports of our work to be submitted to the mayor, or to the governor if the case demanded it. Mitchel and I wrote them together, often occupying long evenings on the job, and occasionally going down to Atlantic City for concentrated work on some difficult summary.

There was another man associated with Mitchel in all these undertakings—Henry Bruère, at that time director of the Bureau of Municipal Research, a private unofficial organization of singular vision and usefulness. A student and a clear thinker, he was perhaps more responsible than any other man for providing Mitchel not only with technical advice but with a philosophy of social action. Certainly during all of Mitchel's career Bruère was his closest friend and collaborator, and in his subsequent work as president and chairman of the board of the Bowery Savings Bank in New York he was a member of that group of thoughtful leaders who, as in every city, are largely responsible for the civic ideas that galvanize our public life.

Bruère was younger than Mitchel and older than I, and the three of us, apart from our youth, had much in common. Certainly in those early days in the McClellan administration, we established a firm relationship of confidence and understanding.

As a result of Mitchel's searching and brilliant investigations Ahearn and Haffen were removed from office by Governor Hughes, and Mitchel then plunged into a study of the borough president of Brooklyn, Bird S. Coler. In the meantime there were countless other investigations of city offices, undertaken either at the instigation of the mayor or directly by the Commissioners of Accounts.

Mitchel's relations with the mayor's office were never easy. He was too forthright and unyielding to work harmoniously with a man endowed with McClellan's suspicious and sometimes autocratic temper. I suspect that if the fascinating quality of Mitchel's youth and the success of his courageous work had not attracted wide public admiration, the mayor might have been tempted to remove him from office. For McClellan was an unpredictable personality. He had cut off his relations with Charles Murphy, the head of Tammany Hall, and was anxious to break the grip of that organization on the city government; but he never seemed to be sure about the kind of system he was going to establish in its place. Many of his appointments were admirable, but he had been brought up in an atmosphere of machine politics, and the conception of the "machine" as a necessary part of a city administration he could never escape. He had no liking for innovation. He wanted to make the existing system as effective as possible, but he had no inclination to change the system itself. At heart he was not a fighter, and he was as temperamentally unequipped for offensive warfare as his father, the Civil War general, before him.

In consequence too many of his appointments were given to former Tammany politicians who had broken with their chief, and McClellan's bitter complaint about their disloyalty when they later reaffirmed their allegiance to the organization showed a streak of naïveté which contrasted strongly with the doctrine of realism he professed.

I remember once when Mitchel and I had one of these ex-Tammany protegés of McClellan on the witness stand, we reduced him to such a pitch of confusion that he could only reply: "I done the best what I knew how." The newspapers picked up the phrase, and in the ensuing public laughter and ridicule we were given to understand that the mayor was not amused.

If McClellan had made a clean sweep of the entire administration instead of the half-break he made with Tammany Hall, if he had done what Mitchel, La Guardia and Wagner did later —appoint the best possible men to all positions and open the doors to new ideas for improving the public service—his record as mayor would have been more creditable.

As it was, he ranks well above the average mayor in the city's history. He had an extraordinary knowledge of the machinery of government; he was honest; and he acted with decision. My own relations with him were cordial, due in part at least to our common Princeton bonds, and I occasionally had lunch with him at his club across Broadway from the City Hall. Indeed once or twice when he talked frankly about Mitchel and the work of the office, I was perhaps helpful in persuading him that the gossip he heard about his Commissioner of Accounts—and he listened to too much gossip—was unfounded. All in all he was a likeable personality, and an unusual figure in municipal politics. He was a scholar at heart with a great fondness for books, and a feeling for culture seldom seen among politicians in the City Hall of New York. The fact that his later years were spent on the faculty of Princeton as a professor of economic history indicates where his talents lay. If he had faults—and his autobiography published after his death shows him at his worst —they were balanced by some agreeable traits.

*

Meanwhile during this period with Mitchel I continued my work at the law school, attending either the late afternoon or the evening sessions. The week-ends were given over to study, and although I had transferred my living quarters from the Henry Street Settlement to a boarding-house on East 44th Street, my days and nights were still crowded, and I was working to the limit of my capacity. But the financial stringency was gone, and that source of anxiety no longer hung over me like a threatening cloud. In June, 1908, I graduated from the law school, passed the state bar examinations and was admitted to practice.

At the end of the year McClellan on his own volition offered to appoint me as an assistant corporation counsel. I really was not qualified for the position, although I doubt if at the time I was troubled by this consideration. I was young and ambitious and I was probably confident that hard work could make up for lack of experience. And I knew I was capable of hard work. With Mitchel's encouragement, therefore—for we were both young and ambitious—I accepted the post, starting my new duties in January, 1909.

For me it was a memorable year. In those days, nearly fifty years ago, the corporation counsel's office had no particular organization and certainly a minimum of discipline, and a young assistant could do about as much or as little work as he pleased. I was assigned to the contract division where there were plenty of cases to try and plenty of advisory opinions to write in reply to city departments seeking light on their legal rights and responsibilities. I was eager for experience and I undoubtedly plunged into the work with more enthusiasm than wisdom. That my record in court was not too disastrous was due largely to the help I received from another young assistant corporation counsel, Francis Martin, who later became the presiding justice of the Appellate Division of the Supreme Court in New York. Two or three years older than I, he knew more law than I did, but we shared a common ambition to learn the trade. We joined forces and together we worked up our cases with infinite pains. I cannot say that we achieved any measure of brilliant success, but we survived, and as I recall it the city did not suffer too materially from our lack of experience.

During this period I spent many nights in the office on the "advisory opinions" which always seemed to pile up faster than they could be disposed of. The recollection of one of these nights is still fresh in memory. A Tammany district leader called by appointment to see me. Like his chief, Charlie Murphy, he was a saloon-keeper, and he had evidently fortified himself for the occasion. I had never met him before, and he turned out to be a veritable caricature of a Tammany boss—the kind of caricature which, a generation before, Nast had drawn so devastatingly in *Harper's Weekly*. He was big, burly and profane, with a cigar in his mouth and a derby hat cocked at a rakish angle on the side of his head. He had obviously heard through the omnipresent grapevine that I was writing an opinion on something in which he was financially interested, and there was no finesse about his approach.

"Young man," he roared, "that's my contract, and I want that opinion written right."

I told him as firmly as I could that the responsibility for writing the opinion was mine, and that as far as I could see there would be no satisfaction in it for him.

He stared at me incredulously. Then with an oath he snarled:

"Well, Mr. College Man, you think times have changed, don't you? But they ain't."

He was wrong. Times *had* changed. Already in New York the tides which had started with Seth Low and the formative generation that preceded him were flooding in, and never again, in spite of administrations like those of Hylan and Walker, would the handling of the city's affairs sink to the levels of Tweed and Croker and Murphy. A new dawn had begun, and we who lived through the groping days of the McClellan regime were conscious of its promise.

*

At this moment accident and good luck once more stepped into the picture to change the course of my fortunes. In the municipal elections in the fall of 1909, Mitchel, running on the reform or Fusion platform, was chosen as President of the Board of Aldermen. With him was elected the entire Fusion ticket with the exception of the mayoralty which as the result of a fluke went to Judge William J. Gaynor, nominated by Tammany Hall. It was obvious that Gaynor was one of the last men that Tammany really wanted, but its leaders were out to win and they took a desperate chance on this doughty old warrior. It turned out to be as unhappy a guess as Tammany ever made, for no mayor in the history of the city ever shook the dry bones of municipal administration as Gaynor did.

The Fusionists had a majority of the Board of Estimate and my name was suggested for the secretaryship of that important body. At the last minute Gaynor offered to appoint me Commissioner of Accounts if the Fusionists would agree to leave the existing secretary of the Board of Estimate undisturbed. It was the consensus of opinion of the reform group that I should accept the post, for Mitchel had made it one of the most important in the city government, and its influence for honest and effective administration was incalculable.

"If Gaynor doesn't play square with you, you can resign," said Mitchel. "Paste your resignation on the outside of your door where he can see it all the time."

So I accepted—in a state of considerable bewilderment and with not a little misgiving. Mitchel's shoes looked discouragingly large.

VI

*

City Official in New York

I HAD never met Judge Gaynor until, early in January, 1910, I was ushered into his office in the City Hall. He had the reputation of being a formidable person, and during his seventeen years on the Supreme Court bench in Brooklyn he had been the terror of the lawyers practicing before him. His bearing was cold and severe. He was sixty-two years old when I met him, but his gray hair and gray beard made him appear older. He had a slight cast in one eye and the effect was disconcerting, because you never could tell whether he was looking at you or a little to your left.

He greeted me in somber fashion and asked me just one question:

"How old are you?"

"Twenty-six, sir," I replied.

He paused for a moment before he spoke.

"That is a handicap which time will soon correct," he said.

Then he gave me my instructions:

"I want you to get after the crooks in this city, and I don't care whether they are members of Tammany Hall or the Republican Party or the Citizens' Union or Dr. Parkhurst's church."

Thereupon he swore me in as Commissioner of Accounts, and I bowed and left the office.

*

In the two and a half years or more that I served as his Commissioner of Accounts I never got any closer to him than this; and most of my fellow-commissioners had the same experience. There was an icy reserve about him which I could not penetrate, an acidulous quality that discouraged easy communication. He never laughed, at least as far as I was aware, and if he ever smiled I never saw it. I knew from casual comments or expressions on his face that he was interested—deeply interested—in my work, and except on one occasion he threw his entire support behind my investigations. Never for a moment did I doubt his essential integrity, or his desire to serve the city to the limit of his ability; but his eccentricities, his prejudices, his ingrained obstinacy, and above all his passionate love of a fight kept his administration in a ferment, and the press and public in a divided state of delighted approval or execration.

It was a rare morning when the papers did not play up a new pungent attack which the mayor had launched against somebody—against Hearst, "meddlers," "noisy scamps," "rag-bag newspapers," clerical reformers and above all Dr. Parkhurst. "He thinks he is pious when he is only bilious," he said about Parkhurst. "He is a man of vast and varied misinformation, of brilliant mental incapacity and of prodigious moral requirements. Self sufficient, all sufficient, insufficient Dr. Parkhurst!" The letters which Gaynor wrote during his administration were classics, usually short and sharp, often whimsical and philosophical, sometimes ill-tempered and cruel. To a prominent woman who complained that girls of the underworld were frequenting Irving Place, he wrote: "You can't tell whether they are bad girls or not. I would not know a bad woman or girl if I should meet one in the streets. How do you know they are bad? It takes a bad person to tell a bad woman." To William J. Schieffelin of the Citizens' Union who stood high in the ranks of the reformers of that era Gaynor wrote: "I could not attach much weight to your letter, for your invariable course discloses a purpose not to help, but to hurt. In fine, I do not care to hear from you on any subject."

Yet beneath this cantankerous spirit lay a consistent social philosophy. Above all he hated to see little people pushed around. He was forever the champion of the underdog, whether it was a prostitute, a small-time gambler, or a bewildered immigrant rabbi complaining that the boys pulled his whiskers. He constantly asked me to make certain that the city marshals, whose difficult job it was to levy on debtors' goods, carried out their tasks without oppression. Once he sent me a letter he had received from a woman complaining that she had been beaten by a policeman. The woman turned out to be a prostitute, and when I casually mentioned this to the mayor, he snapped: "A prostitute is still a citizen." I took her to the precinct station nearest her home and she picked her assailant out of two platoons assembled on parade. When I placed him on the stand, he confessed the charge, and the mayor had him immediately dismissed from the force.

Gaynor in his heart never seemed to care much for the police, especially their third-degree methods and their tendency to arbitrary action. "They are only citizens dressed in blue clothes and brass buttons," he said, "with no right or power, which their fellow citizens do not possess, to arrest without a warrant." But in the end it was his police force which more than anything else proved to be his undoing.

The first year of Gaynor's administration was a high point in municipal progress. His appointments were excellent; with all his eccentricities and testiness he marshalled his team of associates behind impressive standards of public work; and above everything else, he refused to play politics. At the end of his first six months the New York *World* which had been outspokenly critical made this acknowledgment: "No other man

ever accomplished so much in so little time. He has revolutionized the spirit of the city government. The power of his precept
and example has spread throughout the public service." And
on Valentine's Day the New York *Herald* suggested the following exchange of greetings between the mayor and Charles
Murphy of Tammany Hall.

THE MAYOR TO MURPHY
Don't mind what other folks may say,
I love you more and more each day,
No knife can cut our love in two,
You know just what I think of you.

MURPHY TO THE MAYOR
Just hand that love stuff to the birds,
Actions cut more ice than words,
You've passed me out the rinky dink,
It's good that you can't hear me think.

Meanwhile my work as Commissioner of Accounts was going
forward at a driving pace. The office was swamped with investigations. Early in the year the mayor informed me that he did
not intend to appoint the second Commissioner of Accounts
allowed by the charter, and that the whole responsibility was
mine. Evidently in his eyes my youth was not a handicap,
although to me it was an occasional embarrassment. Once when
our office boy was at lunch I happened to sit down at his desk
in the outer office to look at a newspaper. A newly elected
member of the Board of Aldermen whom I had not met came
in through the door.

"I would like to see Commissioner Fosdick," he said to me.

"I am Commissioner Fosdick," I replied.

He looked at me with angry eyes. Then he snapped:

"Look here, young fellow, don't you get fresh with me. You go tell Commissioner Fosdick I want to see him."

The subjects of our investigations were chosen in various ways. Under the charter we had to maintain a continuous audit of the accounts of the comptroller and the chamberlain. In addition we were supposed to examine every three months the accounts of over eighty separate divisions of the municipal government which handled funds, including the many inferior courts. With the limited force at our disposal even an annual examination of these divisions was impossible, and I spent considerable time before the Board of Estimate trying, in part successfully, to secure the services of additional accountants.

Our investigations were also determined by suggestions from the mayor's office or by requests from department heads. Judge Gaynor constantly referred to me letters of complaint which he had received—often anonymous. Across the top he would write in his meticulous penmanship: "See me about this."

My office itself under the charter had an independent responsibility "to make such examinations as the said commissioners shall deem for the best interests of the city," and during the period that I was commissioner I never hesitated to follow a clue which seemed promising. At all times I had a loyal crowd behind me in the office. When Mitchel first came in as commissioner he had been a little suspicious of the personnel, and perhaps rightly so, because many of them were members, at least perfunctorily, of Tammany Hall. They had had to join the organization to get their jobs in the first place, and now they were protected by civil service. But he soon discovered, as I did, that with one or two exceptions—and we got rid of these— they were a group of honest men, and personally I never worked at the head of a more devoted staff. They had been long in the city's service and they seemed to be able, as they said, "to smell a crook" even in unlikely places.

Occasionally an investigation would start as the result of some fortuitous incident. Once my office boy told me that he had been offered five dollars by a stranger to secure a particular voucher which with hundreds of others was at that moment going through the process of audit in our office. We had to study the voucher for some time to discover what was wrong with it —so wrong indeed that somebody would want to destroy it— and it led to the unearthing of wholesale theft.

Mitchel, as Commissioner of Accounts, had made a thorough investigation of the borough governments of Manhattan, the Bronx and Brooklyn, and I determined to continue the pattern by taking up the Borough of Queens. Here we ran into conditions far more serious than anything Mitchel had encountered. Forgery, perjury, grand larceny and various kinds of barefaced theft showed up as a result of the investigation. Dead men and dead horses, or nonexistent men and horses, had places on the city's payroll, and the gang collected the money for their imaginary services. Forgeries of payrolls, time sheets and inspectors' reports, and false affidavits and certificates were common. Systematic assessments for political purposes were levied upon municipal employees, and prior to elections the payrolls were padded with the names of men who never even bothered to appear at their posts.

Immediate action by a grand jury was indicated, but I was unable to secure the kind of cooperation from the district attorney of Queens County which seemed to me essential. With Mayor Gaynor's approval, therefore, I went to Albany to see Governor Charles Evans Hughes. I had never met him before and my first impression of him was not too favorable. His eyes seemed cold, and with his large, reddish beard cut square at the bottom he looked more like a priest of some fanatic sect than like the extraordinary lawyer and executive he was. I started to say that we had both of us gone to Colgate for two

years and had been members of the same fraternity, but if he
heard me he was not interested. He plunged directly into the
situation in Queens County, asking me searching and detailed
questions about the conditions I had unearthed. In the end he
terminated the interview abruptly with the statement that he
would grant my request, that is, he would appoint a special
deputy attorney general to take over the grand jury investigation in Queens County. Nearly twenty years later when he and
I were trustees together on the board of The Rockefeller Foundation I found him a genial associate. Either the years had
mellowed him or my first interview with him had occurred at
an unpropitious moment.

The man he selected for the task in Queens County was
Arthur Train, an excellent trial lawyer who had been assistant
to District Attorney Jerome in New York and who later was to
become known as the author of the "Mr. Tutt" books. Plunging
into his new assignment with all his characteristic verve he
induced the grand jury to return over a hundred indictments
against a score of public officials including two superintendents
of sewers, a superintendent of highways, a borough architect,
a judge of the municipal court, a deputy sheriff and a district
captain. The scene in court when the arrested officials were
arraigned was, as *The New York Times* remarked, "much like
an old time political picnic when the Queens County bosses
were in their prime."

Nevertheless the investigation wound up in a kind of anti-
climax. Governor Hughes was appointed by President Taft to
the Supreme Court bench, and in the following election John
A. Dix, a Democrat, was chosen to succeed him. Train was
eased from his post as deputy attorney general and after that
the Queens gang had things much their own way. A few of the
lesser people were convicted and fined—the judge announcing
openly in court that he would not impose prison sentences—but

many of the indictments were in the end dismissed, or if tried, were thrown out for "lack of evidence." The last case was against a prominent borough official charged with forgery. I appeared as a witness for the prosecution, and the judge, claiming that I had abused the constitutional rights of the defendant when he had appeared before me, gave me a severe tongue-lashing in open court, and threw the case out. This so aroused Mayor Gaynor that he wrote me a letter which he made public, in which in his characteristic fashion he dissected the judge and his decision with cruel frankness. "I do not wonder that you feel discouraged," he said in conclusion, "when your work is frustrated by such a judicial ruling."

Nevertheless, as a result of our findings, charges were filed with the governor against the borough president, Lawrence Gresser, and later he was removed from office, just as his fellow borough presidents, Ahearn and Haffen, had been removed before him. I have always remembered with grateful appreciation the petition, signed, after the departure of Gresser, by nearly a thousand citizens of Queens County, asking me to move to that borough and run for borough president!

*

The yellowing pages of my reports on the investigations made during the years I served as Commissioner of Accounts are still in the city archives. They cover such a variety of subjects and situations that generalized comment is difficult, but perhaps they can be classified under several loose headings. First there were those that related to sheer graft. One of the earliest of these had to do with the so-called "dock masters" of the city's Department of Docks and Ferries who were charged with the duty of collecting wharfage rates for boats or barges landing at municipal piers. Under the existing system, installed by a previous administration to prevent theft, the dockmaster was obliged to punch through a triplicate folder of a ticket. The first folder was sent to the department as a voucher accompanying the report of monies received; the second folder was kept by the dockmaster for record purposes; while the third was handed to the owner of the boat as a receipt.

I started the investigation by subpoenaing as many boat owners as I could find, and succeeded in securing most of their receipts. A comparison of these receipts with the vouchers filed in the department showed discrepancies of a remarkable character. In few cases did the first and third folders of the triplicate tickets agree, and it was evident that they were punched at different times. In other words the amounts of money which appeared on the receipts of the owners of the boats were far in excess of the amounts turned in to the dock department. This leak in the city treasury was estimated to approximate a hundred thousand dollars a year. Three of the dockmasters were indicted, and three others disappeared; and we installed a more adequate system in the hope that the leak could be plugged.

In another case the law provided that "no poor or indigent soldier, sailor or marine who had served in the military service of the United States should be sent to any alms house," but should be provided for in his own home. The Board of Estimate annually included in its appropriations for the Department of Public Charities a sum sufficient for this relief. We subpoenaed thirty-four of these beneficiaries. Sixteen of them testified that the amounts appearing on the vouchers represented sums larger than they had received. Some of them denied also that the signatures on the vouchers were their own. One woman testified that her father was dead at the time his signature was supposed to have been placed on a receipt acknowledging relief.

In another case we encountered the obverse side of the coin

—that is, it had to do with the cupidity of acquisitive citizens trying to mulct the city. Of these two types of graft I always felt that the latter was far more prevalent and more serious. This particular case had to do with condemnation proceedings where streets were being widened and awards made by a commission to compensate the owners of damaged parcels. As Assistant Corporation Counsel I had had some experience with this activity, and I had heard apparently worthy citizens sorrowfully testifying about "the intrinsic value of the old homestead that no money can ever replace," only to learn upon investigation that they had purchased their property within two or three years—indeed, in one or two cases, subsequent to the published determination of the city to take the land. I had heard these citizens testify to the "enormous damage" which a proposed improvement would do to their property, shaving off verandas and cutting houses in two, only to find that the verandas had been added, and even the houses built, after the city had made up its mind to take the property, and with the deliberate intent that they should be shaved off and cut in two. I had even known some of our good citizens to buy up old houses and move them to the line of a street widening proceeding, so as to be able to collect extensive damages.

In the case that came before me as Commissioner of Accounts, one of these citizens—and he was the principal of a public school—had managed to get himself appointed as a member of a condemnation commission. He then proceeded to purchase through some of his teachers acting as "dummies" a number of lots along the street that was to be widened. I was examining on the stand the city's expert who, so it seemed to me, had given unusually high values for certain parcels on this street. He was insisting that the values were not out of line.

Q. "But why did you give a value of $4,553.37 for Parcel Number 13?

A. I gave no such value to that parcel.

Q. But here is your own testimony in the record of the Commission. Look at it."

He stared at the record for perhaps two minutes, and then with a flushed face he said:

"Commissioner, have you a magnifying glass?"

We found him one, and he showed me that the initial digit 4 had originally been 1. In other words he had given a value of $1,553.37 for Parcel 13, and it had been raised to $4,553.37. A careful examination of the record showed a score of forgeries, not only in the original copy of the record but in the three carbon copies on file in the Bureau of Street Openings.

Before we finished with this investigation it led us into a tangled plot that involved not only the public school principal and some of his teachers, but a number of real estate people and a congressman. I gave the facts to District Attorney Charles E. Whitman. "A dirty mess," he called it, and he acted swiftly.

*

Nothing in my time so shocked the city or brought such a sense of sickening despair as the Triangle Shirtwaist factory fire in March, 1911, on Washington Place, Manhattan, in which 147 employees, most of them girls between seventeen and twenty-five years of age, lost their lives. The factory was located on the top floors of a loft building, and the girls, cut off from stairways and fire escapes, and in some cases with their clothing in flames, jumped by scores from the windows to the street below, where their broken bodies spattered the sidewalks. It was a Saturday afternoon and I happened to be in the neighborhood. Nothing that I saw at the front in the First World War seven years later surpassed in horror that dreadful scene. It has haunted me all my life.

It was the old story of blocked fire escapes and locked doors and faulty building construction; and I plunged immediately into an investigation, not of the tragedy itself, for that was in the hands of the district attorney, but of the Bureau of Buildings of the Borough of Manhattan, where I felt one of the deep-rooted causes might lie. It turned out to be a frustrating experience. We seemed to be up against something age-old and hopeless, a long-lingering malignancy for which there was no positive cure.

We subpoenaed as witnesses many of the prominent builders and contractors of the city. The first witness was the vice-president of an iron company who testified that when a question arose as to the thickness of plates in a building which his concern was erecting, a building inspector had offered to pass the alleged defect.

> He said it was worth something to keep his mouth shut about this. I said: "Well, how much?" He said: "It ought to be worth an M but I will take a D." I said: "What do you mean?" He said: "Don't you know Roman numerals?" I told him I didn't remember. He said an M meant $1,000 and a D means $500.

The company official insisted that no money had been paid, but in another case a contractor admitted the general practice of payments to building inspectors.

> Q. By your concern?
>
> A. Not by our concern particularly. I guess by everybody more or less. . . . Our men would say they wanted to put up this thing or that thing temporarily, and so and so, the inspector, would put up a holler, and then he would stay away for a half a day perhaps, and when he came back everything would be all right, and our men would let it go in as expenses on the time sheets.

Another contractor, admitting the practice of payments to inspectors, testified:

> I give them an odd five dollars just the same as giving a tip to a bank clerk or anybody else. It is simply an ordinary thing to give a fellow five dollars or something like that. It is a common thing anyway.

Still another contractor, while refusing to be specific about definite cases, testified as follows:

> . . . Here a little inspector comes up—I call him little because he has not been in the building business as long as I have. He comes up there and says: "Well, you have got to put in forty pieces of stuff," where I think fifteen will be enough.
>
> Q. So you paid him?
>
> A. I wouldn't deny that, but that is so common.
>
> Q. So common that you didn't think anything about it?
>
> A. No. Why should I? I was obliged to. Every builder is obliged to go to them. I am not a squealer. It took a long time for me to learn it. That is the fact. What are you going to do? They can make you more bother. "Give me $10 or $15," they say, "and I will help you $150 worth. If you don't give me this $10 or $15 I will make it so hard for you that it will put you out of business."
>
> Q. I take it then that this particular case is not the only case in your experience where you have found it necessary to give money to building inspectors?
>
> A. No. I have to do it, and so does everybody who succeeds in New York.

Success in New York! The phrase remained in my memory for a long time, but I well knew that the name of any other city could have been substituted—Chicago, Detroit, San Francisco—and the allegation would have been equally appropriate. It was not one administration that was under indictment; it was a system, a way of life, a vacuum in terms of ethical values, which is as old and as difficult to eradicate as human imperfection itself.

To be sure, we separated some of the building inspectors from their jobs, but I felt at the time that nothing really significant had been accomplished, except perhaps a portrayal of the tragic consequences of deficient character in our impersonalized age.

This pessimism was modified by subsequent developments. The Triangle fire became both a symbol and a motivating social force, and it played a dynamic role in launching a number of important programs in the United States, especially in the field of tenement house and factory regulation. It was what we call today a "breakthrough"—although at the time we would not have understood the term—and it placed public policy and the standards of social legislation in America on a new level. The significance of disaster in the evolution of public thinking and governmental practice was never more dramatically illustrated, and the Triangle fire, with all its tragedy and horror, became a mighty symbol of an awakened social consciousness.

*

Another type of investigation which my office made was aimed at what we called "the parasitic boys." No other species of the human family so aroused the mayor's ire. The loan sharks who preyed on city employees and garnisheed their salaries were among this group, and we went after them in vigorous fashion. By the use of subpoenas we obtained information from one hundred city employees, and discovered that the rate of interest charged by the loan agents in these cases, calculated on a per annum basis, ranged from 50 per cent to 400 per cent. Even these figures did not tell the whole story. Some of the loan agents refused to accept part payment, but insisted upon a renewal of the loan each month with the usual charges for legal services. In many such cases confessions of judgment were filed against men who had paid four-fifths of the original loan in renewals. Thus the salary of a fireman who had borrowed $47.50 to pay his wife's hospital bill, and had returned $40 in renewals, was garnisheed for $77, which with fees and interest amounted to $96.49; so that at the end of a year he paid $136.49 for his loan of $47.50.

We subpoenaed all the loan agents who dealt with city employees. They were an unhappy group of men on the witness stand, and in my report to the mayor I published their names, their records and their methods.

One unexpected development grew out of this investigation. We slapped a *duces tecum* subpoena on one of these characters, and the next morning his chief clerk appeared, pleading the illness of his principal, but producing, among other papers, probably through inadvertence, a file of letters relating to so-called "strike" bills introduced into the state legislature to curb the loan sharks. For example, an assemblyman would propose a bill against the evil, and the loan agents, who apparently had some kind of organization, would raise money to pay him off. The bill would then be dropped. The letters named specific people and amounts of money, and we published the entire correspondence, which rocked political circles in upstate New York far more that it did in the city. The incident certainly furnished a fresh illustration of the old rhyme:

> Big fleas have little fleas
> Upon their backs to bite 'em;
> And little fleas have lesser fleas,
> And so ad infinitum.

Another investigation related to the "hangers-on" in the City Hall who were shaking down gullible citizens on the pretense that special favors could be secured from city officials for a consideration. A news dealer who wanted a stand, an auctioneer who wanted a license, a contractor who wanted to get a tenement house violation removed, would pay these "hangers-on" various sums in expectation of services to be rendered. When no result was forthcoming, they generally nursed their grievances in silence for fear of a charge of bribery. But a few complained, and we were able to make some arrests among these parasites. "I think it can be said without exaggeration," I remarked to the mayor in my report, "that there is hardly a department head in the city who does not run the daily risk of being 'sold out' by men who trade upon ignorance and credulity in claiming to represent him."

I was always of the opinion that the police were more gullible than any other body of public servants. They seemed to be obsessed with the idea that any measure beneficial to them as a group could not be obtained without the payment of money. One of the last reports I handed to the mayor had to do with the incidents which followed the passage of a legislative act abolishing the rank of doorman in the police department and transferring the one hundred and ninety-four incumbents of that rank to the grade and privileges of patrolman. The bill had been introduced at the instigation of the police commissioner; and although there was a doormen's association, it had played no part in the passage of the act.

Nevertheless the former doormen got the idea they owed something to somebody, and when a lawyer who had formerly been a policeman began writing them dunning letters on the necessity of their paying their share of the expense in securing the passage of the bill through the legislature they willingly came through with amounts ranging from $25 to $400, apparently dependent upon their individual gullibility. My report denounced the lawyer as a sham and a fraud, and the mayor sent it to the district attorney and to the Grievance Committee of the Bar Association.

*

There was another type of investigation which had to do not so much with graft as with what might be called public security or consumer welfare. The study we made of the extensive traffic in bad eggs illustrates this classification. Dubbed by the newspapers "the rot and spot hunt," it stirred up widespread interest. It developed as a result of an anonymous complaint and took us into the Bureau of Food Inspection of the health department. There is in actuality a legitimate commercial use for rotten eggs: they are employed by tanners to soften leather. But at the time of my investigation they brought higher prices when sold for food purposes, and they were used primarily by public bakers in making pies and cakes.

We started by subpoenaing a number of wholesale egg dealers in the city, and from their books we obtained the names of the bakers to whom rots and spots—a trade classification—were sold. It was an amazingly long list, and I remember that the biggest pie company in New York, popularly known as the "Pie Trust," was among the customers. The bad eggs were sold in cases marked "Not to be used for food purposes," but at the price for which they were purchased they could hardly have been used for anything else. They generally brought about five cents a dozen, although cans of broken rots and spots were sold at three cents a pound.

Some of the witnesses refused to answer questions on the ground that it would degrade and incriminate them, but we had a watertight case, and in my report I published a complete list of the offending wholesale dealers and bakers. I sent the report to the district attorney because one of the health department inspectors—and there were probably others—was shown to have accepted bribes for shutting his eyes to the traffic.

This investigation led us into a study of the sanitary condition of bakeries, and the undertaking was so extensive—we inspected one hundred and forty-five establishments—that I had to bring in special help. Frances Perkins, later Secretary of Labor in the Roosevelt administration, tells me that I gave her the first job she had after leaving college—inspecting bakeries on the East Side. Our inspections covered bakeries of all grades and conditions. With the exception of the so-called factory bakeries, of which there were relatively few in New York at that time, the great majority of bakeries were located in cellars and basements never intended for that use. Many of them had been converted from storerooms for coal, ashes and rubbish without surrendering the original purposes for which the cellars were planned. If they had windows, and few of them did, they opened into shafts, areaways or filthy back yards.

More than half the bakeries visited by our inspectors had broken, dirty floors and filthy sidewalls and ceilings. In twenty-five per cent of the places inspected, the sewer pipe ran through the mixing room, and wherever the pipe was located on the ceiling, the collected moisture was dripping into the mixing vats and over the utensils and unbaked materials. More than fifty per cent of the places visited had no provision for the clothing of the employees, and the clothing removed upon entering the bake shop was found lying about the room—shoes in mixing vats, coats and trousers on mixing boards, and in some cases on the rising dough itself.

Animals were found in more than one-third of the cellar bakeries visited. Cats were seen walking over the mixing boards and through the vats; they were seen sleeping in barrels of flour and even upon unbaked dough. Some bake rooms served as nurseries for litters of kittens. One place revealed a dog and three puppies; there had been seven originally of which four died in the bake room. Some bake rooms contained beds, mattresses, cookstoves, bureaus and baby carriages. Evidences of residence and all in violation of the law!

These were the conditions under which most of the bread was baked in New York City fifty years ago. Although I do not know what has happened in baking conditions since that time, it seems improbable that anything approaching that evil situation could exist today. Perhaps the explosion set off by the publication of our report had something to do in establishing new standards.

Another investigation under the general classification of public security related to moving picture shows which were at that time of recent origin. The building code provided that any building used for public entertainment, which had accommodation for more than 300 people, should comply with all the requirements of the law covering exits and fire appliance equipment. As an inevitable consequence most of the moving picture places maintained a seating capacity of *less* than 300, generally 299, and were subject only to the casual judgment of fire department inspectors on their occasional visits.

The result was chaos. Our inspections covered all the 450 motion picture houses in operation at that time in the greater city, but we made a special study of fifty show places selected at random in Manhattan, Brooklyn and the Bronx. Of these fifty, thirty-six were crowded to the danger point with no protection against fire or panic, and with the aisles so completely blocked by standing spectators that it was impossible in some cases for our representatives to elbow their way into the hall. In most of these places the ventilation was wretched, with no air except such as came in through the front doors. In many places attendants went through the room with large pump atomizers spraying perfumery on the crowd to allay the odor. In most places, too, five and seven persons were occupying three seats between them, sitting on each others' laps. In one place in Brooklyn our inspector reported:

Seats full and about two hundred and fifty standing in the rear and in the aisles. A critical inspection of this place was impossible. The crowd was surging back and forth, pushing and shoving for vantage points of view. Quarrels were frequent. The air was fetid and stifling. This place is without one single redeeming feature.

From this investigation I went on to a study of the Bureau of Violations of the fire department, the unit that was responsible for maintaining the prescribed standard of fire equipment in buildings that came within the law—theatres, roof gardens, loft buildings and buildings used for manufacturing and commercial purposes. It proved to be the largest investigation we ever undertook, involving the physical inspection of over 500 buildings and the examination of 105 witnesses. The conditions we discovered were appalling—obstructed fire escapes, doors opening in rather than out, the presence of combustible rubbish, and the indiscriminate use of inflammable and dangerous liquids. For example—typical of scores—in a seven-story building on East Broadway, housing fourteen different employers and a total of 158 employees, fire exits were blocked on every floor; iron shutters were eaten away with rust; entrance doors and all hall doors opened inward; no fire appliances of any kind had been installed; and the fourth floor, filled with piles of calico garments in process of manufacture, and equipped with beds and a gas stove, was used as the home of the family proprietor.

Scarcely less dangerous were the conditions found in the eighty-five theatres which then existed in Manhattan and the Bronx. In every one of them violations of the building code were discovered. There were never enough axes, or extinguishers, or pails or hose. Some of the theatres had interior exit stairways of wood in violation of the law; in some the exit stairways were old and dilapidated; in one the exits in the gallery led to a peaked roof down which it was necessary to slide to the fire escape; in several the exits were so confused that a stranger could find his way out only with difficulty; in a number the extinguishers were found hidden and inaccessible behind masses of scenery; in several others piles of rubbish had been allowed to collect under the stage and in the scene docks.

Out of this investigation certain facts emerged which threw a sinister light on these dangerous conditions in New York's theatres. Every theatre at that time had to obtain an annual license dating from May 1st. Consequently every April an inspection was made by the fire department representatives to determine the advisability of recommending the new licenses. In the annual inspection of April, 1910, ten theatres were reported by the department's inspectors to be lacking the various fire appliances required by the building code, such as sprinkler systems and extinguishers. Upon the basis of the inspectors' memoranda, reports recommending against the issuance of the licenses were forwarded to the fire commissioner. But within a few days a second series of reports was prepared in which it was stated that a reinspection had been made of the ten theatres, and that the deficiencies had been found to be corrected. The theatres in question, therefore, secured their licenses for the ensuing season.

Our investigation developed the fact that the reinspection referred to in the second reports had not been made, nor had the appliances called for by the building code been installed.

In spite of exhaustive examination we were unable definitely to establish the responsibility for the false reports. Somewhere in a morass of cover-up tactics and perjured testimony the trail faded out.

*

No one can study the issues of municipal government, as I had the opportunity of doing in the years I served as an official in New York, without realizing that while graft and dishonesty are serious and demoralizing factors, the chief problem is waste. The real leak in the public treasury is not the result of peculation but of defective standards of work, poor methods, inadequate supervision and inefficient organization. The difficulties which face a government executive are difficulties with which a private business concern is unacquainted. Our political practice is based on the idea of turning things upside down every four years. A new department head, therefore—such as a commissioner of health or of street cleaning—is faced at the start with this disturbing concept of impermanency. In the four years of his term he must learn the business, keep it going, outline a policy, discover where the leaks are, and take such measures as he can to stop them. By the time he reaches this last step, his term has often expired, and his policies and plans, his half formulated systems, and partially installed checks are swept aside by his successor who must repeat the process all over again.

In my time in the city government there were five different commissioners of street cleaning. I think I can safely say that five different policies were formulated during that period for the final disposition of ashes and garbage. Commissioner Waring bought three steam dumpers for transporting ashes to sea at a cost of $40,000 apiece. His successor decided that they were worthless and discarded them. Commissioner Woodbury resurrected them, claiming them capable of large economies; and after his time they twice suffered death and resurrection. Commissioner Edwards finally sold all three of them for $267.

But despite this handicap of impermanency due to our democratic system, and despite other drawbacks such as civil service which too often protects ineffectual and unwanted employees, it is not only possible but vitally necessary to raise the standards of efficiency in public administration. At least that was the conclusion I came to in my years as Commissioner of Accounts, and on no other issue did I put so much emphasis.

It started in a study of the municipal ferry service when we found that the employees assigned to public ferry boats were far more numerous than those used on the private ferry boats, operating in the same waters and generally carrying many more passengers. For example, the municipal ferry boat *Nassau* of 1396 tons had a crew of twelve, while the Delaware, Lackawanna and Western ferry boat *Ithaca* of 1462 tons had a crew of only seven. The five ferry boats used by the railroad on its Barclay Street line had a total crew of 65, while the crew required to man the two municipal boats on the 39th Street division numbered 75.

As a result of extensive reorganization savings were affected which without in any way handicapping the municipal ferry service amounted to $175,000 a year.

In an investigation of the Bureau of Sewers of the Borough of Manhattan we found that the cost of cleaning sewer basins amounted to $4 a cubic yard. Our analysis showed that at least $1.50 of this cost was chargeable solely to time wasted in loafing. Poor organization and improper methods were accountable for at least a dollar more. We were not successful in reducing the final cost to an ideal level, but we brought it down to about $1.50 a cubic yard, and saved the city approximately $35,000 a year.

We began to get into this type of work so extensively that in 1911 I created a bureau of efficiency as a subdivision of my office, with competent engineers in charge. "I do not claim," I said at the time, "that this new bureau is in a position to make more than a beginning in this activity. It will mean a large force and a great deal of time to take up the plan comprehensively. If with our present force we are able to study two departments a year we shall be greatly encouraged. All we ask is the opportunity to show what the application of efficiency standards can accomplish in dollars and cents."

*

In all this work I had the complete support of Mayor Gaynor. Indeed, without his support the work could never have been done. I do not say that my relations with him were easy, for he was lacking in warmth and affability, and he could be unpredictably irascible. If it had not been for his secretary, Bob Adamson, a former reporter on the New York *World* and an old friend of mine, I do not know how I could have kept this relationship on any satisfactory basis. Whenever I wanted to see him I would call Adamson with the question: "How is the Old Man feeling today?" His answer would be either: "Not so good, Ray," in which case I would postpone my visit, or "Feeling fine. Come on over."

And yet among all of us who served him there was a sense of loyalty which in the early years was real and deep. He had a magnetic quality difficult to define. He was without fear, unmoved and unflinching in the face of public clamor, and dogged in the support of his convictions. There was another factor, too, in our attitude toward the mayor—a feeling of something like compassion; for in August, 1910, he was the victim of an attempted assassination as he stood on the deck of the *Kaiser Wilhelm der Grosse* at Hoboken, embarking for a brief vacation in Europe. His assailant was a mental case, a discharged employee of the dock department who had haunted my office for weeks with his alleged grievance. Gaynor was shot in the back of the neck and the bullet remained in his throat for the rest of his days, often racking him with spasms of coughing. He nearly lost his life, and when he returned to his office after two months of recuperation we were all of us inclined to overlook his increased acerbity, although toward the end of his term his weakened physique and his growing impatience with opposition affected the quality of his judgment.

One of my difficulties, and a source of some embarrassment, was the fact that Gaynor and Mitchel almost from the start had little liking for each other. With his open, direct, and independent mind Mitchel could not possibly understand a man like Gaynor, and made little effort to do so. Gaynor on his part was suspicious of Mitchel's ambition, and when he referred to him in a newspaper interview as "the boy in a summer suit"—due to Mitchel's penchant for light gray suits even in winter time—the war really started. In an angry outburst Mitchel lashed out at the mayor's ideas, habits, and "his little dog Spot," whom Gaynor had casually mentioned in a recent letter, thus giving the newspapers a field day and projecting a canine into public notoriety thirty years before F.D.R.'s Fala achieved his fame.

During Gaynor's illness, Mitchel, as president of the Board of Aldermen, became acting mayor, and one of his first moves was to direct me to investigate police activities at Coney Island, about which he had received a complaint. Wide open conditions of vice and immorality were discovered, and Mitchel and I both appeared before the grand jury. The result was the dismissal of a police inspector, and the indictment of a police captain, a sergeant and ten patrolmen, together with eleven keepers of disorderly houses.

When Gaynor returned to the City Hall from his recuperation he immediately sent for me and demanded an explanation of the incident. He was furiously angry—not at me, because I had acted under orders, but at Mitchel who, he claimed, had "usurped" his authority. Although he himself frequently criticized the police, he was sensitive about criticism directed at them by anybody else. Moreover he had a theory of what he called "outward order and decency," and he was suspicious of people who probed into vice. "They have evil minds," he said, "and it is none of their business."

In only one instance—and it was a few months after I had been appointed commissioner—did he ever interfere with an investigation which my office had undertaken; but that interference almost led to my resignation. The investigation had to do with an alleged improper relationship between Dr. Daniel C. Potter, a former Baptist minister who had an important position in the comptroller's office, and a group of Roman Catholic charitable institutions which, together with other denominational groups, were receiving subsidies from the city for the care of homeless children. I was asked to undertake the investigation by the comptroller, who was himself a Catholic, and the request was emphatically endorsed by Judge Gaynor.

I had taken testimony from only about half a dozen witnesses when the mayor directed me to drop the investigation. He said it was being misunderstood by our Catholic friends and it wasn't worth-while to start a religious war over the matter. Bewildered by his change of front, I argued strongly that to stop the inquiry and leave the accuracy of the charges and counter charges undetermined would be unfair to the parties concerned, and would involve my office in the suspicion that we were open to political or ecclesiastical pressure. But the mayor was adamant and the investigation was halted.

Mitchel who had strong ideas about the independence of the

Commissioners of Accounts' office thought I ought to resign, and argued the matter forcefully. In my uncertainty I went down to Princeton to get Woodrow Wilson's advice, although, knowing his temperament, I was inclined to believe that he would endorse Mitchel's opinion, in which case I was prepared to retire. To my surprise he took the contrary line. It was a matter of judgment between points of view, he said, and the mayor as my superior officer had made the decision. The responsibility did not rest on my shoulders, and he thought I would be foolish to make an issue of the matter by resigning. With an eased conscience, therefore, I accepted his advice.

A few months later the dispute erupted again. A movement was started to appoint Dr. Potter to the Board of Ambulance Service, and the mayor, who had only recently returned from his recuperation following the attempted assassination, rather weakly, so it seemed to me, swung his influence behind it. He asked me to give him a statement that my investigation, as far as it went, had shown no grounds for criticism of Potter, and when I somewhat angrily declined, he in turn lost his temper, and our interview terminated in an acrimonious exchange.

That night I married Winifred Finlay in Montclair, New Jersey, a Wellesley graduate of charm and radiance to whom I had been engaged for over a year; and we left on our wedding trip uncertain whether my position as commissioner would be waiting for me when we got back. But apparently the mayor quickly forgot the incident. Ten days afterward he sent me a telegram asking whether it would be possible for me to advance the date of my return home in order to undertake an investigation of the Board of Elections, so that the findings would be ready for the state legislature when it convened a month later. Of course we came back, and I remember that that particular investigation was one of the most difficult and complex of any I ever handled.

Thereafter for nearly two years I managed to get along with the mayor as well as any of his commissioners did. He had our respect and in a certain sense our admiration, but never our affection.

*

In retrospect the years I served as Commissioner of Accounts were more arduous and exhausting than any other period in my life. We were continually at war on many fronts, and there were no intervals of relief. A man who enlists in the public service, if he does his duty, must reconcile himself to a fighting career. With us one investigation followed another, and often half a dozen were being simultaneously developed. I examined all the witnesses and wrote all the reports except those relating to our current audits. In many cases the reports were followed by reorganizations, dismissals or indictments, and consequently a great deal of subsequent work was necessary. There were constant conferences in other departments of the administration, and my appearances before grand juries were frequent. I remember one day, indeed, when I had to appear before three grand juries, in Manhattan, Brooklyn and Richmond, on three different sets of facts. As our reports to the mayor were always given to the press, my contacts with newspapermen were continuous, and some of the lasting friendships of my life grew out of this association. I used to see the City Hall reporters on the morning papers at five o'clock almost every afternoon, and I often managed to squeeze in an interview with the afternoon press reporters some time during the morning. My wife frequently declared that she might as well have married a doctor because the telephone bell at our home rang all night long.

On top of this work which crowded my days I accepted many invitations to speak before various kinds of groups—citizens' committees, local schools and colleges, political clubs and church organizations. Early in his administration Mayor Gaynor agreed to speak at an evening service in a Methodist church in the Bronx, and he asked me to go with him and tell the audience about the work I was doing. At the conclusion of the meeting he said to me: "I think it would be helpful if you took time to do that whenever you can." I adopted his suggestion, and while it added to a burden that was almost more than I could carry, I felt that it was a useful contribution to public education in the problems of municipal government.

Although I prepared the outlines of my talks with care I always spoke extempore, and today, except for a few addresses that were printed at the time, or are preserved in newspaper files, I am unable to recall precisely what my message was. I do remember, however, that I was concerned about the responsibility of citizenship for creating an atmosphere in which honest and effective government could develop; and one address on this theme which I made before an association of manufacturers has survived. In it I said some harsh things about the encouragement which business interests gave to laxity and even dishonesty in the conduct of the city's affairs. "The moral level of a government cannot rise above the moral level of the citizens behind it," I said. ". . . The bitter phase of the work of a conscientious public official is that the fight, to so large an extent, must be waged against his own people."

My advantage in making a speech like this was that I could support these obvious generalizations with concrete facts which we had dug up in our investigations, and I never hesitated to do so. Indeed one of my talks, according to a newspaper account, bore the title: "Success in New York"—the phrase which a witness had used to justify his "gifts" to building inspectors. "Here we have the true secret of the situation," I said, "the hurrying greedy rush for success before which even our civic ideals go down."

There certainly was nothing original about this kind of preachment. It goes back at least to Plato and his simple statement: "The basis of good government is citizens who are good men." But perhaps in the era of the Gaynor administration, when the corruption of municipal officials was the chief target of attack, it did no harm to underscore the other aspect of the problem, and remind the public that the insidious foes of honest government were often the "good people"—the contractors, the manufacturers, the landlords, the business men—who tried to obtain by pressure or purchase special favors to which they were not entitled. "In the last analysis," I said, "it is *they* who determine the character of government. They set the tone. They are the responsible parties."

*

As I reached the midyear of 1912 I began to realize with increasing clarity that due perhaps to his declining health the momentum with which Judge Gaynor had started his administration was falling off. He was involved in a row with the newspapers over the conduct of the police department and other issues, and his growing unpredictability and belligerency were beginning to thwart his own high standards. At the same time I was conscious, as of course I had been from the start, that there was no permanent career in the type of municipal work that I was doing, and that in a sense I was in a blind alley which led to no precise goal or future. For a man without independent means, this can be a disturbing factor, and when that summer an opening developed in Detroit which promised, among other things, the utilization of my training as a lawyer, I accepted it. It seemed at the time like a welcome escape from the New York years in which I had driven myself so relentlessly.

When I told the mayor of my decision, he gave expression to the only commendation I ever had from him. "I shall be sorry to have you go," he said simply, and we parted on a friendly basis. The date of my resignation was fixed a month off, so that I could clean my desk of current investigations.

The last report I submitted to the mayor—and we printed it in a pamphlet—was a slashing attack on billboard advertising in New York City, replete with many photographs of the scandalous conditions that existed. These billboards were often "double deckers" and "triple deckers," and on upper Fifth Avenue they confronted Central Park across the street for blocks, stretching from south of 96th Street north to 110th Street. They defaced Riverside Drive all the way up to Dyckman Street, and Grant's Tomb was almost surrounded by them. Central Park West in Manhattan and Eastern Parkway in Brooklyn were ruined from an aesthetic point of view, and the equestrian statue of George Washington in the Plaza at the entrance to the Williamsburg bridge was hidden behind strident claims to the virtues of various beers, soaps and movies.

My main attack in this report was directed at the court decisions which defeated the efforts of the city authorities to remove the billboards. "Aesthetic considerations," said one court, "are a matter of luxury and indulgence rather than of necessity, and it is necessity alone which justifies the exercise of the police power to take private property without compensation." Said another court with nonchalant finality: "This is simply an attempt to protect the aesthetic sense, hence invalid." There seemed to be something almost sacrilegious about such decisions, a kind of blind desecration, a denial of the age-old claim of beauty to a place in the lives of men. It was at this that I struck with emphasis in my report.

Years later my friend, Bob Moses, who has done so much to protect the aesthetic values of his time, told me that when he was a postgraduate student at Columbia University, a copy of my report on billboards came into his hands. I like to think that perhaps the seed of that final report fell on fertile ground; and I like to believe, too,—although this is an area where cause and effect are indeterminable—that the work that was done for decency and honesty in the government of New York nearly half a century ago was not without some consequence in the years that followed.

VII

*

European and American Police Systems

THE venture in Detroit proved abortive. I was asked to assist in the legal and financial reorganization of a large concern, and while I never thought of it as anything more than a stepping stone, it became obvious in less than a month that the company was too near the brink of bankruptcy to be salvaged. Just as I was returning to New York I received a letter from Woodrow Wilson, who had been nominated for President the preceding June, asking me if I would serve as comptroller and auditor of the finance committee of the Democratic National Committee. "I should myself feel greatly honored," he added in a warm and gracious sentence, "that a former pupil of mine, who has so distinguished himself in a position of trust, should turn to me at this time."

Without a moment's hesitation I complied with his request, for while I had always thought of myself as a Republican of the progressive stripe, I believed that in Woodrow Wilson the country would find inspiring leadership of a new and unique kind. Until election time, therefore, I had offices in the old Fifth Avenue Hotel in New York, the headquarters of the Democratic National Committee. At Wilson's direction we introduced, for the first time in the party's history, a strict budget system, with lines of accountability definitely established, and with periodic audits. In following this activity I visited the party's offices in Cleveland, Cincinnati, Pittsburgh, Chicago, and St. Louis. Our methods came as a shock to the old guard of the Democratic Party. They were not used to that sort of thing and they doubtless put it down as one of the inexplicable peccadilloes of the man to whom in more disparaging moments they referred as "that Princeton professor."

It was an interesting lot of people stationed at the headquarters in New York. William G. McAdoo was there, later Secretary of the Treasury—tall, lean and incisive; and Josephus Daniels, afterward Secretary of the Navy, with his North Carolina accent, his black string ties, and his genial friendliness; and the affable Henry Morgenthau, whom we immediately dubbed "Uncle Henry" and who subsequently served as our Ambassador to Turkey. Billy McCombs was also there—the tragic figure whose promising career was brought to an end by ill health and an ill-adjusted temperament. And then there was a tall, slender, handsome young fellow of great charm—a year older than I was—a man of whom we were all deeply fond. We called him Frank or Franklin. Twenty years later we called him Mr. President.

Wilson himself occasionally dropped in at the headquarters, and some of us went down to Princeton to get his advice. It was a time of intense excitement, especially when Theodore Roosevelt was shot by a would-be assassin, and Wilson temporarily suspended his campaign. The night before election Wilson spoke before a madly cheering audience at Madison Square Garden. He was hoarse and tired, and the meeting was not the kind of occasion for which he was adapted or which he particularly enjoyed. But he acquitted himself magnificently and sent the crowd away with the feeling that a new kind of intelligence had been recruited to serve the public interest.

With the close of the campaign I found myself confronted with a number of possible openings. District Attorney Whitman renewed an earlier offer to appoint me as a special assistant in the trial of Lieutenant Charles Becker of the police department, which promised to be, as indeed it became, one of the most sensational murder cases in the history of the city. But this seemed to me to lead to no concrete goal, and I declined. The governor-elect of New York, William Sulzer, wanted to appoint me chairman of an investigating commission which would serve the state as the Commissioners of Accounts office was serving the city; but this would have taken me back into public life again, and after my five years experience it held no illusions. Two or three attractive business offers developed, but business did not in any way appeal to me. I was interested in law and government, and in my heart I cherished the somewhat nebulous notion of a law practice which would enable me to concern myself with the problems of government without the necessity of holding office.

It was at this moment that John D. Rockefeller, Jr. approached me with a suggestion which after considerable deliberation I accepted. In brief he wanted me to make a broad study of police organization in Europe for the Bureau of Social Hygiene which he had recently created. I had first met Mr. Rockefeller in 1910 when he was chairman of the special grand jury in Manhattan investigating the so-called white slave traffic. A trim, youthful-looking figure, eight or nine years older than I, he had called at my office to discuss the problems growing out of his grand jury experience. The findings of the jury had profoundly disturbed him, and in his earnest way he was searching for some method by which what was then euphemistically known as "the social evil"—as if there were no others—could be continuously and scientifically studied. Thereafter I had seen him on two or three occasions, and once I had been the speaker at the annual dinner of his Bible class.

The result of his deliberations was the formation of the Bureau of Social Hygiene, and one of its first steps was to send Abraham Flexner to Europe to study the methods in various countries of controlling prostitution. Flexner's book, *Prostitution in Europe,* is even today one of the great classics in its field. He came back from Europe with the idea that the regulation of prostitution is so intimately related to efficient police organization that until that problem was solved there was little hope of advance in the field which he had been studying. It was this thinking, therefore, that led Mr. Rockefeller to ask me to undertake the investigation. I had had an intimate acquaintance with the police department of New York, and my experience seemed to provide the necessary background.

I estimated that it would take me a year to carry out the assignment—six months in field work and six months to write the book; and because it promised to be an interesting experience I decided that I could afford that amount of time. If I had known that it would take two years instead of one to finish the task, and that I would then go on for another two years to a similar study of police organization in America; if I had realized that this specialized interest would lead in turn to a government assignment on the Mexican border, and later, by a natural step to similar duty in Washington in the First World War; if I had foreseen that the path from Washington would take me into an entirely new concept of governmental activity—the League of Nations—I doubt if I would have had the courage or the desire to wander so far from my original pattern.

Early in January, 1913, my wife and I sailed for Europe, and we were gone for ten months. My first stop was Scotland Yard where I spent nine weeks getting an intimate acquaintance with British concepts and methods of police organization. I carried letters of introduction which opened all doors not only in London but in every European city which I visited, and everywhere I was most hospitably received. The Home Secretary arranged for an office for my use in Scotland Yard where I could see the inside working of the system, and this was the practice in almost every city I went to, even in bureaucratic Berlin, where I had a room in the headquarters on Alexanderplatz. My itinerary took me to practically every large city in Europe except those in Russia. I tried to obtain permission to visit St. Petersburg and Moscow, but when the imperial Russian authorities—for these were the days of the empire—learned the nature of my errand, I was politely informed that such an inquiry would be impossible, which indicates, perhaps, that what we think of today as Communist suspicion and intransigence have their age-old roots in Russian character and custom.

In every city I visited I tried to see the police in actual operation. I went on patrol with the London "Bobbies" and watched their courteous procedures in arresting and arraigning prostitutes and drunks. I listened to them testify in the police courts and occasionally in Old Bailey. I saw them handle with the greatest good nature and gentleness crowds of violently disposed suffragettes. "Now lady," I heard one of them say, as he picked up his battered helmet from the ground, "if you do that again I shall be obliged to take you into custody." I saw a large squad of them standing unmoved and apparently unobservant as well-aimed stones were being hurled at them by a group of strikers. When ordered to charge they did so calmly and deliberately. Scorning to use their truncheons—the only weapons they carried—they rolled up their rubber ponchos and with these implements beat back their assailants. The disorder was effectively quelled and nobody was hurt.

In Berlin where methods of crime detection had been highly developed I joined the squad of specialists created to deal with the *next* murder (there were less than a dozen murders a year in Berlin at that time); and when the anticipated crime occurred I watched the careful scientific analysis by which it was promptly solved. In Budapest I went with a group of detectives when they raided an illegal gambling establishment and an unregistered house of prostitution; and in Paris I had many opportunities to watch the *Brigade de Sûreté* in its daily work with important felonies.

During my study I met some extraordinarily interesting and able people attached to the various police forces. Sir Edward Henry was at that time Commissioner of Police in London. A university graduate, he had spent his entire life in police work—in India, South Africa, and later as head of the Criminal Investigation Department of Scotland Yard. He had introduced from India the fingerprint system of identification, and there was scarcely a problem in police theory or practice which he was not equipped to handle. Karl Ritter von Brzesowsky, president of the police force of Vienna, was another outstanding man —a university graduate who had served for twenty-eight years in various police posts before he had been appointed to his present position. A man of charm and wide cultural interests, he and I kept in touch with each other for several years, and his photograph was on my desk long after the First World War had rung down the curtain between Austria and the United States.

Another interesting figure was Alphonse Bertillon, head of the Criminal Identification Department of the police force of Paris. In 1883 he had introduced his system of anthropometry, or bodily measurements, as a means of criminal identification. It was based on the fact that the dimensions of certain bony portions of the human frame do not vary between adolescence and old age, and Bertillon employed this principle as a primary method of classifying criminals, although he used fingerprints as a sub-classification. When I was in Europe a bitter struggle was being waged between this method and Sir Edward Henry's fingerprint system, and I listened to many fiery arguments from the likable Bertillon. The inability of the Paris police to discover the perpetrator of the theft of *Mona Lisa* from the Louvre was the final blow to the anthropometric system, and Bertillon died the following year. It seems that the thief had been in the hands of the Paris police on a previous occasion when his fingerprints, along with his measurements, were taken. Fingerprint impressions were left on the frame of the picture, but his record in the file was not found, because measurements rather than fingerprints constituted the primary classification. As a Paris newspaper satirically commented: "Unfortunately this discourteous thief neglected to leave his measurements at the scene of the crime." Under the Henry system his identity could have been established in a matter of minutes.

The outstanding impression I received from my study in Europe was that police administration there was a distinct career which attracted the best brains obtainable. With few exceptions it was divorced from politics. Its elaborate training schools for recruits had no counterpart in the United States. Its methods of crime detection were based on scientific procedures far beyond anything that was known in America at that time. As I said in the conclusion of my book, *European Police Systems:*

> The European police department is on the whole an excellent piece of machinery. To its construction a high order of creative intelligence has been devoted; in its operation an equally high order of intelligence is constantly employed. . . . [It] bears an excellent reputation. Scandals are infrequent. With few exceptions both officers and men have the confidence of the public. It is only occasionally that one hears of dishonesty. Even suspicions of dishonesty are not common. The police are not associated with dishonesty in public imagination.

Perhaps the most important safeguard against police corruption is negative in character. The European police are not called upon to enforce standards of conduct which do not meet with general public approval. There is little attempt to make a particular code of behavior the subject of general criminal legislation. The high moral standards of a few people are not the legal requirements of the state. . . . The distinction between what is criminal and what is merely vicious is on the whole clearly drawn . . . and the functions of the police are not confused with those of the church, the school, and other organizations and influences by which civilization is advanced.

*

In the middle of 1914 I went back to Europe to have my manuscript read by the police authorities in London, Paris, Berlin and Rome. I wanted to be certain that the factual basis of my narrative, as distinct from its elements of judgment and interpretation, was unquestionably accurate. While in Rome, at the request of Arthur Woods, police commissioner in New York City, I succeeded in making an arrangement with the Ministry of the Interior by which the fingerprints and photographs of Italians arrested for serious crimes in New York would be sent to Rome to determine whether the defendants had had previous criminal records in their home country. If so, under United States laws, they could be deported. This agreement worked admirably under the Woods' administration, and was continued, so I understand, in later years.

My book was published at the end of the year, and while it was widely reviewed in the United States it seemed to excite more interest in Europe. My friend, Henry A. Moe, of the Guggenheim Foundation, tells me that when he first enrolled in Oxford as a Rhodes scholar in 1924, he was given two books: Sir Henry Maine's *Ancient Law,* and my book on European police! It was translated into a number of languages, and while time and two world wars have now rendered it out of date, it was, I think, the first systematic attempt to paint on a broad canvas the workings of the police systems of an entire continent. "It is surprising," said the *New Statesman* of London in its review, "that no one should have thought of writing this book before."

Coming back from Europe in 1914 the ship on which I was traveling was rammed by another boat in the English Channel during a fog, and we were transferred to a German liner, the *Imperator*. Among its passengers was Theodore Roosevelt, who was returning from the marriage of his son, Kermit, in Spain. Several times I had heard him speak on public occasions, but I had never met him. Learning from a mutual friend that I had been studying police systems in Europe he invited me to have dinner with him in his stateroom. I was the only guest. As I entered the room he rose from his chair, shook me warmly by the hand, and exclaimed in his falsetto voice: "Fosdick! Dee-lighted! I hear you have been looking into police methods in Europe. I have always wanted to know about them. Sit down and tell me everything. Now when I was a police commissioner in New York . . ."

What followed was the most fascinating monologue I ever listened to. It continued during the dinner and through the evening. Except for an occasional question I never said a word. Early in the proceedings he left the police field entirely. One topic would suggest another and he never came back to his point of departure. His police experience in New York suggested the policing of the Panama Canal, and from that he jumped to a great variety of subjects, talking with the animation and vivacity which were so characteristic.

I remember that he told me among other things of his difficulties with South American republics, of his relations with the Vatican, of his talks with the German emperor and his opinion of the German army. It was as enjoyable an evening as I ever spent, and when I rose to go he again shook me warmly by the hand and said with his staccato emphasis: "Fosdick! I appreciate this very much. I always wanted to know how Europe managed its police!" He was entirely sincere, and I am certain he was unaware of the fact that I had scarcely spoken a sentence during the evening.

We reached quarantine in New York harbor too late at night for the passengers to disembark, but Roosevelt and a few friends were taken off in a private yacht and I was invited to go with them. As Roosevelt stood on the yacht, with the side of the massive ship towering above him, and the searchlights focused on him, every deck and every porthole were lined with faces. With his sense of the dramatic, he took off his hat and waved it again and again with a youthful enthusiasm, while the passengers and the crew answered with a burst of cheering such as I have seldom heard. It would have been impossible for Woodrow Wilson to do this; he would have found it ostentatious and distasteful. But with Roosevelt it was a spontaneous outpouring of his own inner ebullience; it was part of the magnetic charm which gave him so wide a following.

Just as I was finishing the police book Woodrow Wilson asked me to take the position of Commissioner of Immigration at the Port of New York, with headquarters at Ellis Island. I had no desire to return to public office and I declined. Whereupon the President wrote me urging my reconsideration of the matter. "I should not deem myself faithful to my public responsibilities," he said, "if I did not make a very earnest effort to open your mind again on the subject, and to turn it toward acceptance, so strongly do I feel that you are the very man we need for just that place." He asked me to come to Washington to see him if I had further doubts.

With a heavy heart I went to the White House. I knew from

long experience how irresistibly persuasive he could be. And it was as I expected. He reverted to his favorite theme of "Princeton in the Nation's service." He drew a vivid picture of what Ellis Island could be made to be. Here hundreds of thousands of immigrants every year got their first impression of America. It must be a good impression—an impression of America at her best. The tawdry surroundings of Ellis Island could be transformed into a kind of laboratory of human relations. We could make these future citizens feel that they were indeed coming to a new home—a home that was glad and proud to welcome them, and that would do everything within its power to unite them with the family of democracy. The job required high imagination and patience. It was a challenge—a worthy challenge to a Princeton man.

I do not know how I escaped his spell. I am sure I was not entirely articulate. He was courteous as always, but I could sense his displeasure, and I left the White House feeling that I had sinned against the light. Even today, more than forty years later, my conscience occasionally troubles me when I recall my stubborn refusal.

*

The problems of police administration as they affected the lives of human beings in modern society had become for me a fascinating study, and while I was finishing my book I was chosen as associate editor of the *American Journal of Crime and Criminology*, through whose columns I tried to develop public interest in the studies of criminal methods and criminal psychology which were being carried on in European universities by such experts—then unknown in America—as Hans Gross, Alfredo Niceforo and R. A. Reiss. In such circumstances Mr. Rockefeller's suggestion that I undertake a survey of the American police problem appealed to me, and I entered upon it with enthusiasm.

In the course of the inquiry I visited every city in the United States with a population of 100,000 or over. My European book gave me easy access, and I had the same hospitable reception which I had received abroad. The contrast between the situation on the two sides of the Atlantic was disillusioning. As I traveled from east to west across the continent I could not help remembering the conscious pride of European cities in their police, and the atmosphere of public confidence in which they carried on their work. I recalled the unbroken record of rectitude which many of their forces maintained, and their endeavor to create, with the aid of expert leadership, a maturing profession. I remembered, too, the infinite pains with which the police administrators were trained and chosen, and the care with which the forces were shielded from political influence.

And what did I find in the United States in that study of over forty years ago? Perhaps a paragraph from my book can best summarize the situation:

In America the student of police travels from one political squabble to another, too often from one scandal to another. He finds a shifting leadership of mediocre calibre—varied now and then by flashes of real ability which are snuffed out when the political wheel turns. There is little conception of policing as a profession or as a science to be matured and developed. It is a *job*, held perhaps by the grace of some mysterious political influence, and conducted in an atmosphere sordid and unhealthy. Instead of confidence and trust, the attitude of the public toward the police is far more often than not one of cynicism and suspicion, expressing itself, occasionally, in violent attacks which are as unjust as they are ineffective. In the interim between these spasms of publicity the average police force sinks in its rut, while crime and violence flourish.

There were mitigating factors, however, which tended to cancel out some of my harsh comment. In the first place I found that American police were overwhelmed with a volume of crime which would have broken the backs of even the best forces in Europe. In the year that I was abroad, London with a population of seven millions and a quarter had nine murders. That year Chicago, one third the size of London, had 105, while New York City had over 200. Indeed New York and Chicago each had annually more murders than the whole of England, Scotland and Wales put together. Equally significant were the burglary statistics. New York and Chicago had eight times the number of burglaries that London had; and even cities like Detroit and Cleveland far exceeded London in this category of crime. Robberies or "hold-ups" showed an even more amazing disparity, with London's annual quota of approximately twenty matched by New York's average of 900. Continental statistics were difficult to obtain due to dissimilar definitions of crime, but it was obvious that Europe's figures were far below ours.

In the second place, Europe's police dealt with homogeneous populations with long established traditions and fixed patterns of social habit; while American police, on the other hand, were called upon to enforce the same laws among a score of races and maintain a standard of conduct in a population coming from radically diverse environments. As I said in my book: "To see a London 'Bobby' at work, dealing with people of his own race who understand him and whom he understands, is to learn a larger sympathy for his brother officer who walks the beat in New York, Chicago or San Francisco."

Nevertheless, with all allowances for the peculiar conditions which made our police task so difficult, America, forty years ago, had little to be proud of. The achievement was sordid and unworthy, and our progress, such as it was, had fallen far behind our needs. We had failed in the elemental responsibility, laid on all peoples who call themselves civilized, of preserving order in their communities. If the frankness of my book disturbed the complacency of many citizens—and the countrywide outcry that greeted its publication indicated that it did —that was the purpose I had in mind in writing it.

As I say, this was forty years ago, and I have had no contact with the police problem in the decades intervening. But my old friend and associate, Dr. Luther Gulick, whose life work has been given to governmental affairs, tells me that the situation has vastly improved. The rise of state police systems and of the Federal Bureau of Investigation has been accompanied in many parts of the country by new standards in municipal police work, and while America is still overburdened by its volume of crime, and there is still much to be done if our methods and effectiveness are to keep step with our problems, the old days that I knew are apparently gone—days when in a few cities the entire police personnel changed with an overturn on election day, when fingerprints were filed in the order in which they were taken because there was no one in the department who knew how to classify them, and when policemen on patrol duty in the streets smoked cigars!

*

It seems odd to say that my work for the next three years was determined by a Mexican bandit, but it is true. His name was Pancho Villa, and his raid across the border in March, 1916, had consequences which reached into many American lives. That summer our entire National Guard was hastily mobilized on the Mexican border, and complaints began to pour into Washington about the evil and demoralizing conditions surrounding the camps. The newspapers carried lurid stories of lack of discipline, drunkenness and the rise of venereal disease. Newton D. Baker, who had only recently been appointed Secretary of War, was much disturbed, and one day early in July he sent me a telegram asking me, if possible, to come to Washington to see him.

I had first met Baker on some legal business in 1909, when he was City Solicitor of Cleveland, and I was Assistant Corporation Counsel in New York; and later during the Wilson campaign of 1912, I had had several conferences with him. A graduate of Johns Hopkins University, he was, like Woodrow Wilson, a scholar in politics, and between the two men, as I was later to discover, were strong ties of mutual respect and affection. He shared with Wilson a deep social insight, a supreme ability to articulate his ideas in felicitous words, and a superb courage. In addition he had what Wilson did not possess, at least to the same degree: a singularly serene and gracious mind. The President in 1913 had tried to appoint him Secretary of the Interior, but Baker had felt that his first allegiance was to the mayoralty of Cleveland to which he had recently been elected. Now in 1916 Wilson had finally persuaded him to enter his cabinet. Short in stature and frail in physique, he was to prove himself a giant of strength in the titanic struggle which was so soon to overwhelm the nation. When I took the train for Washington on that hot day in July, I could not foresee that I was entering upon an intimate friendship which would last over many years.

Baker had in mind a challenging suggestion. In brief he wanted me to go to the Mexican border as his personal representative and find out just what the situation was. Was it as bad as it was being painted? "Let's first get the exact facts," he said, "and then we can come to a conclusion as to what, if anything, we ought to do." Within a week, therefore, I was on my way to the border, preceded by military orders to General Frederick Funston, the regular army officer in command of the entire area, giving me complete access to all types of army installations.

I could not have asked for a more cordial reception than I

received at Funston's headquarters in San Antonio. And yet there was a quizzical twinkle in the eyes of the general and of some of his fellow officers. They never put it in words but their implied question was what did this new Secretary of War think that soldiers were like. Men were men and "sissies" were not wanted in the army. If anyone supposed that human nature could be changed, particularly in the fighting forces, he was headed for disillusionment. Indeed, Funston, whom I came to like very much, bestowed on me the nickname "Reverend." It was not that he confused me with my brother Harry, for Harry was not known in army circles at that time. But he assumed that anybody interested in such an errand as mine, and whose report to the Secretary of War would undoubtedly be geared to some impracticable ideal, was probably a professional "do-gooder" to whom an ecclesiastical title should be attached. It was as "Reverend," therefore, that I was passed on from one army command to another along the Mexican border from Brownsville, Texas, to western Arizona.

What I found out in that five-weeks trip was recorded in my confidential report to the Secretary of War. It was an almost unrelieved story of army camps surrounded by growing batteries of saloons and houses of prostitution. Ten new saloons to accommodate the troops had opened in Laredo in the month before my visit, and others were being planned. In other parts of Texas new saloons had sprung up on the roads leading to the camps and even on property immediately adjoining the military establishments. In still other places temporary shacks fringing the camps had been erected for the sale of liquor to the soldiers. In Douglas, Arizona, a prohibition state, liquor was freely and openly sold to the troops in so-called "resorts."

As for prostitution, town after town was enlarging its facilities to meet the military demand. "Crib" buildings, similar to the vicious type which I had seen in San Francisco and New

Orleans during my study of police systems, were being erected in many of the red light districts, and according to the police large numbers of prostitutes from all over the country were flocking into such centers as San Antonio, Laredo and El Paso. The red light districts at night, particularly on pay-day nights, were crowded with hundreds of troops, and drunken riots which were not infrequent had to be suppressed by the Provost Guard. Meanwhile the venereal disease rates were soaring.

The difficulty with the situation, as I told the Secretary of War, was that no uniform policy in relation to this situation had been developed by the army, and the ideas and attitudes of the divisional and camp commanders showed the widest variation. Most of the regular army officers, including Funston, shrugged it off as a hopeless problem, but occasionally a camp commander would take the initiative. In Columbus, New Mexico, the town authorities, at the request of the army officials, had created two restricted districts—one for white soldiers and one for colored soldiers—located on the edge of the encampment. On the other hand, one or two of the National Guard commanders—notably General O'Ryan of the New York militia—rigorously used his military police to put saloons and houses of prostitution out of bounds for the troops. Many enlightened citizens in places like El Paso, for example, were concerned about the growing demoralization of their communities, and looked in vain to the top army command for light and leadership.

In my report to the Secretary I recommended that the War Department take a definite stand "in the interest of the efficiency of its troops" against the unrestrained excesses of prostitution and the saloon. "Under present conditions," I said, "every commanding officer deals with it as he sees fit, without relation to anything that any other division is doing. What is needed is a strong word from Washington." I advocated that all "crib" sections be put out of bounds. "The Provost Guard could starve out these vicious areas in a week." I suggested close cooperation between the army and the municipal authorities in enforcing existing laws, and I recommended that if a community proved recalcitrant or bowed to the powerful forces behind these evils, the troops be moved to another site.

The "strong word" from Washington was immediately forthcoming. Secretary Baker sent my report, through Funston, to all commanding officers on the Mexican border. "I am entirely satisfied," he wrote, "that the time has come when the health of the army must be safeguarded against the weakness that derives from venereal disease and the excessive use of alcohol." He endorsed my suggestion that unless communities cooperated in preserving more wholesome conditions, "the troops be removed to other places"; and he ended his letter with the sentence which rattled around the ears of the commanders on the border: "I want you to realize that I will support and sustain every effort you make for the accomplishment of the object set forth." The letter was supplemented by a general order.

Baker was no novice in this field. He had been mayor of a large city, and had dealt with these problems for years. As he said in his letter, he realized that "gradual and wise restraint and restriction are more effective and more permanently helpful than sudden and spasmodic attempts at complete suppression." But he knew, too, that there was no excuse for a wide open community and that determination and vigilance were the price that had to be paid for reasonably decent conditions.

For me he had another suggestion: would I return to the border to talk not only with the army people, but with the mayors, the chiefs of police, and the citizens, and underscore the new thinking and the new directives of the War Department? On the long, dusty train ride back to Texas—for there were no commercial airplanes in those days—I began to sort

out some of the impressions I had received in my trip along the
Rio Grande and beyond. I remembered the five thousand troops
encamped just across the railroad tracks from Columbus, New
Mexico, and the way they used to come to town every evening
—almost in a body—to escape the monotony of camp life. And
what did they find when they came to town? There were no
moving picture shows and no pool tables; there was no place
where they could read or write letters; there were no homes to
which they could go; there wasn't even a newsstand where they
could purchase a magazine or a newspaper. The only attractions
in town were a few disreputable saloons and a red light district.
These institutions had the field all to themselves; there was
nothing to compete with them.

I remembered, too, that in most of the camps there was no
athletic equipment of any kind—no baseballs, bats or mitts, no
footballs, no basketballs, no playing fields or courts of any kind.
And there were no books or magazines, either, and sometimes
when the train stopped at a crossroads a group of soldiers would
come aboard and ask the passengers if they had any reading
material they could spare—even a newspaper. I remembered
how the train crews used to lock the doors of the coaches as we
approached some of the stations because otherwise the soldiers
would come in and drink up all the ice water. I remembered
the utter boredom and dejection with which groups of men in
uniform would walk the streets of the town or village near their
camp, in a pathetic hunt for diversion or for any normal or familiar sight or sound. And I recalled, too—and it was the one
bright spot in the picture—the imaginative beginnings of the
work of the Army and Navy Branch of the Y.M.C.A. in supply-
ing athletic equipment for some of the army posts. It was a task
far beyond their limited funds and was totally inadequate to the
need, but it was at least an affirmative gesture in an otherwise
melancholy environment.

"The situation has improved on the Mexican border," I wrote Secretary Baker on my return to New York. "The cribs are closed, at least for the moment, and so are most of the fly-by-night saloons on the roads to the camps. But you and I have had enough experience in city government to know that this *verboten* approach isn't going to accomplish a great deal. It's *part* of the answer, but it isn't the whole answer, although in terms of precedence it may have to come first. The real question to which as yet we have *no* answer is what are we going to substitute for the things we want to drive out. We can't operate in a vacuum. We're up against a competitive situation here, and something on a pretty ambitious scale will have to be done."

Baker picked up the challenge with enthusiasm. "Come on down here," he wrote, "and we'll put our feet on the desk and talk it over." That fall, therefore, he and I had two or three long conferences in his office in the War Department. We thought we were talking about the Mexican border. In fact, although we were unaware of it, we were discussing ways and means of normalizing the life of the American soldier in the greatest war in which the United States, up to that time, had ever been involved.

VIII

*

Training Camps in
World War I

THOSE of us who crowded into the Capitol on the evening
of April 2, 1917—and few of us are left—to hear Woodrow
Wilson deliver his great war address before the joint session of
Congress will never forget the impact of his moving eloquence.

> We shall fight for the things which we have always carried near-
> est our hearts—for democracy, for the right of those who submit
> to authority to have a voice in their own governments, for the
> rights and liberties of small nations, for a universal dominion of
> right by such a concert of free peoples as shall bring peace and
> safety to all nations and make the world itself at last free.

Forty years later it is difficult to recapture the mood of dedication and crusade which his words inspired. The nation was
united behind a compelling ideal. Before us stretched a shining
prospect, and it seemed as if our generation by some divine
providence had been specially chosen for great and determining events.

A few days later I ran into Lillian Wald in the railroad station
in Washington. With Jane Addams she had gone to the White
House on a hopeless mission, and there were tears in her eyes
and she looked distraught. Placing her hands on my arms in a

characteristic gesture she said: "Raymond, this is wicked, wicked. It must somehow be stopped." She was thinking of the long future and saw it in a different and perhaps truer perspective; and I have always regretted the impatience and exasperation with which I shook her off. But at the moment I had little time for such thoughts, for Baker had sent for me, and I was on my way to make a study of military training camps in Canada.

Back again in Washington, a few weeks later, I reported to the Secretary, and we drew up a plan, which we discussed with the President, for the creation of a Commission on Training Camp Activities. In later years, with his characteristic generosity, Baker was inclined to give me the credit for the genesis of the idea, but while I may have contributed to his thinking by my reports on Canada and the Mexican border, it was his grasp and creative imagination which put the plan together. He had been mayor of a large city, and as a result of a lifetime of work with social agencies he had a sympathetic understanding of the problems of youth. "We will accept as the fundamental concept of our work," he wrote me, "the fact which every social worker knows to be true, that young men spontaneously prefer to be decent, and that opportunities for wholesome recreation are the best possible cure for irregularities in conduct which arise from idleness and the baser temptations."

The Commission on Training Camp Activities on which I served as chairman was launched, therefore, with the single purpose—and again I use Baker's words—"of rationalizing as far as it can be done the bewildering environments of a war camp." It was a commission of nine members representing different interests or specialties which we thought might prove useful: Lee F. Hanmer, Thomas J. Howells, Joseph Lee, Malcolm McBride, John R. Mott, Charles P. Neill, Lt. Col. Palmer E. Pierce, and Joseph E. Raycroft. Shortly thereafter, at the suggestion of the President, the Secretary of the Navy, Josephus

Daniels, appointed a Commission on Training Camp Activities to serve the Navy, and I became the chairman of this commission also, although there were some variations in personnel between the two bodies. However for all practical purposes the two organizations were one, and they turned out to be the most completely harmonious and certainly the most devoted and hard working groups with which I was ever associated. Around their efforts in the next two years was built what the *Survey Magazine* later called "the most stupendous piece of social work in modern times."

We were organized before the Military Draft Act was passed and before the camps had been created for the reception of the troops. Starting in a small office in the State, War and Navy Building, with my secretary and myself as its only occupants, we shortly were moved to larger quarters in the old Patent Office Building, then to a four-story apartment house near the War Department, and finally to a building which the government erected for us on Virginia Avenue—a building which, alone of all the temporary structures of the First World War, is still standing today. Beginning with one secretary we ended with a staff numbering in the thousands, located not only in Washington, but across the country and in Europe.

The complexion of our early work was determined—unexpectedly for me—by two sections of the Military Draft Act: sections 12 and 13, which were to have far reaching and unforeseen consequences. They prohibited the sale of liquor to men in uniform, and they gave the President the power to establish, around all military camps, broad zones in which prostitution was outlawed. At the request of the Secretary of War I appeared before the committees that were framing the act and testified about the conditions I had found on the Mexican border. As a result of a directive by the President the responsibility for overseeing the enforcement of these two sections of the law was given to the twin Commissions on Training Camp Activities. I would have preferred to have the positive side of our work take precedence over the negative aspects, but there was no choice, and we were launched into a resounding battle.

Our first problem was personnel. Fortunately as head of our new Law Enforcement Division we secured the services of Bascom Johnson, attorney for the American Social Hygiene Association. With his advice we recruited a group of forty young men—mostly lawyers—who were given commissions as lieutenants in the Sanitary Corps of the Surgeon General's office. Johnson became a major, and our approach to the problem, therefore, was not through civilians, but through men in uniform who could speak effectively for the armed forces. We divided the country into ten districts, each in charge of an officer who directed the activities of our fixed-post agents in army and navy camps.

The first movement in the campaign was a vigorous letter which Secretary Baker sent to the governors of all the states.

Our responsibility in this matter is not open to question. We cannot allow these young men, most of whom will have been drafted to service, to be surrounded by a vicious and demoralizing environment; nor can we leave anything undone which will protect them from unhealthy influences. . . . From the standpoint of our duty and our determination to create an efficient army, we are bound, as a military necessity, to do everything in our power to promote the health and conserve the vitality of the men in the training camps. I am determined that these camps, as well as the surrounding zones within an effective radius, shall not be places of temptation and peril.

The War Department intends to do its full part in these matters, but we expect the cooperation and support of the local communities. If the desired end cannot otherwise be achieved, *I*

propose to move the camps from those neighborhoods in which
clean conditions cannot be secured.

Baker's letter had an electric effect, and under the pressure
of local opinion some of the more sordid places began to dis-
appear. But it was by no means a uniform movement, and our
law enforcement officers whose primary job was "to prod the
communities" reported the existence of considerable skepticism
in regard to the serious intentions of the Federal government.
Mayors and sheriffs were asking whether this was not an
"idealistic program" put out for popular consumption. Even
army and navy officers questioned it. A general in charge of a
southern camp boldly wrote to the Board of Public Safety of a
neighboring city to the effect that a segregated district was the
best way to handle prostitution and the way most satisfactory
to him.

It took sharp measures to bring home to the local communities and the armed forces that the War and Navy Departments
were in earnest. Seattle, Washington, and Birmingham, Ala-
bama, were put out of bounds for soldiers and sailors until the
two cities cleaned up. Philadelphia, which perhaps gave us more
trouble than any other city in the United States, was finally
brought to terms only when Secretary Daniels put in a large
squad of marines to patrol the streets. San Antonio, Texas,
succumbed when Secretary Baker threatened to move the
troops. New Orleans, whose notorious red light district, covering twenty-eight city blocks, had not been disturbed in more
than half a century, put up a strenuous fight, and the mayor of
the city made two trips to Washington to argue with us about
"the God-given right of men to be men." It was not until
November, 1917, that the district was ultimately closed, and
the incident was noted throughout the country as a final and
complete indication of the government's attitude. Never there-

after was its sincerity in this matter questioned.

Once the tide began to turn, communities that were not included in military zones and were thus under no legal obligation to conform started cleaning house. Our argument had been not primarily one of morals, but of military necessity, for in those pre-penicillin days venereal disease was a far more crippling disability than it is now. We therefore hammered home, through the agency of a Social Hygiene Division which we created, the historic drag of this affliction on the efficiency of fighting forces. "Fit to fight" became a slogan which swept across the country, and by the end of 1917 I was able to report to the Secretary of War and the Secretary of the Navy that every red light district in the United States had been closed —a hundred and ten of them; that the venereal disease rate was the lowest in our military history; and that drunkenness among the troops on leave no longer represented a serious situation.

Of course the problem was a constant one which required eternal vigilance, and our Law Enforcement Division was active throughout the war. We found that the so-called "charity girls" who haunted the fringes of the camps were often carriers of venereal disease; and to meet this problem we added a section on women and girls under the inspired direction of Mrs. Jane Deeter Rippin, whose organization included nine district supervisors and nearly 150 field workers, all of them trained women, stationed in the vicinity of the camps. This activity created another problem—the question of the custody and rehabilitation of the girls whose commitment to institutions was found necessary. The jails were full, and the local authorities were unable to handle those sent to them by the courts. I remember a personal inspection of a woman's prison in Newport News, Virginia, where every single inch of floor space on three floors was covered with mattresses in an attempt to provide for the inmates. At Baker's request, the President gave us $250,000 from his war emergency fund to add additional institutional facilities, and we set up in our Commission a new section on reformatories and detention houses, under Mrs. Martha Falconer, to guide us in this difficult field.

*

All this work was absorbing and at times spectacular, but my real concern was the positive part of the program which I had dreamed about on the Mexican border, and in which Secretary Baker so deeply believed. At the first meeting of our Commission in April, 1917, I brought forward a tentative plan to invite the cooperation of three organizations to help in providing an adequate leisure-time program for the troops in the training camps: the Y.M.C.A., the American Library Association, and the Playground and Recreation Association (afterward known as the War Camp Community Service). We had come firmly to the conclusion that we wanted to work through existing agencies, and that we would create additional machinery only when necessary. The Y.M.C.A., after its experience on the Mexican border, was ready with an extensive program to build and administer the club houses and recreation centers we wanted in the training areas. The American Library Association could supply the millions of books, magazines and newspapers that would be required. The War Camp Community Service could develop the social and recreational assets of the neighboring cities, towns and villages to which the soldiers would naturally go when on leave.

At this first meeting we made a miscalculation which in my opinion was to have unhappy consequences. Baker and I had assumed—and I think that most of my associates on the Commission shared the assumption—that the approach of the Y.M.C.A. to its work in the camps would be nonsectarian. We thought that it would represent an American contribution without relation to creed or any other divisive factor. Indeed its unique position was recognized by the President's executive order issued after our meeting in which he characterized the organization as "an adjunct to the Service." It was with dismay, therefore, that I learned that the Y.M.C.A. had no real Catholic representation on its newly-formed War Work Council. My reaction was that it was an inadvertence, but I was told that the omission was "a necessity." Secretary Baker, who was as disturbed about the development as I was, immediately called a conference in the War Department, and made a strong appeal to the Y.M.C.A. representatives to have the decision reversed. He pointed out that otherwise it would be necessary to admit to the training camps a Catholic organization, probably a Jewish organization, and perhaps, indeed, other branches of the Protestant faith, like the Unitarians, which were not affiliated with the Y.M.C.A. The result would be a sectarian emphasis out of keeping with the work to be done or with the spirit of unity and cohesion which the government desired above all else to inculcate in the new army.

But the Y.M.C.A. representatives could not be swayed. They said that however much they might themselves desire it, they could not carry their wide-flung constituency with them. Under the circumstances we seemed to have no choice, and we decided that the Knights of Columbus, a Catholic organization, whose application for admission to the camps was pending before our Commission, should be included in the program.

I have always believed that the decision was inevitable but unfortunate. This is not said in any disparagement of the work of the Knights of Columbus or of the Jewish Welfare Board, whose representatives came into the training camps to share the activities of the Y.M.C.A. But in later months when I saw the three emblems—"K of C," "JWB" and "YMCA" so conspicuously displayed on huts, stationery, and even boxes of candy, I felt that this stratification struck a discordant note in an army whose soldiers were fighting as Americans, not as Catholics, Jews or Protestants. Nevertheless these three organizations did a superb job in providing the clubs (generally called huts) and other recreational centers and activities not only in the training camps of the United States but in the areas behind the lines in France.

Early in our work, another organization—the Y.W.C.A.— came forward with the imaginative idea of building in each camp a "hostess house" where the soldiers and sailors could meet their families and their girls under normal homelike conditions. The idea was received by the General Staff with a hoot of derision, but I had seen the mothers, sisters, and sweethearts of the troops standing desolately around the windy corners of the camps, or sitting on planks or cracker-boxes in the rain, waiting to see their men. It seemed to me that a hostess house, located near the entrance of the camp, with its comfortable appointments, large fireplaces, and adequate cafeteria, would be a profoundly normalizing influence in the environment of the troops. In spite of considerable military opposition based on a general dislike of having women "cluttering up the army," we tried it out at the training camp at Plattsburg, where it was an immediate and dramatic success. "Someday you will wear a halo," said a gruff old general to the Y.W.C.A. hostess, as he admitted his conversion to the "newfangled feminism" which he had strongly opposed; and the news spread so rapidly that soon I began to receive indignant telegrams from commanding officers in the various camps, the general tenor of which was: "Where is my hostess house?"

Equally effective and almost as dramatic was the work of the American Library Association in building well-equipped libraries, with attractive reading rooms, in all the large army and navy camps in the United States. They were staffed with experienced librarians, and as I told the House Military Affairs Committee: "Here [in these libraries] any book that a man wants can be had, whether it's a particular detective story or a technical book on engineering. Or if a soldier just wants to browse through the shelves he can browse. Or he can read the magazines and newspapers. Or if he wants to, he can find a comfortable chair to go to sleep in."

The work of the War Camp Community Service in mobilizing the hospitality and recreational facilities of the towns in the neighborhood of military establishments was another spectacular performance. The soldier on leave—even if his time off is limited to an hour or two—has an instinctive desire to get out of camp and "go to town." I saw it on the Mexican border and we knew it would be true of the new cantonments. With a high degree of imagination, therefore, the chambers of commerce, boards of trade, Rotary Clubs, churches, and fraternal groups, were organized behind a far flung attempt to make the communities attractive to the troops. There were club houses where the soldiers and sailors could write letters, play cards or read, billiards and pool places, gymnasiums, shower-baths, informal dances, and, above all, an opportunity to visit in friendly homes. "Take a soldier home for dinner" became a national slogan, and on Sundays in a single community as many as five thousand men were thus entertained. The facilities of over two hundred cities and towns were mobilized behind this multifarious program, with thousands of volunteer workers enlisted in the enterprise.

In all this work, carried on through private agencies both inside and outside the camps, the costs were borne by the agencies themselves, which raised millions of dollars for the purpose from private contributions. It took another generation and the outbreak of another war to obtain public support for the idea that club houses and books and many of the other factors that make for a rounded life within the limits of our military establishments are an essential part of the nation's direct responsibility toward its troops.*

*

Meanwhile, apart from its task of coordinating the work of the private societies, the Commission on Training Camp Activities was engaged in pursuits which could not be farmed out to an existing agency, but which represented an essential supplementation of the total program. For one thing, we were asked by the War Department to run the post exchanges in the new camps—stores where the troops could buy anything from candy, cake, doughnuts and milk to razor blades, magazines, newspapers and stationery. Inasmuch as there were from eleven to sixteen of these post exchanges in each camp, the undertaking represented a gigantic business responsibility, requiring the services of men specially trained in merchandising. We chose these men with scrupulous care, and the enterprise, which involved many difficulties and headaches, was carried to a successful conclusion.

Another of the Commission's projects involved the building and operation of the forty-two Liberty theaters that were erected in the camps, seating from one thousand to three thousand people. For the physical construction including scenery, drop-curtains and special lighting apparatus, Congress appropriated $1,500,000, although it required several appearances before the congressional committees to break down resistance to what was regarded as an unnecessary "frill." Our main task, however, was to organize a circuit or booking office

---

* In World War II the United Service Organizations (the USO), a group of private societies, carried on the same work in the communities adjacent to military establishments and centers which in World War I had been handled by the War Camp Community Service.

to keep the theaters in constant operation. For that purpose Secretary Baker appointed Marc Klaw, the theatrical manager, to membership on the Commission, and we selected a special committee to assist him made up of men like David Belasco, Lee Shubert, Arthur Hammerstein, George M. Cohan and Irving Berlin. A regular booking office was established, and theatrical companies were engaged and routed from camp to camp on a percentage basis of the gross box-office receipts. The cordial cooperation of the theatrical profession is shown by the fact that the leading actors and actresses of Broadway played at the Liberty theaters in such well-known current successes as *Fair and Warmer, Turn to the Right, Here Comes the Bride, Her Soldier Boy* and *Furs and Frills.* Vaudeville and movies were also included in the booking arrangements.

To raise funds to enable the theaters to start operations and to finance companies for the camp circuit, the Commission launched the so-called Smileage Book campaign, and booklets containing coupons exchangeable for tickets for the troops at the camp theaters were placed on sale to the public. It corresponded to the advance sale of theater tickets—good until used. Although I was somewhat skeptical about this last venture, it turned out to be enormously successful, bringing in around $3,000,000, and making the Liberty theaters one of the outstanding sources of entertainment in the military establishments.

Still another venture of our Commission was an idea we borrowed from the British army: the appointment of an athletic director in every training camp. Far more than we did, the British understood the relaxing and therapeutic effect of vigorous games, and only a month earlier, at the conclusion of the dreadful struggle for Vimy Ridge, they had had their men playing football almost before the battlefield was cleared. I had, myself, in the early days of the war, seen the invigorating effect of a baseball game on an exhausted squad of raw recruits returning to camp after a long hike. We came to the conclusion, therefore, not only that athletic supplies in quantity were necessary for the new army, but also that the administration of a carefully planned program should be in the hands of competent experts in each camp.

The program was in charge of Joseph E. Raycroft, a member of the Commission, and the results were beyond our expectations. "Never before in the history of this country," wrote a newspaper sports editor, "have so large a number of men engaged in athletics. Every kind of sport is involved—football, baseball, basket ball, volley ball, push ball, medicine ball, soccer, track and field athletics, and particularly boxing. Everybody's boxing, even the mountaineers and the boys from the farm who never saw a pair of boxing gloves in their lives. Men are learning to get bumped and not mind it. They eat it up." That was the spirit and the kind of army we wanted.

One final activity of our Commission deserves mention, and it was an activity in which I was especially interested. Four years earlier when I was in Europe—and this, of course, was before the war—I was fascinated by the singing of the German regiments as they swung along the country roads on their practice marches. There was a spontaneity and lift to it, and one got the impression that it brought a relief from tension and eased the long miles under heavy packs.

"Why shouldn't our army sing?" I said to Baker as I recounted my impressions.

"Let's give it a try," he replied, "although I warn you the suggestion will not be enthusiastically received by the General Staff."

With this encouragement we developed the idea of placing a carefully selected song leader in every army and navy camp

in the country. As a matter of precaution we first tried it out in
a small ambulance corps camp in Pennsylvania. I had already
talked to the commanding officer about the proposal, and he
had expressed an interest in it. "Magnificent success," he wired
me after two weeks. "Nothing like it in my experience." And
from General Leonard Wood, a few weeks later, came the
message: "There isn't anything in the world, even letters from
home, that will raise a soldier's spirits like a good catchy marching tune."

Not even the hostess houses caught on so rapidly. Under the
spirited leadership of Lee Hanmer, a member of the Commission, we recruited our staff of song leaders, and within weeks
they were assigned to the camps. The singing generally started
in a barracks, a recreation hut or in one of the Liberty theaters,
with the song coach on the platform; and often there would be an
awkward beginning—a reluctance on the part of the soldiers
to let themselves go. The leader generally began with *Tipper-
ary*, the favorite British military song, which was popular here
in America at the time. Then he would get the boys to singing
Madelon, the French marching song (with English words).
Then the old favorites would be called for—*John Brown's Body*
(they afterward often used the words of the *Battle Hymn of
the Republic* to this tune), *Old Black Joe*, *Swanee River* and
Roll Jordan Roll. And of course ultimately the army sang *Over
There, Keep the Home Fires Burning, There's a Long, Long,
Trail, Keep Your Head Down Allemand*, and *Pack up Your
Troubles in Your Old Kit Bag*. The stuttering song, *K-K-K
Katy*, was another favorite and

> Good morning, Mr. Zip, Zip, Zip,
> With your haircut just as short as mine.

As one of the song leaders reported, "singing seemed to

spread through the camp like a fire." It was soon discovered that a single song leader was not enough, and regimental and company leaders were selected from their own outfits and given a course of training. What the doughboy sang troubled him little. He had no need to relate his song to anything in the world but his own free-swinging soul, and he chose surely and well— sturdy old hymns for his more solemn moments, national anthems for ceremonial needs, old favorites for sentiment's sake, and for relaxed periods, gloriously bawdy songs like the extemporized verses of *Mademoiselle from Armentières*, which he sang in France. "The memory of those batteries," wrote an officer later, "singing as they hiked to drill each morning, noon, and before retreat, will be cherished as one of the most inspiring incidents of Camp Taylor."

My chief memory of this activity goes back to a night at Camp Meade when thousands of men, led by a song coach standing on a thirty-foot platform, and supported by massed military bands, sang:

Mine eyes have seen the glory of the coming of the Lord;
He is trampling out the vintage where the grapes of wrath are
    stored.
He hath loosed the fateful lightning of His terrible swift sword.
His truth is marching on.

Tears were streaming down the cheeks of tough, old General Joseph E. Kuhn, the commanding officer. "Never in my life," he said to me, "have I heard anything like this." And I remember another scene—in France, east of Chateau-Thierry—when an American regiment came swinging down the road to reinforce a dangerously sagging position at the front. As a kind of stunt they had fastened to their helmets bunches of the poppies that grow wild in French fields, and the song they sang with joyous abandon as they marched was:

> Hail, hail, the gang's all here;
> What the hell do we care now!

It has always seemed odd that there was no such singing among our troops in the Second World War. But the mood had changed. For us World War I was a high adventure, a crusade with a compelling purpose. But World War II was a grim job that had to be done, and it enlisted nothing like the eagerness or the fervor of the earlier struggle. Moreover in the period between the two wars the weapons had become far more deadly. You don't sing when you toss block-busters on darkened cities or drop atomic bombs.

*

President Wilson described the function of the Commission on Training Camp Activities in better words than I can. "The Federal Government," he wrote, referring to the Commission, "has pledged its word that as far as care and vigilance can accomplish the result, the men committed to its charge will be returned to the homes and communities which so generously gave them with no scars except those won in honorable warfare."

From the start the President was deeply and personally interested in our work, and I was probably closer to him during this period than at any other time. He frequently wrote me letters about our activities and I often conferred with him at the White House. Although I was responsible directly to the Secretary of War and the Secretary of the Navy, in this one respect, at least, the President never bothered about official channels. He would ask me to come to see him or he would write me personally with suggestions or complaints that had been brought to his attention. Often these letters he typed on his own typewriter at night. He was concerned, for example, about the problem of race discrimination in the armed forces at Newport News. At another time he thought that we were not giving sufficient attention to the new possibilities of moving pictures. One of his letters, I recall, had to do with an actress whom he had seen at Keith's theater the night before. The light touch of vaudeville always relaxed him, and he was a frequent attendant at Keith's. His suggestion was that this particular actress might be a successful addition to our theater program in the camps. I am sorry I cannot recall her name, and his letter to me has disappeared. We booked her, of course, and as I remember it she proved to be in great demand, although her artistic temperament involved us in endless difficulties. Perhaps I should add that her name was *not* Elsie Janis, who later in France endeared herself to the entire American Army.

The person who really gave zest and direction to our Commission was Secretary Baker. He was the most satisfactory man to work with whom I have ever known. Endowed with a crisp, incisive mind, he had a power of analysis and a capacity for lucid statement which shone through every letter he wrote and every speech he made. I remember sitting up all one night with Colonel Leonard Ayres, chief of the statistical division of the General Staff, working on a complicated statement that had to be ready for the Secretary's signature in the morning. I don't recall what it was about, but it was a complex tangle of facts that proved difficult to unravel and clarify. Tired out but feeling a bit triumphant we laid our product before Baker. It was a subject with which he was completely unfamiliar. "Well, boys," he said after he read it, "that's all right, but if you don't mind, as long as it's going out over my signature, I'll put it in my own words." Calling his stenographer, and never glancing at our draft again, he rapidly dictated a statement that was so much clearer and better organized than ours that comparison was odious. "What's the use?" Ayres whispered to me as we left the room. "Nobody can keep up with *him*."

Baker looked like a quiet type of student, but his looks were deceptive. Beneath a scholar's mien he had a will like iron and an ability to say "No" in a soft tone that left no doubt in the hearer's mind that the question was definitely settled. Perhaps the fact that he was the son of one of Jeb Stuart's tough old troopers had something to do with the matter. The spirit of decision was never ostentatious, but everybody knew that Baker's hand was on the rudder. They were no pigmy figures, those men with whom he was surrounded in the War Department. The Army does not turn out that type of man. There were Bliss and March, as Chiefs of Staff, both of them powerful characters—the latter, especially, endowed with dynamic energy and drive. There was Crowder who ran the draft act, and Crozier in charge of the Artillery. There was Pershing overseas who spoke from the shoulder and was accustomed to authority. And among them moved Baker, physically a little man, who never was ruffled and who never raised his voice, but who intellectually was the acknowledged master of them all.

It was indeed an amazing performance. Here was a little fellow who came from Cleveland, relatively unknown outside of Ohio. In his first interview with the press he was put down as a spineless pacifist who would last but a few months, and the nickname "Newty Cootie" was given to him in derision. By sheer force of character, by the incisiveness and clarity of his mind, he not only gained the support of the Army, but he mastered the administration of the largest collective enterprise in which this country up to that time had been involved.

We who were part of his official family and saw him at close range knew the stuff he was made of. He was the type of man who never wanted credit when things went right. On those occasions it was always somebody else who was responsible— it was Pershing, it was Bliss, it was March. But if things went wrong, as they frequently did in the conduct of so gigantic an enterprise, then as Secretary of War he insisted on assuming entire responsibility. The Leonard Wood incident is a case in point. Pershing did not want him overseas, and Baker, whose single policy was to support Pershing, issued an order detaching Wood from his division when it went to France. From one end of the country to the other condemnation rained down on Baker's head for keeping a gallant officer at home. A word from Baker that it was done at Pershing's request would have quieted the storm, for the country was anxious to support the commanding general in the field, and would have been inclined to forgive in him even what they might have believed was a mistaken policy. One night I said to Baker:

"Why on earth don't you give the country the truth about this business?"

"Pershing has troubles enough of his own," he replied, "and what's a Secretary of War for if it isn't to take the gaff?"

That was Baker. He was always serene, never excited, never harrassed. Even when things were blackest—when for example he was himself the target of cruel, baseless charges, and the speeches in Congress rang with abuse—he never lost his temper or his equanimity. He was entirely without cynicism. His spirit was cast in too large a mold for pettiness or vanity. In those midnight hours when what he laughingly called his "kitchen cabinet" foregathered in his office to discuss the events of the day, he was at his best. With his feet on the desk and a fresh load of tobacco in his pipe he would throw off administrative cares and take on the role that really suited him—a scholar interested in books and ideas, a philosopher who hated the pomp and circumstance of the task allotted him, and who had the rare capacity to sit back and contemplate himself and the world with quiet humor.

Always he avoided the limelight. He was one of those rare figures in public life who preferred anonymity. When with others of his official family I came back from France with him on the *George Washington* in May, 1919, the ship carried over 6000 troops, and we went aboard from a lighter in the harbor at Brest. The troops had preceded us and as we stood at attention at the head of the gangplank while the band played the national anthem, I was conscious of hundreds of faces peering down from the vast wall of the ship—the faces of doughboys eager to see the "Big Chief." It reminded me of that moment five years before, when Teddy Roosevelt, under identical circumstances, had evoked such spontaneous enthusiasm. But Baker never looked up and we were piped aboard without a gesture on his part.

"What's the matter with you?" I demanded. "Why didn't you wave your hat? Didn't you see they were itching to cheer you?"

"I was afraid they would," he replied.

*

My relations with the Secretary of the Navy, Josephus Daniels, were always cordial but never as intimate as with Baker. Daniels was a man of sterling qualities and high ideals, and there was such an affectionate, fatherly attitude about him that those of us who worked with him regarded him with genuine fondness. But he was an indifferent administrator and he lacked the crispness and decision of Baker. Often the same problem arose in relation to both the Army and the Navy commissions and it would be necessary for me personally to consult the two secretaries. From Baker I could always get an immediate and definite answer, framed in words that admitted of no misunderstanding. Crossing to Daniels' office on the other side of the State, War and Navy Building, I would be met affably and courteously, but more often than not with the reply: "Raymond, come in and see me about this tomorrow. I want to think it over." And inevitably tomorrow would lead to other tomorrows. Sometimes when the delay proved embarrassing I would take the matter up with the Assistant Secretary of the Navy, Franklin D. Roosevelt—Frank, we called him in those days. A young man of great personal charm, he seemed to have something of Baker's capacity for decision, without the maturity or the scholarly background of the Secretary of War. Certainly he was of genuine help to me in my relations with the Navy, and while at that time I did not know him as well as I knew him later, we occasionally played tennis together on the White House court.

I remember particularly my concern over the fact that the venereal disease rate of the Navy was considerably higher than that of the Army, and I was confident that the discrepancy was due to the Navy's failure to install the system of medical prophylaxis after exposure—a system which had been enforced in the Army for several years. My presentation of the case to Daniels, however, got me nowhere. He felt that prophylaxis was, as he expressed it, "an invitation to sin" which he could not countenance. My argument was that the "sin"—if there was any—lay in the Navy's neglect of a scientific weapon to check the incidence of venereal disease. One day Daniels said to me, as if in despair, for I was pressing him hard, and so were the Navy doctors: "I wish I didn't have to make the decision." A few days later he left on an inspection trip, and Roosevelt was Acting Secretary of the Navy. I immediately took the situation up with him and told him of Daniel's remark.

"In that case," he said, "I'll make the decision myself," and he signed the order. Its effect on the venereal disease rate was soon apparent.

As a matter of fact, Daniels, so far from resenting it, appeared greatly relieved by Roosevelt's action. He was always loyal to his young associate, and while Roosevelt, in his talks with me, was occasionally critical of his chief—for the same reasons that I was—it was obvious that the two men held each other in respect and affection.

Another man entered my life at this time—an engaging young chap, slightly younger than I, whom Daniels had appointed as a member of the Navy Commission on Training Camp Activities. His name was Richard E. Byrd and he was a lieutenant not long out of Annapolis. He had injured his leg in a gymnasium accident, and much to his chagrin had been disqualified for active service. Consequently he landed a "desk job" in our Commission and we made him Executive Secretary.

He turned out to be a ball of fire, full of ideas and energy, eager, tireless, and up to his ears in work. But always in the back of his mind was the consuming ambition to get back into active service—particularly into the recently developed aeronautical branch of the Navy. Finally by dint of persistence he got the doctors to pass him and joined up with the new air pilots training base at Pensacola. I let him go with genuine regret, for we had become close friends, a friendship that became firmer with the years and lasted until his death in 1957. Nobody could have foreseen in those early days that this slim, handsome, ambitious young lieutenant would write his name in immortal letters, and take an airplane to both ends of the planet where no airplane had ever been before.

General Peyton C. March, the Army Chief of Staff, was another arresting figure with whom I had considerable contact. Appointed to his position by Baker early in 1918, after the war was well under way, he brought to his task an almost incredible energy. He worked sixteen hours a day and he expected his associates to keep the same pace. He was tireless, ruthless and abrupt, and the conventional amenities did not occupy much of his time. Baker once laughingly remarked that his chief job was to go around with a cruse of oil and a bandage to fix up the wounds which the General had inflicted. On the margin of March's first despatch to Pershing, Baker scribbled: "A perfect example of how not to send a message to General Pershing."

My own relations with March got off to a stormy start. Shortly after he took office he sent for me and without any preliminaries demanded to know how many athletic coaches and song leaders we had in the camps. I told him and he snapped:

"We're not running a circus or a grand opera. Take them out."

Never did my civilian status prove more useful. I didn't even try to control my temper.

"Those men were put there by the authority of the Secretary of War," I told him, "and they'll be taken out by the same authority." And I left the room.

"From what zoo did you get *him?*" I growled at Baker. He smiled indulgently and said: "I'll handle it." And I never heard of the matter again.

Just the same, in spite of these rough edges, and perhaps in part because of them, March's contribution to the war effort was outstanding. Nobody who was in a position to see the inside working of the machinery could fail to appreciate the vitalizing effect of his indefatigable vigor and despatch. Probably he had few friends in the War Department, but he had the respect of everybody. After our first clash, my relations with him were amicable enough, and as I saw him during the relaxed midnight hours in Baker's office, I realized that in addition to his rapier-like glance, he had an engaging grin. I doubt if he ever cared much about the work of our Commission; at least it never interested him. He gave his sympathies to too great an extent—so it seemed to me—to the old school of "drill 'em till they drop," not realizing that the new army was quite different from the regular army with which he had been associated. He never understood or approved of my civilian status. As an old army man it bothered him, and indeed it was not until World War II that the place of civilians with the armed forces was definitely regularized. Baker felt—and I agreed with him—that the civilian status of our Commission was essential. Certainly in my trips to the training areas in the United States, and later in Europe, I found I could talk with complete freedom and frankness to privates and generals alike, a freedom and frankness that would have been impossible if I had had military rank.

March asked me teasingly one day whether I would like to be a colonel, and when I replied in the negative, he said:

"How about the rank of brigadier general?"

"No," I responded, "I'm not interested."

"Why not?"

"Well, for one thing," I said, "I would have to be polite to a major general."

He recognized the thrust and responded with his grin. "I never can figure out where you belong," he said. Later in France this point bothered even Pershing, but he handled it without too much difficulty.

*

In the spring of 1918, with our troops pouring into France by the thousands, Baker and Daniels thought that I ought to go to Europe to see the new conditions of environment and operation in army and navy installations. I therefore sailed early in May and immediately reported to General Pershing's headquarters at Chaumont. I had first met Pershing on the Mexican border, and had briefly seen him in Washington after his appointment as commander-in-chief. He always seemed like a grim, stern, preoccupied man, and certainly the burdens of responsibility which he carried would have crushed anyone whose inner strength was less than his. I used to wonder whether the personal tragedy which he had so recently suffered while on the Mexican border—the loss of his wife and three little daughters in a disastrous fire at the Presidio in San Francisco—had permanently cast a shadow over his spirit. There was no light touch about him, no escape into gaiety, no spark, no compelling personal magnetism. He always seemed taut, tense and restless—never relaxed—and as I wrote my wife at the time: "When he talks to you he walks around the room, never sitting still for a minute." One was immediately conscious in him of an iron streak, of a determination that bordered on stubbornness, of an impatience that was restrained with difficulty, and of a habit of command.

He was a rigid disciplinarian, given to rough words in inspecting a unit of troops, where he often seemed more like a top-sergeant than a commander-in-chief. If there was a button unbuttoned or a rifle that was not clean, he could spot it. "Do you call yourself a soldier?" This was his rasping question which he hurled at privates and officers alike. In consequence, the word that he was coming to inspect a division struck terror into the hearts of the entire outfit. Once when he inspected a military hospital the nurses and doctors flocked down to welcome him as he came in through the front door. "Attention!" he called out sharply. "Back to your posts! This is a military organization!" This rebuff was long remembered in the Medical Corps.

He had one fault conspicuously odd for a military commander: a lack of a sense of time, so that he was habitually late at many of his appointments. As I watched him at work and talked with his frantic aides it seemed to me that his tardiness was due to a stubborn determination to finish the job on which he was engaged—whether it was a letter or a conference —before he went on to the next assignment in his crowded day. But the result was sometimes disastrous, and I knew of divisions of troops that stood in line for hours in the rain, waiting for Pershing's appearance.

That he was generally unpopular with the troops goes without saying, although few of them ever saw more than a rapidly moving profile. Joffre was idolized by the French army and was known affectionately as "Papa." If Pershing was ever characterized by a nickname other than "Black Jack," it was couched in short and ugly terms that rose from plodding columns of American troops. Once when he was quoted, erroneously, as saying that he would take Metz if it cost a hundred thousand lives, the unanimous comment of the army was: "Ain't he a generous guy!"

And yet when all the criticisms are totaled, the fact remains that he had the character and drive that whipped an army into shape and compelled his men to work to the limit of their strength—cursing him, perhaps, but respecting him. I always thought that his appearance had something to do with this feeling of respect. With the possible exception of Pétain he looked the part of a commander-in-chief more than any other general I saw in France. Foch resembled a college professor, deep in thought; Joffre was a roly-poly with an infectious smile; Haig was a gentleman of dignity and reticence. But Pershing from the standpoint of appearance was the ideal soldier—handsome, erect, physically tough, and with the mark of leadership written indelibly on his face and figure.

My own relations with him were from the beginning cordial,

for in spite of his austerity he could be gracious and consider-
ate. He gave affection to few and certainly he never gave it
to me; but he was always frank and honest and appreciative
of the work in which the Secretary of War was so interested.
His loyalty to Baker and the administration in Washington was
absolute and unequivocal. "You may be assured that you can
count on every possible support from the American Expeditionary Force," he wrote me after our first interview, and he
immediately followed it up with letters of introduction to commanding officers and by assigning a military car for my use
and giving me the coveted "white pass" which took me to all
parts of the allied operations. The only stipulation he made
was that I must wear a uniform if I went into the front lines.
"Otherwise," he said, "if the Germans should put over a raid
and catch you in civilian clothes, they would give you short
shrift." When I was at the front, therefore, I wore a private's
uniform or a Red Cross uniform or whatever I could find or
borrow.

It was, of course, my first contact with actual warfare, and
in the three months that I was in France I saw it at first hand.
I confess I was unprepared for its brutality and waste, and
over the years I have tried, perhaps unconsciously, to forget
it as far as I could; but the memory of the poison gas cases,
the shell-shock hospitals, the scream of wounded men, and of
the ghastly forms of human death is with me yet. "The thing
that hits you between the eyes," I wrote to a friend at home,
"is the utter stupidity of war as a method of settling anything.
Even with victory running our way, a battle is at best a blun-
dering, chaotic, stupid business. As you watch it your mind
revolts against the idea that this is the accepted and time-
honored technique by which *homo sapiens,* on the pinnacle of
creation, settles his little differences."

The thing that seemed to redeem the business, at least in

part, was the spirit of the boys—the doughboys. "You can't imagine what an impression they are making on the French," I wrote my family. "They are the greatest lot of sheer boys you ever saw. Every spare minute they stage a ball game or some athletic event, and the French are constantly gasping at their exuberance and tirelessness. When they are not throwing a baseball they are playing with children—the younger the better. They are the idols of all the mothers in the villages where they are quartered because of the attention they shower on the babies. You see a big, strapping six-footer marching along with a two-year old girl on his shoulders, or half a dozen fellows performing monkey stunts for the benefit of two or three small youngsters."

My main job overseas, as Baker and Daniels defined it, was to see how adequately in relation to need the Y.M.C.A., the Knights of Columbus, the Jewish Welfare Board, and the Salvation Army were handling their responsibilities; and I followed their activities from the army and navy bases both in England and France right up to the front-line trenches. I was also asked to check the activities of the Red Cross in relation to the troops—their canteens, hospitals, dressing stations and dugouts—although this society did not come within the jurisdiction of the Commission. As I reported to Washington, I found the work of the Red Cross superb—an excellent piece of planning and organization. Hardly less effective was the work of the Y.M.C.A., although at the request of General Pershing it had embarked on a project of doubtful wisdom—running the post exchanges for the army—a project which later brought it a considerable measure of embarrassment and misunderstanding.

Oddly enough, the Salvation Army was by far the most popular organization with the troops. "Night before last," I wrote home, "in a dugout just back of the first line, I found two Salvation Army lassies serving hot coffee to the soldiers. The German shells were thundering over our heads with a noise like freight trains and exploding far in the rear of us, and our own batteries were replying all around us with crashes of sound that seemed to rip the air but down in the dugout the lassies were unperturbably dishing out the drinks. As a matter of fact they had no business to be there and were subsequently ordered to the rear, but the incident is typical of their work."

But the mistake we had made in allowing a multiplication of social agencies to serve the troops was glaringly apparent. As I told Baker: "Every new organization means additional transport space, a new set of contacts with the army, increased congestion in fighting areas, and another unit of non-combatant personnel that is necessarily acquainted with the movements of the troops." Moreover an unhealthy spirit of competition was beginning to creep into the work of the societies. They all wanted to get to the front, in part because of its spectacular and dramatic value, and in part, too, because the work there seemed more urgent. Consequently there was an uneven development of the field work, with many areas neglected. The army was fighting a war and failed to give the societies the benefit of its supervision and control. "I do not believe that the present policy of *laissez faire* can much longer be maintained," I reported to Baker. "The army, through trained representatives, will have to assume some responsibility for the coordination of all this work, and take some positive part in shaping its course. Otherwise we are headed for some unhappy consequences."

Before I left France I had a talk with Pershing about the matter, but although he agreed with my diagnosis, and regretted the multiplicity of agencies—for which of course he was not responsible—he felt that there was little that could be done in the way of army control during the progress of the fighting. I remember at this interview he was disturbed by a letter which he had received from Clemenceau, then prime minister of France, in which the Tiger had strongly objected to the policy of repression that the United States army command had adopted in relation to prostitution. "Total prohibition of all regulated prostitution in the vicinity of American troops," Clemenceau wrote, "has had for result, in spite of measures of prophylaxis and discipline taken by the American authorities, the increase of venereal diseases among the civilian population of the neighborhood." He went on to advocate the establishment of licensed houses of prostitution. "Should the American High Command see this question in the same light," he concluded, "I will put my services at its disposal, in providing, in concert with the Minister of the Interior, for the creation of special houses of this kind."

Pershing believed strongly that the allegations on which the letter was based were untrue.

"This is the work of some of his prejudiced army medical officers," he said. "They've fooled the old man. Just the same," he continued, "this is too hot for me to handle. It's above my head. You're going back to Washington. Give this to the Secretary of War."

Two weeks later I handed Clemenceau's letter to Baker. He read it through twice, and then said with a half smile:

"For God's sake, Raymond, don't show this to the President or he'll stop the war."

I do not recall just what steps Baker took, but the American policy of suppression remained unchanged both for the Army and the Navy. Neither Baker nor Daniels had any sympathy for the Continental position on prostitution; and when I was in France, after the Armistice, at Pershing's request I sent for Major Bascom Johnson and fifteen of his best officers in the

Law Enforcement Division of the Commission on Training Camp Activities, who acted in an advisory capacity in some of the more troublesome spots at army and navy posts and stations, both in France and England.

In spite of my strong reaction to what seemed to me the stupidity and futility of war I came back from France with the feeling that I belonged to my generation and that my generation was in the trenches. However barbarous war might be I could not escape the responsibilities of my time. With all the sacrifice and heroism which I had seen at the front, I could not live easily with my conscience if I did not share in the challenge. I had just passed my thirty-fifth birthday, but I was still within the range of the draft act. When, therefore, a month later, my number was reached and I was called before my draft board, I refused to claim either exemption or deferred classification, and I was certified as physically fit. My idyllic dream was shattered by Baker who without my knowledge claimed exemption for me. "If the various phases of our war work are to be effectively developed," he wrote me, "some of us must sacrifice our ambitions to serve in the uniformed ranks, and the activity that you are carrying on is of a kind that will not admit of letting you go." At the bottom of his letter in his own handwriting he wrote the word *Orders!* And as the soldiers used to say: "That was that."

*

The army command in France was strongly of the opinion that the war would see its climax in 1919, and all plans were geared to that end. But in the late summer of 1918 Germany and Austria began to crack, and the armistice of November 11 was upon us almost before we could grasp what was happening. The fighting seemed to be over, but the big problem of delay and demobilization loomed ahead of us. Baker thought that my permanent headquarters should be with General Pershing, and by rare good fortune I was assigned, early in December, to the S.S. *George Washington* which was carrying President Wilson and his associates to the Peace Conference in Paris. Secretary of State Lansing and Henry D. White, two of the United States commissioners were aboard, together with John W. Davis on his way to his new ambassadorship at the Court of St. James, and the whole galaxy of experts who had been recruited by Colonel House to advise on the new treaty. Some of them I already knew; with many of them I formed an enduring friendship.

That trip, for me so completely accidental, was a memorable experience. For the only time in my life I kept a diary, and even today I read it with a feeling of excitement. History was in the process of being made. The curtain was rising on a new era in the human story. Wilson, accompanied by his attractive and charming wife, was thoroughly tired out when he came aboard, but the long, deliberate trip— we went by way of the Azores—seemed to rest him. I had a number of talks with him, and as usual he spoke with the utmost frankness. "Fosdick," he said slowly, as if thinking out loud, "if we can create a League of Nations, we will at last do something that the world has been dreaming about for generations." As he developed the idea it seemed to me that he was again the teacher and I was once more a student in his seminar at Princeton. And I felt myself deeply stirred, as I so often did in his classes, by his clarity, his vision, and his great moral power.

At another time, I found him concerned about the spread of Bolshevism—"a poison" he called it. Its absolutism repelled him, and he quoted Jefferson's pledge of "eternal hostility against any form of tyranny over the mind of man." Wilson called himself a liberal, but liberalism must be more liberal than ever before, if civilization is to survive, he said. Conservatism he defined as the policy of "make no change and consult your grandmother when in doubt." "Those who argue for the *status quo ante bellum*," he added, "or for any other *status quo*, are like so many vain kings sitting by the sea and commanding the tide not to rise." In my diary I said, following one of these talks, "I think his mental processes function more easily and logically than in any other man I ever met, and the compelling power of his personality is tremendous."

My diary for the last night of the trip is in these words: "We had our last movie tonight—Geraldine Farrar in an excellent film. At the end, just before the lights went up, a group of fifty bluejackets who had gathered unseen in a corner of the dining room, sang 'God be with you till we meet again.' They sang it softly, in splendidly modulated voices, while we all stood. The President was visibly affected. His head was bowed and I could see tears in his eyes. At the end we all joined in 'Auld Lang Syne.'"

Wilson's welcome in Paris was accompanied by the most remarkable demonstration of enthusiasm and affection on the part of the Parisians that I have ever heard of, let alone seen. His train from Brest was purposely delayed and arrived at ten o'clock in the morning. The rest of us came through on a fast train that got in at six in the morning. The parade over a four-mile drive consisted merely of eight horse-drawn carriages, preceded by a handful of hussars of the guard. Wilson and Poincaré rode in the first carriage. Troops, cavalry and infantry, lined the entire route, and tens of thousands of persons fought for a glimpse of their hero. The streets were decorated with flags and bunting, and huge banners bearing the words *Welcome to Wilson* or *Honor to Wilson the Just* stretched across the roadways from house to house.

I was at a window in a building on the corner of Rue Royale

and the Place de la Concorde. The carriages approached at a trot. We could hear the cheers across the Seine. Wilson was smiling and waving his hat. The noise was deafening. It was all over in a minute and we heard the cheers rolling up the Rue Royale to the Madeleine. The troops started to march, but the crowds broke through and for an hour the Place de la Concorde was a riot of color and enthusiasm. I noticed twenty or thirty British soldiers marching with the sign: "The British—vos Alliés de 1914–1918." "I hope this is not symbolic of trouble at the peace table," I said in my diary.

My diary ends on a somber note. "Tonight," I wrote, "the boulevards of Paris are still celebrating. An American can have anything he wants today; he owns the city. The girls even try to kiss him on the streets. I wonder—and the thought keeps coming back to me—what will be the greeting of the French when the Peace is finished and Wilson comes to go home. I wish it could be guaranteed that their affection for America and the Americans would be as real and as enthusiastic as it is today. Poor Wilson! A man with his responsibilities is to be pitied. The French think that with almost a magic touch he will bring about the day of political and industrial justice. Will he? Can he?"

*

Pershing greeted me cordially at his headquarters in Chaumont. He looked older and grayer than when I had seen him five months before, and the lines of care and anxiety were etched more deeply on his face.

"I think we'll have to give you a title," he said, reminiscent of General March's perplexity, "and I propose to appoint you as my civilian aide. I don't know exactly what it means," he added with a smile, "but it sounds all right."

He gave me offices at Chaumont and also at his Paris headquarters, 45 Avenue Montaigne, and suggested that I spend as much of my time as possible with the troops in the field. "I want to know exactly and in detail how their morale is standing up and what the weak spots are," he said. As I look back on it now after forty years I wonder at the temerity with which I undertook the assignment which to General Pershing must have seemed highly irregular. Of course any reports that I made to him were supplemented by those of his own inspectors attached to his staff; but my experience in the United States had been that either through timidity or inability to get the doughboy point of view the reports of army inspectors frequently failed to reflect the whole situation.

My first task was to find out what was happening in the field. With my old friend, Colonel Leonard Ayres, assigned as a military aide, I made a series of trips by car, covering hundreds of miles and ranging from Coblentz where our third army had its bridgehead on the Rhine, down through our second army area stationed north of Toul, and south and east of Paris where the widely flung units of our service of supply were stationed. Because I wanted to find out how our allies were handling their problem I visited the British sector centered in Cologne, the Canadian sector in Bonn, and the French sector in Metz and Mayence. The battle areas, especially north of Verdun and in the Argonne, with their hastily buried dead, and with guns, bayonets, helmets, cannon, and ammunition scattered in the wildest disorder, were scenes of indescribable destruction. East and west of the Hindenburg line, the ground had been so churned up and fought over that even the military graves and their occupants had long since disappeared. "It makes one think of the surface of the moon," I wrote home. "The only figure that comes to my mind is that of a gigantic spoon furiously stirring a liquid earth until it becomes frozen or rigid, and then sprinkling over the top of it bits of wood,

steel, bones, rags, and other debris." And my letter continued
with these words:

> At nine o'clock in the evening, in absolute darkness, and with a
> slight rain falling, I climbed a sign post at what appeared to be
> a crossroads. To my surprise I found that we were in the city
> square of Noyon—where Charlemagne was crowned and Calvin
> was born. Around us on every hand lay the ruins—the cathedral,
> the city hall, all the houses, now just crumbling piles of brick and
> stone with no human being within miles. Even the dogs have left.

My reports to General Pershing were as precise and specific
as I could make them, and the following paragraphs illustrate
the topics with which I bombarded him.

Back pay. In spite of the efforts of the Army authorities it is still
possible to find, particularly in the hospitals and among casual
outfits, hundreds of cases of men who have not been paid for
three or four months. Moreover, this matter is apparently not
confined to casual groups. For example, on January 26th, Company B. of the 341st Labor Battalion, stationed at Varennes, consisting of approximately 250 men, had not been paid since
September 30, 1918. Some units in the 308th Field Artillery,
stationed near Dijon, within two weeks received back pay for
three months. I heard of similar cases from men in the field, but
I mention only those which were verified through responsible
officers.

Lighting facilities, such as candles, etc. The importance of this
point is, I believe, paramount. I have come across many outfits,
both in the 2nd Army and in parts of the 3rd Army, that had a
very limited supply of candles, or no candles at all. As it gets
dark between half past four and five the men are unable to read
or play games or have any entertainment. In some cases the last
mess was served in the dark because of the lack of any light. To

men living in dugouts, as many of the 2nd Army are living, the supply or lack of candles may mean the difference between good and bad morale.

Wood. There seems to be a noticeable absence of wood for fire in parts of the 2nd Army and elsewhere.

Mess. At many points, noticeably in the 2nd Army and to some extent in the 3rd, mess is still served in a mess line out-of-doors. The men stand in a single line regardless of the weather and are served as their turn is reached. After being served they sit or stand where they can, sometimes in the rain. Many of the men attempt to take the food to their billets, but complaint is made that it is often cold before they get it there.

Uncertainty of plans for returning home. It is unnecessary to remark that the thing uppermost in the minds of the troops is the desire to return home. This question dwarfs all others and has apparently become in some parts of the Army almost a mania. Rumors, often of the wildest sort, fly from group to group, and the troops seem to vibrate between hope and despair according to the latest report which they can obtain. These rumors often have to do with the future use of the troops, and I have heard in various parts of the Army from the soldiers that they expected to be sent to Russia, that they expected to be sent to the West Coast of Africa, that they expected to be used to rebuild the devastated areas of France, that they expected to have to quell uprisings in the Balkan States, etc. In other words, it is the indefiniteness of their status that seems to worry the men almost as much as their enforced sojourn in France. I have been told many times by men in the Army that if they could only know authoritatively that they were going to return on approximately a certain date, the fact that the date was four or six months off would not be half so demoralizing as the recurrence of hope and despair that must inevitably accompany the present state of uncertainty.

Assuming that it is not possible to forecast with any degree of accuracy the probable date of sailing of specific units, would it not be possible to use every conceivable channel—general orders, chaplains, "Stars & Stripes," welfare agencies, etc.—in keeping the troops informed on the following points:

a) the policy of the Government with regard to the return and demobilization of the A.E.F.,

b) the varying amounts of shipping available for troop transport,

c) the actual progress of demobilization by number and organization,

d) the probable future rate of demobilization.

Conditions North of Toul. I doubt whether anything can permanently be accomplished to maintain the morale of parts of the 2nd Army as long as this body of troops is located in its present desolate situation. Thousands of them are living under conditions of great hardship and discomfort in the area that was fought over north of Toul. They are billeted in villages that were destroyed during the war or in dugouts that were constructed during the fighting, surrounded on every hand by desolation and waste. I believe that the morale conditions in some of the smaller detached units of these troops are really serious. They live in the mud, they eat in the mud, they sleep in the mud. They are leagues from human habitations save those of soldiers, and the country for miles around consists of far-stretching seas of mud, crossed by water-filled trenches, fenced into long strips by endless wire, dotted with graves, littered with the debris of battle, and showing here and there the remains of dead horses. In one case I found a Commanding Officer of a small detached unit, a Lieutenant, in a mental state bordering on hysteria.

Obviously this suggestion is made in ignorance of military requirements, but it is apparent to a casual observer that to preserve the morale of the men in these parts they should be moved at the earliest possible moment.

I had expected that my frankness would startle General

Pershing, but although, as he said, he had never before dealt with a civilian in army matters, he accepted my reports with every evidence of appreciation. He was indignant over the news that some of the units of the army had not been paid for months, and, as I afterwards learned, he rode his staff hard, not only on this item, but on other matters which I brought to his attention or which he learned from his own army inspectors. We had several long discussions about my recommendations, and he wrote me a personal letter expressing his satisfaction. "Your experience," he said, "will greatly strengthen me in my very sincere desire to improve and maintain the highest morale among our troops until the day of their discharge."

One of my recommendations inspired a degree of misgiving on his part. I had not realized when I went to France after the Armistice—and I am sure Baker knew nothing of it—that Pershing's staff, with an immense army at its disposal, was contemplating a program of extensive and intensive drill and tactical training, in order to profit by the errors of the Meuse-Argonne offensive. It was hard for the staff to close all the special schools that had been in full operation at the time of the Armistice, getting ready for the campaign of 1919. The fighting was over, and during the delay in sending the troops home, a golden opportunity was presented to make real soldiers out of civilian recruits.

Into this situation I stepped unwittingly. It seemed to me that the general order which had gone into effect on January 1, 1919, prescribing twenty-five hours of drill a week, was creating havoc among the men, and I so reported to General Pershing.

Most of the men in the Army are not looking forward to any career as soldiers, [I said]. They did not get into the Army because they had any special predilection for soldiering. They

answered the nation's call in the time of crisis and gladly made
themselves part of a great war machine. But now that the crisis
is over they turn instinctively to their peace-time habits of mind
and are impatient with any attempt to continue unrelieved the
military tasks for which most of them have no natural fondness.
In other words, the motive is gone out of the whole business, and
the ideal of perfecting themselves in the profession of arms is not
to them an acceptable substitute. To see a Battery that has fired
70,000 rounds in the Argonne fight going listlessly through the
movements of ramming an empty shell into a gun for hours at
a stretch, or training the sights on an enemy that does not exist,
is depressing enough to watch, and its effect on the spirits of
the men is apparent. They seem to wilt under it. The same is
true of infantry drill in the muddy roads, up and down which
columns of American soldiers trudge listlessly and without spirit.
As one Lieutenant expressed it, it would only need a contagious
word or two, and his whole outfit would throw down their guns
and run like a pack of schoolboys . . .

Obviously the men of the American Expeditionary Force will
submit cheerfully and gladly to any kind of hardship or any hours
of labor during wartime, but when the deep and impelling motive
for work and sacrifice—that of helping to win the war—is with-
drawn, other motivating forces have to be substituted.

I am conscious of the impertinence of a suggestion of this kind
coming from a civilian, and I would not venture to broach it except for my knowledge of what the British are doing in their
Army of Occupation. Two hours a day, in the morning, is the
maximum required. There is no formal tactical drill of any kind.
"We only aim to keep our men physically fit," the Chief of Staff
told me. The rest of the time is given up to mass athletics, sports
and educational work, together with such details of military
duties as may be necessary. In other words, the British aim to
keep their men continually busy, but military drill forms only a
small proportion of their duty.

I asked the Chief of Staff in Cologne what would happen if the schedule of drill were extended to cover perhaps five hours a day. "Why frankly we would have a mutiny," he said. "The soldiers would think that it was being done just to take up their time and would see the needlessness of it. These men are not professional soldiers,—they are citizens who have been turned into excellent fighters for the time being, but who are looking forward eagerly to their civil occupations. It would break the back of the Army to insist on more drill than we give them now."

Pershing was troubled about my recommendation, but two or three weeks later he withdrew the general order. However, I suspect that it was not my argument, but a quiet word from Baker, that effected the result.

*

Meanwhile the problem of which I had become aware five months earlier remained unsolved: the army exercised no control over the private societies, and the field was spottily developed. Whole units of troops were either inadequately served or not served at all, while in other places there was competition and duplication between the agencies, particularly between the Y.M.C.A. and the Knights of Columbus. "One can go through such villages as Grandpré, Marcq, or any of the points of the Northern Argonne Section," I wrote General Pershing, "and not find a single representative of any of the agencies, or even so much as a baseball, a bar of chocolate, or a magazine."

As a matter of fact this problem in the end proved insoluble. The whole basis of operation had been inadequately conceived; and while the army profited enormously by the services of the private societies, it was not until World War II that a really satisfactory arrangement for this aspect of the work was evolved.

But the American Expeditionary Force itself, under the prodding of Pershing, and through the drive and energy of General Avery D. Andrews, head of the G–1 section of the General Staff, eventually did a remarkable job of its own. Adopting the plan which we had devised in the United States of detailing inspectors or welfare officers to each of the areas into which the country was divided, the A.E.F. thoroughly and systematically covered the field. Its program involved educational, athletic, and entertainment features. A university was established at Beaune with ten thousand students; ten thousand more were attending French and British universities; and roughly 130,000 men were at Post Schools, corresponding to our elementary and high schools at home. In athletics the figures showed millions of individual participants. Under the heading of entertainment, moving pictures, professional talent, and particularly amateur shows were utilized in all parts of the army. "It represents a new emphasis in the management of an army," I wrote Secretary Baker, "at least, an *organized* emphasis, and the results are bound to show themselves in the future conduct of military affairs in the United States."

In my final report to the Secretary of War, written just before I left the service, I came back to the subject of the private agencies.

I have come increasingly to the belief, [I said] in two years of intimate association with this work, that the sectarian basis underlying much of it is fundamentally wrong. None of the societies, of course, works exclusively for its own constituency. Their facilities and privileges are open to all regardless of faith, but the auspices through which these privileges are extended are in some cases sectarian. The tendency of this arrangement is to stimulate rivalries and a jockeying for position that are disheartening to witness and discouraging to cope with. To see the representatives of these different agencies vying with each other in an attempt to make a last good impression upon the returning troops, bringing prominently into the foreground their respective emblems and insignia, is to despair of the whole system of social work in the war.

And I went on to say:

If we ever have another war to fight or another emergency of this kind to meet, I believe that far better results will be obtained not only by eliminating religious stratification of the sort just mentioned, but by reducing to the lowest possible minimum the number of organizations working directly with the troops in camp or in the field.

As a matter of fact, I am inclined to go a good deal further. I believe that we have reached a point in the development of much of this social work in the Army where it can safely be intrusted to the Government to operate. This might not apply to such specialized activities with women, as the Y.W.C.A. has been carrying on, for example, or to a program of hospitality outside the military reservations such as the War Camp Community Service has been conducting in the civil communities adjacent to camps. But it certainly applies to all the work which directly touches the troops within the training areas or on active service in the field. I am strongly of the opinion that the leisure time program of the Army of the future can best be carried on by the Army itself, whether it be in posts or cantonments. The successful experience of the Army officers at home and in France in handling complex entertainment and educational programs fully justifies this belief. There is no logical reason why all this work which the societies have been conducting and which is intimately related to the spirit and morale of the troops should be left to the discretion and ability of private agencies, collecting their funds from private sources. Morale is as important as ammunition and is just as legitimate a charge against the public treasury.

Secretary Baker had my report printed with the foreword that the Secretary of War was "substantially in accord" with my statement. It aroused considerable opposition among the societies, and thereafter it lay forgotten in the files of the War Department for twenty-one years. In 1940, with a new war threatening, it came into the hands of General George C. Marshall, Chief of Staff, whom I had met as a young major on Pershing's staff in Chaumont. He christened it the "Fosdick Report," and as such it became one of the factors in the creation of the Special Services Division through which the Army assumed full responsibility for much of the work that in World War I had been left to private initiative. It was a pity that Baker did not live long enough to see the fruition of the ideas which he had set in motion and to which he had given such loyal support.

*

I said good-bye to General Pershing in France with some regret, for nobody could watch him at work without realizing what an unusually strong and sturdy character he was. He was so forthright, so stubbornly honest, so determined to make the army an implement worthy of the American tradition, that one was inclined to overlook his tough and stormy methods. In spite of the blinding light of publicity in which he lived, there was no vanity about him, no element of self-seeking, no Cromwellian complex. In an atmosphere that might have ruined a lesser man he kept his head and his sense of balance. And he mellowed with the years. During the twenties I occasionally used to call on him in the old State, War and Navy Building where as General of the Armies he had an office which in spite of its elaborateness seemed somehow empty and forlorn, for there were no papers on his desk demanding to be read, and no more important decisions to make. On one such visit he gave me his photograph which he had inscribed "To my war time comrade and friend." "Those were good days, weren't they?" he said, but his eyes were the sad eyes of an old man who looks back on a life that is closed.

My parting with Baker was a real wrench. "I am sorry to go," I wrote him from New York, "but principally I regret leaving *you*. We have been in intimate contact since 1916, and I guess I have seen you at all hours of day and night and under all sorts of conditions. I have worked with many men in my life, a few of whom I have admired immensely. I am sure you will think me guilty of no exaggeration when I say that my association with you has been a supreme experience."

Baker replied:

There is a traditional belief that friendships are only made in youth. Those who defend this thesis do so on the ground that when men have come to mature years interest discolors acquaintance and makes friendships infrequent if not impossible. Those who write on this subject in the future, however, will have to admit the exception which arises when men of mature years are profoundly interested in the same thing, and that not a personal and selfish interest but a public interest. I am quite sure that deep friendships are engendered by that kind of service, and if I am called on for my proofs, I will confidently tell of the feeling I have for you, growing out of these splendid years of real service together.

IX

*

The League of Nations

A LIVING thing is born." With these words Woodrow Wilson presented the preliminary draft of the Covenant to the Paris Peace Conference in February, 1919, in one of the most impressive speeches of his career. And indeed it was a living thing—not the organization itself, as Wilson thought, for its life was brief and its end darkened with failure. What linked it to an enduring future was that it embodied in constitutional form the long hopes of mankind for peace and a rationally organized world. In the march of history it was a forward thrust of unprecedented scope and speed, involving marked changes in international relations—changes of approach, changes of technique, changes particularly in public attitudes and convictions. On the foundations of the League another organization has since been built, and still other structures may succeed the present one; but the pattern of world-wide unity through constitutional forms which Wilson traced in his speech at the Quai d'Orsay that cold February afternoon has become firmly woven into the thinking of mankind.

The excitement and exhilaration of those days are reflected in the rather ecstatic letters I wrote my family from Paris—letters which my wife assiduously collected and preserved, and which constitute a sort of personal diary of the period. "Wilson has captured the imagination of the common people all over the world," I said, "and he has put his great ideal across. . . . He will stand out in the future like a shining flame when the other men of his time have been forgotten. . . . I suppose he will be cursed all over the lot by the brethren of the Republican Party and by many of the Democratic Party; but those two parties will be in their graves, dead and happily forgotten, long before the figure of Wilson grows dim in the imagination of the world."

In my wildest dreams it never occurred to me that I would have a part in the new organization, but in May, 1919, two days after I landed in New York from France, Frank Polk, Acting Secretary of State, called me up to say that the President, who was still in Paris, wanted me to accept the position of Under Secretary General in the League of Nations. The Annex of the Covenant of the League provided that the Secretary General should be Sir Eric Drummond of the British Foreign Office, and the idea at that time was that there should be an American and a French Under Secretary General. Jean Monnet, who over the years has had a distinguished career in France, was chosen for the latter position.

For me the President's offer could not have come at a more inopportune moment. I had been in France for eight months out of the previous twelve, and it was difficult to face the thought of once more leaving my family. I had a four-year-old daughter who was occupying an increasing share in my thoughts and dreams, and the critical postwar shortages abroad made it inadvisable to take the family with me. Moreover I was not at all sure that I was the man for the job. I felt that I was ill-prepared by previous experience for so unique an undertaking. In my uncertainty I talked with Newton Baker. "Where in the world," he asked, "would anyone find experience in running a League of Nations?"

I came to believe, therefore, that it was a call to service from which I could not escape—a chance to play a part in a brave,

new world; and encouraged by a long and detailed cablegram
from Colonel House, I sailed for London, the League's temporary headquarters, late in June, exchanging greetings with
the President by wireless in mid-ocean, he having left Brest
the same day I left New York. "It is rather exciting," I wrote
my family from the ship, "for there is something new stirring
in the world today, and the adventure and hope of it are in the
air."

Sir Eric Drummond and Jean Monnet were already in London when I arrived, and they had taken over an inconvenient
mansion as temporary quarters for the League—Sunderland
House in Curzon Street, formerly the home of the Duke of
Marlborough, a garish, ornate building, splashed with gilt, and
with the ceilings painted with cupids and water nymphs. It
seemed like a singularly inappropriate building for a sober institution like ours, but in postwar London it was the only thing
that could be had. I could not foresee that the name *Sunderland
House* would come to symbolize in the minds of many of us
not only the beginning of life-long friendships, but the first blue-
print stage in the architecture of what we fondly hoped was a
new world.

For both my colleagues I formed an immediate attachment.
Drummond, an Oxford graduate, had been in the British Foreign Office for many years, and was a prominent member of
its staff at the Paris Peace Conference. Monnet, who had real
financial genius, had been head of the French supply organization in London during the war. We were all young; Drummond
was just over forty; Monnet was thirty-one, and I was thirty-six;
and we were embarked on a venture where there were few
signposts and no beaten paths.

The world has moved so fast in the last forty years that it is
difficult today to comprehend the lack of knowledge and experience which handicapped us as we set about the task of
creating an international secretariat. Nothing like it had ever

been done before. The Covenant provided for an Assembly, a Council, and "a permanent Secretariat," and it was obviously the intention that the Secretariat should be the eyes and ears of the League, the branch that never adjourned and was always in session—collecting facts, analyzing data, keeping in touch with the specific functions outlined in the Covenant, and submitting its recommendations to the Assembly and the Council.

Our first decision—and it was Drummond's idea—was that the Secretariat should be an international civil service rather than a group of national representatives, and that its members should receive their appointments not from their own governments but from the international authority. Although the choice of Monnet and myself had been somewhat in conflict with this principle, we determined that future appointments should represent this ideal of a civil service, international in its structure, its spirit and its personnel. As I wrote Newton Baker at the time: "The members [of the Secretariat] must be divorced from their allegiance to their respective governments. They serve only the League."

As it turned out, this decision had far-reaching consequences, not only with the League of Nations but with the United Nations which followed it. It was a revolutionary step, and we were repeatedly warned that it could not succeed. But when, years later, the historian of the League, Frank Walters, came to write the account of that period, he had this to say about our experiment: "Throughout the existence of the League the Secretariat was held, by universal consent, to be an instrument of the highest efficiency. Taken as a whole, its members, drawn from over thirty countries, differing in language, religion and training, worked together in a spirit of friendship and devotion. They developed a corporate sense, a pride in the reputation and record of their service. . . . Never again can it be maintained that an international civil service is bound to be a failure."

Our next step was to determine what functions, given by the Covenant to the Assembly and the Council, would have to be implemented by definite machinery established in the Secretariat. For example, where the Covenant spoke of mandates or specific social questions, did that involve the necessity of definite sub-divisions in the Secretariat to handle these new responsibilities? We came to the conclusion that it did, and we organized a series of sections each with a director at its head. It was a distinguished group of people who were thus, in those early days, brought into the service of the Secretariat—men like William Rappard, Sir Arthur Salter, Erik Colban, Joost van Hamel, Bernardo Attolico, Paul Mantoux, Pierre Comert, Arthur Sweetser, Huntington Gilchrist—and a woman, too, Dame Rachel Crowdy, who became head of the Section of Social Affairs. They were the pioneers, these early officials of the Secretariat—able, resourceful, confident and devoted—and I am convinced that their influence is alive in the international thinking of today, multiplied perhaps beyond all power of measurement and computation.

*

It seems strange to recall that in those first few months we worked under such a sense of urgency. We confidently believed that the treaty would be quickly ratified by the powers, and that the first meetings of the Assembly and the Council would take place that autumn. Consequently there was no time to be lost, and we were absorbed by questions of procedure, agenda, and many other problems for which there were no precedents. One of the topics of discussion was whether the meeting of the Assembly or the meeting of the Council should come first. Another point had to do with the admission of the press. I find among my papers a memorandum I gave Drummond which I headed somewhat ambitiously: "Tests or Standards to Measure

the Growth of the League in the Direction We Want it to Go."
Among my "tests" were the following:

1. Mandates which shall not be cloaks for annexation.
2. Publication of them before final acceptance, in order that
   discussion may be provoked.
3. Publicity to meetings of the Council and the Assembly.
4. Appointment of impartial persons as chairmen of the Saar
   Valley Government Commission, and of the Danzig Commission.
5. Early meeting of the Assembly.
6. Consideration at such an early meeting of the question of
   the admission of Germany to the League, the question of
   disarmament, and the question of conscription.
7. Character and quality of the Permanent Court of International Justice and its judges.
8. The League to keep scrupulously clear from assuming any
   duties assigned by the Treaty to the Principal Allied and
   Associated Powers.

On the last point I felt deeply. It was already apparent that
the Treaty contained vindictive clauses which were bound to
make trouble in the future, and which probably could not be enforced. The responsibility for carrying out these harsher measures lay with the Allied and Associated Powers rather than with
the League, but influences were at work, even in that early
period, to give the League a wider degree of oversight. "There
are plenty of people over here," I wrote Newton Baker, "who
would like to have the League now assume responsibility for
the Reparations Commission and the other punitive measures.
But this, it seems to me, would be a ghastly mistake. Let's steer
clear of these things and give ourselves time to establish our
work in the confidence and conscience of the world. The

League stands for disarmament, for peace, for international
justice, for the protection of backward peoples, for a better
standard of living, for the relief of suffering, for the fight against
disease. Let's stick to that program and let the other crowd see
where they get with theirs. . . . If the League succeeds, it will
be because its emphasis has been positive and creative, rather
than repressive."

Of course problems of this kind were scarcely the responsibility of the Secretariat. It would be the Council and the Assembly that would determine these issues; but in those days
when the provisional Secretariat was the only part of the
League in existence, the discussion of these momentous questions could scarcely be avoided. In retrospect it seems as if
Drummond, Monnet and I, who constituted what was called
the "cabinet" in that initiatory period, spent our days and nights
in consultation. "We eat and sleep in terms of the League's
present status and future development," I wrote home, describing a conference that had lasted all afternoon and well into the
night. "And of course we do a lot of speculating on how soon
it will become a really effective instrument."

Yesterday [I continued] Drummond, in something of a philosophic mood, was inclined to stress the *inevitability* of the
League. That is, he feels that with the fast-developing interde-
pendence of the world as an economic unit, time is running on
our side, and the sheer necessities of the situation will force the
growth of some kind of world organization even if we were to
muff this particular attempt.

Monnet and I were inclined to qualify this point of view. We do
not feel that time is running on our side, except in the sense of a
future too remote to be of advantage to this generation or the
next. This generation is in a race with international anarchy, . . .
and Monnet and I stressed the point that the world has very

little time in which to set up the framework of international government and *establish the habit of teamwork*. We have far too little time to do a good job before the strains and stresses come. And the danger—the really frightening danger—is that before the nations have learned how to play ball together, they will be overwhelmed by some new emergency—like a football team that has to meet its strongest opponent at the beginning of the season when it is only half trained.

That is why it seems to us that the present job is so urgent—so immediately compelling—and of course Drummond agrees completely with this. It was a grand debate . . ."

Evidently during this provisional period, the finances of the League were somewhat straitened, although my recollection of the matter today is dim. However I find that I wrote my wife: "Confidentially the League is broke, and it may be a month or two before I can draw a salary. The question hinges on the illegality of nations advancing money to the League until the Treaty is ratified. Drummond expects to be able to work out some solution, but in the meantime we are asked to live on faith. This may be all right for Drummond and Monnet, but it's going to be a little tough on me. . . ." But in a few weeks I was able to reassure her: "The League has at last gotten some money —borrowed it from the French government—and we have paid salaries for July."

During this period of the organization of the Secretariat we had the advantage of the advice and judgment of two remarkable men—Lord Robert Cecil and Colonel House. Both had been members of the League of Nations Committee of the Paris Peace Conference, and with the exception of Woodrow Wilson they had a deeper and more detailed knowledge of the evolution of the Covenant than any other delegates. They were close friends, and both, of course, were loyal supporters of the President.

Lord Robert Cecil was a tall, lean man with stooped shoulders and a kindly face. He had one of the keenest minds I had ever encountered, and he was profoundly interested in our preparatory work in setting up the Secretariat. We gave him an office in Sunderland House and we went to him for advice on all kinds of questions. "Cecil will undoubtedly be Great Britain's representative on the Council," I wrote my wife, "and he will have tremendous influence in shaping the League. If Colonel House represents the United States, as I assume he will, there will be two men, with similar views, in a powerful position to mold the future."

Cecil had been responsible for the inclusion in the Covenant of Article XIX, which had to do with the "reconsideration of treaties which have become inapplicable and the consideration of international conditions whose continuance might endanger the peace of the world." "We must try to keep things *fluid*," he used to say to us, "capable of continuous revision, so that injustices don't crystallize." As it turned out, unfortunately, in the twenty years of the League's history Article XIX was never invoked.

Colonel House was in London all that summer, working on the question of mandates in a committee under the chairmanship of Lord Milner. I had first met the Colonel in 1914 when I crossed the Atlantic with him just before the outbreak of the war. Dudley Field Malone, a mutual friend, had introduced me to him at the gangplank, and because we shared a common interest in Woodrow Wilson I saw a good deal of him not only during the trip, but later both in Berlin and at his apartment on East 66th Street in New York. He was a small, frail, courteous, bright-eyed man with a gentle voice and winning manners. He had dignity, simplicity, personality and charm. He made friends easily and he had a rare capacity for establishing rapport with his auditor, punctuating his sentences with "that's

true, that's true." With me, at least—and I am sure with others
—he was at all times amazingly frank in his comments on men
and events, and he had an engaging habit of prefacing his confidences with the phrase: "This is graveyard." My relations with
him were periodic and never really intimate, but in one phase or
another they extended over nearly a quarter of a century. I
was truly fond of him, and so, I believe, were most of the people who were at any time associated with him. Never for a moment did I question his fundamental loyalty to Woodrow Wilson. Even after the tragic break between the two men in 1919,
and in the years that followed Wilson's death, I never heard the
Colonel speak harshly or bitterly of his former friend. He dis-
agreed with him in some of his policies, but his tone was one
of continued admiration and affection—and of sorrow, too.

And yet from the beginning there was something about the
Colonel that was perplexing. It was a kind of vanity that sometimes broke through his urbane surface, a love of power that
was not always well concealed. I think that like most political
figures he liked the *feel* of power in his hands, but in his case the
trappings of power interested him not at all. Display was re-
pugnant to him, and anything that smacked of ostentation was
alien to his character. I am sure he was not averse to being
known as the power behind the throne, but he preferred to be
an unseen power. I remember he once gave me tickets to an
Army-Navy football game where he was supposed to sit in the
President's box. When he arrived at the stadium, he announced
that he was not going to the game, but would stay in the car
until it was over, and would then join the President. "The
President and his party have to go from the Army side to the
Navy side between the halves," he told me, "and I hate all that
ballyhoo." For more than two hours, therefore, he sat by himself in the car, safe from reporters, photographers, and the pry-
ing eyes of 60,000 people.

Nevertheless the trace of vanity remained, almost adolescent in its naïveté—a confidence, far too thinly veiled, that his influence was unrelated to his proximity to the throne. It never betrayed him into arrogance, and I cannot say that it was strong enough to distress his friends; but it was sometimes disconcerting. I suspect it was to this that I was alluding when I wrote my wife in August: "I spent today in the country with Colonel House at his place on the South Downs. . . . He is delightful to work with, as always, although as you know from what I told you some years ago he has his peculiarities. But so, I suppose, have we all. Anyway he is fighting a great fight [on the mandate question], and I am with him and the President to the finish— whatever it may be."

A month later I wrote her this: "The Colonel seems a bit worried over some newspaper story about an alleged break between Wilson and himself. He showed me some cablegrams which he and the President had exchanged over this and other matters. The cables seemed cordial and even affectionate. It's undoubtedly another wild rumor . . ."

*

Our sense of urgency in organizing the Secretariat and bringing the League into existence was stimulated by another factor which colored all our thinking. We were only a few months away from the close of the war and Europe was a shambles. The battlefields ranging from the Channel to the Swiss border had not yet been cleared, and over the old gun positions the torn camouflage still flapped in the wind. The economic situation was chaotic beyond description. Broken down transportation systems, shortages of raw materials and food, paralyzed industrial production—these were some of the threads of cause and effect which were so twisted that nobody seemed to know how to start unraveling them. There was mass starvation east of the Rhine, and the diseases of malnutrition were spreading at an alarming rate. Herbert Hoover with whom I had talked on a visit to Paris early in the summer was decidedly pessimistic. "Coal and food," he said, "where will it come from?" He talked undramatically and drily—just figures and statistics—but the total picture was all the more vivid because it was made up of cold facts.

"I confess I am frankly frightened," I said in a letter, written in the late summer of 1919, to my old associate in the War Department, Frederick Keppel, "when I see what forces this war has let loose. We seem to be faced with a disease which is perhaps too deep to be healed by a peace treaty. A new spirit is needed and where is it coming from? The immediate future is going to make a demand on human capacity in terms of knowledge and wisdom and tolerance and understanding such as no generation has ever had to meet before; and in all the ignorance and intolerance and hatred in the world today I don't see the intellectual and spiritual reservoirs from which the demand has any chance of being met. . . ."

It was during this gloomy period that the great victory parade was staged in London. Americans, French, Italians, Czechoslovaks, Japanese, Chinese, Portuguese, and thousands of Britain's own troops marched in the seven-mile route which ended when the King took the salute in front of Buckingham Palace. "It was a thrilling and deeply moving spectacle," I wrote my family, "and yet in a sense terribly depressing."

The American troops came first, headed by Pershing on a spirited horse which danced all over the street; but Pershing is a superb horseman and it was obvious that he was enjoying himself. Our troops were truly magnificent. They evidently had been carefully picked and drilled. They were all six footers, and in new uniforms and freshly varnished helmets they marched past with the snap and precision of West Point cadets. . . .

Foch headed the French troops, riding on a quiet, little horse. He looked neither to the right nor to the left. French soldiers always seem to me to be indifferent marchers, but today in their battle-worn uniforms and with their long, menacing bayonets they looked like the tough, gallant soldiers they are.

But it was the British troops that really swept the crowd off its feet in an emotion such as I have never seen. The hundreds of thousands of people who were packed along the curbs wept more than they cheered. Everybody was in tears. Particularly when the broken ranks of the Old Contemptibles swept by—the men who fought at Mons and the First Battle of the Marne—a sob broke from the crowd that you could hear way up the street.

They called it a Victory parade, but it was the saddest thing I have ever seen, because it was really a funeral march for 5,000,000 Allied soldiers who are buried on the Continent. I don't suppose there will ever be a sight like that again. . . .

At the end we walked back to Sunderland House in a pretty grim and sober mood. So much depends on the League of Nations. The obstacles in the way are really frightening, but somehow or other it has got to be made to work. . . .

*

It is hard to realize how isolated we were that summer in London from the tumult that was stirring in Washington. We knew, of course, that some of the Senators were looking at the Covenant with jaundiced eyes, but that anything really serious could happen to it did not enter our calculations, at least in the early weeks. "I can't imagine that Lodge's noisy crowd is going to get very far in its efforts to put the President in a hole," I wrote home, "but it will be a relief to have that hurdle behind us. Colonel House is a little worried, but feels that the President

will win out in the end. . . ." Judging from my letters it was not
until mid-August that we suddenly became alarmed, and with
me it was both alarm and anger. My poor family must have
suffered from my vehement and bitter letters. "The Senate
hasn't learned a thing from the war," I wrote. ". . . It would
seem as if we had had enough of blood and barbed wire and
no-man's land, but evidently not. So we are passing on to the
future another and more fearful sacrifice. Great God! If the
people at home could see what this means, they would regard
any attempt to use the League as an instrument to win an
election or beat Wilson as the most terrible kind of sacrilege,
and would lynch at the first lamp post anybody who tried it."

Meanwhile Europe, aghast at the possible catastrophe, and
not too familiar with the divided responsibilities of the American form of government, watched the scene with incredulous
eyes. To them the President had been the spokesman of America
in a flaming appeal for an ideal that had captured the imagination of the world, and it seemed inconceivable that he would be
repudiated by his own people.

As the crisis deepened in Washington the plans of the Secretariat for the coming meetings of the Assembly and the Council
ground slowly to a halt. Until the decision of the Senate was
definitely made other nations hesitated to go forward in
ratifying the Treaty, and the activities which we had so confidently expected to develop in the fall had to be indefinitely
postponed. It was at this juncture that the International Labor
Office, which had been established under a special section of
the Treaty, and had only indirect connections with the League,
decided to go ahead with its initial meeting scheduled, by a
definite clause in the Treaty, for Washington in October, 1919,
although the Office was still awaiting the acts of ratification
which would bring it formally into existence. To this meeting,
fraught with embarrassment and possible danger, Drummond

despatched me to represent him and the Secretariat, and I arrived in Washington about the middle of October. By that time
Wilson had taken the stump for the League of Nations with
disastrous personal consequences. Like a soldier in battle he
had fallen on the field—in Pueblo, Colorado—had fallen with
the cry that echoed down the years that followed: "My clients
are the children; my clients are the next generation."

Two letters which I wrote my family at the time illustrate the
situation as I saw it. "Over everything in Washington," I said
in the first letter, "hangs the shadow of the President's illness.
The lines of Walt Whitman's poem keep running through my
head: 'Where on the deck my captain lies.' And truly the ship
is without a captain, and its precious cargo of hopes for a
saner world is in dreadful jeopardy."

In the second letter I made this comment: "After nearly a
year's absence the atmosphere in Washington seems strangely
different. Of course it was obvious in 1917 and 1918 that the
Republicans didn't like Wilson, and I shall always remember
how T.R. [it was at a private dinner in New York] referred to
the President as 'the gray skunk'; but T.R. was never given to
understatement about his political opponents. Anyway, the
Republican dislike of Wilson here in Washington has changed
to open hatred. In spite of the fact that he is a desperately sick
man they still hate him, and the comments you hear at the
capitol or in hotel lobbies are almost unbelievable. To hear
people talk you would think that Wilson was the chief enemy of his country. It is dreadful to come back from Europe
where his name is revered and find this vitriolic feeling at
home."

The months that followed in Washington were for me an
unrelieved nightmare. I was in intimate touch with the State
Department, with Colonel House, with Newton Baker, with
some of the Senators, and with many newspaper men. We were

shadowed by a double tragedy: first, the attitude of Senator Lodge and his bloc, who saw the League of Nations only as a unique opportunity to crush the President; and second, the crippling illness of Wilson which shut him off from outside contacts and deprived us of leadership at a time when we needed it most. We might have survived one or the other tragedy. We could not survive both.

Lodge turned all the resources of his able mind to the task of defeating the Covenant, and it must be admitted that his strategy was brilliantly conceived. No proposal in our time has ever had such overwhelming public support as the League of Nations had in its early stages. Thousands of resolutions urging immediate ratification of the Covenant were passed by educational associations, college faculties, state and local bar associations, fraternal organizations, church groups, chambers of commerce, and all kinds of clubs, societies, and public meetings. In June, 1919, the League to Enforce Peace which was leading the fight, and of which ex-President Taft was chairman, made an analysis of editorials on the Covenant appearing in American newspapers for the preceding week; out of approximately 1,200 editorials, 1,100 favored its adoption. At the same time the *Literary Digest* made a poll of the nation's press which showed overwhelming support for the League of Nations. Organized labor and farm organizations were almost solidly behind it. Sixty-four out of the sixty-eight farm papers supported it. Thirty-two state legislatures had passed resolutions favoring the entrance of the United States.

The correspondence and memoirs published in the last thirty-five years show the craft and acumen by which Lodge beat back this enormous movement. "The situation must be treated with great care," he wrote to former Senator A. J. Beveridge. "I do not think it would be wise for us at this stage . . . to confront it with a blank negative. . . . We must proceed with caution."* To his associate and collaborator, Senator James E. Watson, he was even more frank. When Watson protested that with public opinion running so strongly in its favor the League could not be defeated, Lodge replied: "Ah, my dear James, I do not propose to defeat it by direct frontal attack, but by the indirect method of reservations." According to Watson, "he then went on for two hours—going into the details of the situation that would thus be evolved, until I became thoroughly satisfied that the Treaty could be beaten in that way." **

And that was the way it was beaten—by a series of sniping attacks, first on one flank and then on another of the League of Nations; attacks on details of the arrangements, attacks based on suspicion of other powers, principally Great Britain, attacks made on the ground that the Covenant was not strong enough and thus had little hope of stopping future wars, attacks made on the ground that the Covenant was too strong, and thus jeopardized national sovereignty. Sometimes the attacks were deliberately dishonest. Senator Spencer of Missouri, for example, in a widely publicized address, stated that the Secretariat of the League would require 185,000 employees, whose salary roll would amount to $460,000,000 a year. He further made the estimate for "printing (exclusive of labor), plants, furniture, office equipment, attendance of witnesses at hearings, etc." of $500,000,000 per annum. Unavoidable extras would swell the total of the Secretariat's annual expense account to $1,194,592,090. His final argument was that inasmuch as the United States was the richest country in the world, our taxpayers would have to pay the bulk of the bill. "Whatever our Senators lack," I wrote Drummond "—and I concede they are lacking in many things—as a loyal American I protest they

---

* Quoted in *Henry Cabot Lodge: a Biography*, by John A. Garrity, New York, 1953, p. 350.
** Watson, *As I Knew Them*, Indianapolis, 1936, pp. 190–191.

are not lacking in imagination!"

Perhaps Lodge's most effective argument was that all he was trying to do was to "Americanize" the Treaty. "The reservations are purely American in character," he said. To many people to whom the new internationalism was at best a somewhat disturbing concept, this statement of Lodge, repeated and underscored, brought a degree of reassurance. Why not Americanize the Treaty? What possible objection could there be? The difficulty, of course, was that this idea was predicated on the ill-defined supposition that America had a special, preferred place among the nations of the world, and that she could do what she would be unwilling to have other nations do. What if the British Parliament had begun to "Anglicize" the Treaty, the French Chamber of Deputies to "Gallicize" it, and the Japanese to "Nipponize" it? One can imagine with what burning indignation we would have reacted to such a procedure, and how absurd and self-defeating it would have been.

But in those days Americans did not stop to analyze the implications of the Lodge proposal. There was a degree of immaturity in our ideas and thinking. All through the debate in the Senate ran the intimation, often openly expressed, that if the other nations wanted us in the League they would have to take us on our own terms. We were striking an attitude which we would quickly and hotly have resented in any other power. We were acting like a spoiled child in the family of nations; only we surrounded the process with lofty phrases like "protecting America's destiny," or "guarding our independence of action," or "Americanizing the Treaty," oblivious to the fact that of the thirty-two nations which had signed the Treaty, only the United States felt the necessity of attaching reservations to its ratification.

In the end the American people became confused, and as time went on they grew tired of the wrangling and the long-drawn-out delay. The traditional isolationism of the country seemed to take on a second growth, and the weeds of postwar apathy and disillusionment began to spread. As I said in a letter to my father: "Lodge and his crowd have played on all our prejudices and whipped up all our fears, until people everywhere are beginning to wonder whether this League may not be the instrument of the devil, cunningly designed by foreign politicians and sold to our idealistic and gullible President!"

*

There is a widespread belief, which has now become almost a part of the folklore of America, that the responsibility for the defeat of the Treaty lay entirely at Wilson's door. This dictum, handed down by a few observers, has apparently been accepted, and it is expressed in these words by one of the close students of the period: "A few conciliatory gestures by the President would have sufficed to win the two-thirds vote necessary for ratification."

It has always seemed to me that this point of view was an over-simplification. That the President made some tragic mistakes, both before he went to Paris and later, that during his illness he was poorly advised if he was advised at all, that the impairment of his vitality affected the quality of his judgment —all this is true. What is overlooked, it seems to me, is the temper of the opposition and the emasculating character of some of the fourteen reservations which the President was asked to accept. The reservations were not mere verbal interpretations, nor were they advanced in any bargaining spirit. "Take it or leave it," Lodge's lieutenant told the Senate, "that or nothing." And what did the reservations do? They offered a grudging, suspicious cooperation under conditions which would have made the League a far less effective instrument, if indeed they had not crippled it. In effect they asserted in belligerent tones the ultimate supremacy of the American Congress over any international organization of which the United States was a part. They denied the validity of the votes of the British dominions: Canada, Australia, New Zealand, South Africa and India; they laid down a formidable list of untouchable "domestic" questions from which the League was sternly warned away—questions which had often proved to be fruitful sources of international dispute; they asserted that the Monroe Doctrine, whose integrity Wilson had specifically protected in the Covenant, was not subject to "arbitration or inquiry"; they served notice that we would not necessarily abide by agreements relating to limitation of armaments; they stipulated that no citizen of the United States should be appointed to any branch of the League's activities without the approval of the Senate; they cut the heart out of the collective security provision of the Covenant—Article X—which had so aroused the enthusiasm of the smaller nations at the peace conference. As if this were not enough they demanded in the preamble that these obfuscating reservations be accepted in writing by at least three of the four following nations: Great Britain, France, Italy and Japan.

In an analysis of the reservations which my associate Arthur Sweetser and I wrote at the time, we made this observation: "It is preposterous for us to think that we can enter the League of Nations on a specially privileged basis, free of many of the obligations binding other nations, or that these other nations have no particular points or principles which they too would desire to have excluded from the operation of the League, once this policy of national self-seeking prevailed. . . . We cannot refuse other countries what we demand for ourselves, and if we assume that we have no higher duty than to look after our own interests, we cannot deny the same assumption to other Powers."

I did not see at the time, nor have I been able to see in the years since, how the President could have accepted all the Lodge reservations. "If the United States makes a reservation," Sweetser and I wrote, "allowing it to increase its armament at its own good pleasure, what possibility is there that we shall ever bring about the gradual disarmament of nations for which this war was largely fought? If we reserve the broadest kind of questions as within our domestic jurisdiction, what right have we to protest if France makes a similar reservation for the German Rhineland, or Italy for the Adriatic? Once we get into that sort of thing, there is no end to the outcropping of selfish exceptions which the militarist and reactionary forces in all nations are only too anxious to make."

This was the point of view strongly held at the time by many of us, friends and supporters of the President, although Colonel House came ultimately to believe that the reservations should be accepted. But the Colonel was ill during much of this period, and he seemed distraught and uncertain. I remember one night Attorney General Thomas W. Gregory and I had dinner with him at the old Shoreham Hotel in downtown Washington. He was playing rather inconclusively with a number of ideas, and as we walked away afterward Gregory said to me: "The Colonel just doesn't understand the animus of the Senate." What we hoped for during these controversial months was that some basis might be found for interpretative reservations on which the President and the Senate could agree—interpretations of various sentences in the Covenant which would accompany the acceptance of the treaty and which the President could communicate to the other signatory powers. This would have been in keeping with the draft of just such interpretative reservations as the President himself had outlined and had handed to Senator Hitchcock, the Democratic leader of the Senate, before he started on his tour in the West.

But it was not to be. In retrospect, it seems to me that in spite of our recurring hopes for some break, the cards were stacked, and no variation of the play, except a complete surrender by Wilson, could have changed the result. Certainly this was Newton Baker's firm belief, and he kept in touch with the situation day by day in the greatest detail.

Of course it is interesting to speculate on what the outcome would have been had the President not been cut off from contacts with friends and advisers and the opportunity for conference. Could a formula have been worked out which, while not completely satisfying either side, would have safeguarded the League from the effect of some of the more crippling reservations? Was Wilson right in believing that it would be better not to go in at all than to go in in so scuttling a spirit? If the Republicans had won their point with the President would they have succumbed to the temptation to "Americanize" the operations of the League as they had "Americanized" the Covenant?

History is an account of what has happened and it leaves tantalizing questions like these to unresolvable dispute. The written evidence proves, I believe, that Lodge never intended that the reservations should be accepted. He was bent on the complete defeat of the Covenant. The newspapermen with whom I was in close association, particularly Dick Probert, head of the Associated Press in Washington, and Richard Oulihan of *The New York Times*, were fully cognizant of the strategy. I remember Probert telling me that if at the last moment the President's opponents in the Senate thought there was any danger that he might *accept* their reservations they would add one that would make it impossible for him to do so. And they did. Evidently in a moment of uneasiness as they approached the final vote in March, 1920, the irreconcilables added the fifteenth reservation—the so-called Irish amendment—expressing sympathy for the aspirations of the Irish people for a government of their own choice. The utter cynicism of the reservation was unbelievable. Here were the Senators shouting a warning to the world to keep off the coattails of Uncle Sam. In their reservations they dared any nation at its peril to lay a hand on anything we chose to term a domestic question. And then they added a reservation which was a direct attack on England's policy toward Ireland, and pretended to assume that Great Britain would be willing to signify in writing its acceptance of the proposal.

I do not believe the Irish reservation had any effect on the President's decision, for he had already come to his conclusion. But it threw a sinister light on the tactics of the anti-Wilson forces in the Senate in their determination to kill the League.

*

I think of those frustrating months in Washington as being one of the most difficult periods of my life. "To have to stand by," I wrote my father, "and see the wrong thing done when the right thing seems so obvious is exhausting business. Those dreadful memories of dead men hanging on barbed wire won't let me sleep. Must this thing happen again?"

I keep saying to myself [I continued]: "You have this thing out of perspective. Whether we join the League or not isn't as important as you imagine." But it doesn't do any good. I *know* it is important. It is perhaps the single important decision of our generation. Of course, the League may not work, but it is the only thing that stands between us and another war—the only hope we have, frail as it may be. Its opponents offer no alternative. They are intent on killing *this* plan, but they haven't a single idea to put in its place; and as Wilson said out West: "The world cannot breathe in an atmosphere of negations."

My feeling of bafflement during those unhappy months was

heightened by the uncertainty of my own position in Washington. At the conclusion of the meeting of the International Labor Office in November I would naturally have gone back to London, but Secretary of State Lansing strongly counseled against it on the ground that it would arouse additional antagonism on the Hill, particularly since under the seventh reservation my appointment as Under Secretary General would be subject to the approval of the Senate. With Drummond's consent, therefore, I stayed on in Washington, keeping in touch with the fast-changing developments. "I am most anxious not to embarrass the President," I wrote Drummond, "or the cause of the League here at home, but I hate this pussyfooting policy which keeps me here in Washington where I am not wanted, because the only responsible official to whom I can get access—the Secretary of State—is afraid to have me go back to London."

In January, 1920, the situation reached a crisis. The necessary number of ratifications of the Treaty having been filed, the first meeting of the League's Council was called in Paris. Prominent on the agenda of the meeting was the approval of the appointments already made to the Secretariat. Wide publicity was bound to be given to the fact that among those appointments were half a dozen Americans, one of them an Under Secretary General, and Senator Borah was lining up a new attack on the President, based on the charge that he had "jumped the gun."

In my perplexity I called at the White House to see Joseph Tumulty, the President's secretary, an old friend of mine, and at his suggestion I wrote a letter to Wilson, outlining the whole situation. I told him of the Americans who had already been appointed—Arthur Sweetser, Manley Hudson, Huntington Gilchrist, Howard Huston, and one or two others. "I have naturally hesitated," I said, "to intrude on your illness with such a detail as this, but the question concerns others than myself, and may have important consequences. . . . What would you advise me to do?"

Two days later I had the following letter from Tumulty:

> The President has carefully read your letter of the 14th of January, and has asked me to say to you that he feels he cannot decide the question it contains as he thinks it is one which should be left to you and the gentlemen associated with you to take counsel together and determine in concert what it is right to do.

I have often wondered whether my letter ever got through to the President in his sick-room. The words of his reply sounded like him, but the message was completely at variance with the flashing, decisive spirit of the Woodrow Wilson I had known. In any event, I felt that without his positive support I could not myself assume the responsibility of continuing in the position of Under Secretary General, and in this opinion Newton Baker and Frank Polk, the Under Secretary of State, strongly concurred. Colonel House was ill in the South and I could not reach him; and I did not ask the advice of Secretary of State Lansing, because he was an excessively timid man and I knew in advance what his answer would be. I therefore cabled my resignation to Sir Eric Drummond. "It is a sorry, agonizing mess," I wrote my associate, Huntington Gilchrist, in London. "My only satisfaction in resigning is that it releases me from the burden of silence. I can now speak my faith before the world."

*

Early in March, 1920, I sailed for London to finish up some odds and ends at Sunderland House, and it was during my absence that the Treaty was finally defeated in the Senate, a consummation long anticipated.* I was in a depressed mood,

* The Treaty had first been defeated in the Senate on November 19, 1919.

and on the way over on the boat I tried, in a letter to my wife, to sum up the shattering experiences which in so brief a time had overwhelmed the high faith with which my generation had entered the war in 1917.

> . . . I remember writing you nine months ago from the *Aquitania* when I was going over to take on the new job. The hope was so real and the chance for a decent world seemed so vivid and tangible. And now it is all washed up and the adventure is gone. I don't care about myself in this business, as you know. I shall certainly be happier practicing law at home than living a lonely life in Europe. And I have never had any illusions of special competence for the job; and the title "Under Secretary General" has always seemed a bit grandiose.

> But I do care deeply and, I confess, passionately about America's desertion and the chance we've missed to make this world a fit place to live in instead of a place to fight in. We had the most unique opportunity that ever came to any generation and we weren't wise enough to see it or big enough to take it.

The friendly atmosphere of London had changed in the five months of my absence. Public opinion in England and on the Continent was now colored with resentment and distrust. The insulting character of the Senate debate, the provocative tone of the reservations, the belief that the obligations contracted by the President could be lightly repudiated, our repeated assertions that Europe would have to take us on our own terms or not at all, the continuous taunts at Europe's helplessness by such men as Senators Johnson and Reed, our easy assumption of "moral superiority"—all this had left a bitterness that was deep and in some cases really violent.

"It's hard to be an American in Europe these days," I wrote my brother Harry from Sunderland House, "hard to hold your chin up." And to Newton Baker I wrote: ". . . Do you remember those boys we saw in that hospital east of Paris just a year ago? And those other boys who were coughing their lungs out in that gas hospital? They didn't die to pave the way for a bigger and better war in which their sons or grandsons could die. And yet that is where we seem to be heading. . . ."

Coming back to New York on the S.S. *Baltic* early in April, I wrote this final letter to Drummond:

> I want once again to thank you for your generous understanding during these difficult and humiliating days. We Americans on the Secretariat will not soon forget it. It has been a privilege to be associated with you, and if for reasons beyond our control some of us must now leave the work, we take with us the proud memory of a gallant beginning in a great cause under your leadership.
>
> And the cause is by no means lost. Rather the fight has just begun—a more difficult fight than we imagined ten months ago. In the United States the issue never can be settled until it is settled right. I am an American and I want to see my pride in belonging to America justified by her willing acceptance of the role she must play if the world is to be saved from shipwreck. For of this I am convinced: If through ill will or ignorance or apathy we fumble this chance to establish a definitized system of international relationships, another generation will wade through agony and blood before the chance comes again.
>
> Once more let me thank you for your words, both expressed and unexpressed, during these dark days through which we have lived together.
>
> My loyal and affectionate greetings to you and all my associates on the Secretariat.

X

✳

The Law Years

DURING the Civil War my grandmother kept a small account book in which she occasionally jotted down items about the weather or her own feelings. The day after the battle of Chancellorsville, so disastrous to the Union cause, although she made no mention of the battle itself she wrote this revealing phrase: "Broken in body, mind and spirit."

In some such mood I came back from Sunderland House to New York. I was physically exhausted, disillusioned and heartsick. The only bright light on the horizon was that I could at last realize the ambition which had beckoned for years—to establish myself in the practice of the law. Ever since I had left the office of Commissioner of Accounts I had followed a bypath, and while during this process my training as a lawyer had proved invaluable, I was not anchored in the law as a profession.

When, therefore, shortly after my return, an old friend, James C. Curtis, who had been Assistant Secretary of the Treasury in the Taft administration, suggested that we join forces in establishing a law firm, I eagerly accepted. We added a third partner, Chauncey Belknap, a young man just back from the army, who earlier had served as secretary to Mr. Justice Holmes in Washington; and the firm Curtis, Fosdick and Belknap was launched on its sixteen-year career, with offices during most of that period at 61 Broadway, New York. I was not too certain what contribution I would be able to make to the new firm, and I hung out my shingle with some feeling of trepidation. My first client was John D. Rockefeller, Jr.

Thirty-five years later I brought out a biography of Mr. Rockefeller in which I attempted to paint a portrait of that remarkable man, and there is little that I can add to the picture. He was—and is—a person of great sincerity and integrity, with a lively sense of social responsibility. Combined with this was a modesty of spirit rare in one brought up in his circumstances. There was nothing dogmatic or opinionated about him. His position in the world of finance gave him no feeling of power or even of assurance. He hated the hollow deference paid to wealth and the obsequiousness of timid minds. He wanted to be convinced, not deferred to. "The only way you can help me," he said to me at our first interview, "is to tell me at all times exactly what you think." This statement was soon put to the test, for shortly afterward he sent me the draft of an important letter which he had prepared and on which he asked me to comment. The style of the letter did not seem to me to be particularly happy, but after all a man's literary style is something of an intimate possession, and I did not feel free to change it. I made one or two suggestions relating to clarity and returned the letter. The next time I saw him he handed it to me across the desk.

"Mr. Hughes," he said quietly, referring to his former counsel, "would never have allowed me to send a letter like this."

I got the point, and thereafter in all the many years of our association, our relations were characterized by the utmost frankness. Coming from such differing backgrounds, we naturally brought with us points of view which did not always coincide. For one thing, in my social philosophy I was considerably farther to the left than he was. For another, he was a Republican and I was an ardent Wilsonian Democrat. Again,

I believed deeply in the League of Nations, while he, following the line of the Republican Party, looked upon it, certainly in the early twenties, with some misgiving. But he was a man of immense tolerance, and while we sometimes argued over our conflicting ideas in a frank and even bantering mood, each of us had a respect for the integrity of the other, and we never allowed differences of opinion to be a barrier between us, or to interfere with the work which we did together.

During that first year he urged me on several occasions to give up my law firm and come into his office as his associate, but I resolutely declined. Above all else I wanted independence and freedom, and in no profession, I believe, can these objectives be maintained as readily and naturally as in the law. A lawyer is his own master. In relation to the clients who come to him he can be as rigorously selective as he pleases. He is not responsible for their political or economic opinions, nor are they responsible for his. He can identify himself with the social causes that appeal to him without involving those whom he serves as counsel. His intellectual life and interests can be as unrestricted and uncoerced as he chooses to make them.

This was important to me at the time because the war and Sunderland House had exposed me to a traumatic experience which had cut across the whole pattern of my life, and I wanted to share freely with my generation the new ideas and interpretations which seemed to be coming into their own. Writing later to Newton Baker who had suggested my name for an academic post in the Middle-West, I said: "For the time being my line of duty lies in connection with the work which I have mapped out for myself here in New York for the next five or ten years. I have established a practice which has every promise of good results. It gives me an independence of action and thought which I desire more than anything else on earth. It affords, too, an opportunity to serve specific causes in which I am deeply interested. It gives me some leisure for study. It allows me to give my family and children the kind of environment and education that I have always wanted for them. It opens the way for future activities of a public sort which I confess I cherish for myself. All in all, my life has fallen in happy places and I would be most reluctant to alter it."

*

My work for Mr. Rockefeller proved to be of infinite variety and fascination. I represented him on the boards of some of the companies in which he was financially interested; I developed a plan by which he could keep intimately in touch with the problem of industrial relations in the business concerns largely controlled by the Rockefellers; I served as an adviser in relation to many of his personal philanthropic projects; and more important than anything else, at least to me, I became a trustee and a member of the executive committee of the various foundations established by the Senior Rockefeller: The Rockefeller Institute for Medical Research, the General Education Board, The Rockefeller Foundation, the Laura Spelman Rockefeller Memorial, the International Education Board,* and later, the China Medical Board, Inc., and the Spelman Fund. My function in this arrangement developed over the years into a liaison responsibility—to insure that there was no overlapping or duplication in program, and to help interpret the work of the various boards to each other. If all this type of activity seems like a far cry from the ordinary work of the legal profession, I remind myself of a remark of a Chief Justice of the United States: "The business of law is humanity, and the function of law is to promote the good life."

This is scarcely the place to discuss the breath-taking activi-

* Created by Mr. Rockefeller, Jr.

ties of these foundations, or their stupendous scope and sweep. What I remember most forcefully about those early days was the impact of the wide scholarship and eager imagination of the officers of the boards—men like Dr. George E. Vincent, Dr. Wallace Buttrick, the Flexner brothers, Simon and Abraham, and above all Dr. Wickliffe Rose. I still recall the dramatic meetings at which Dr. Simon Flexner, director of the Rockefeller Institute for Medical Research, would outline in his quiet voice the step by step approach to the problem of cancer, or to the development of some new hypothesis in relation to scarlet fever. It was like a giant picture puzzle in which each small fragment of knowledge, however irrelevant it might seem at the moment, would eventually find its proper place in the ultimate design. "There is no such thing as useless knowledge in medical research," he used to say. "Ideas may come to us out of order in point of time. We may discover a detail of the façade before we know too much about the foundation. But in the end all knowledge has its place."

Wallace Buttrick, president of the General Education Board, was another challenging figure, one of the great educational statesmen of his generation. On the wall of his board room was a gigantic map of the United States, stuck with various colored pins to indicate the location of all the important institutions of higher education in the country—both white and Negro. With a pointer in his hand he would walk up and down in front of the map telling us in intimate detail of the conditions at each place, and where the need and promise lay. He had had but little formal education, starting his life as a brakeman on a railroad, but he was brilliant in his common sense, and in his uncanny comprehension of human nature. Once when a brash college president presented an unitemized request for $576,500, Buttrick, who, better than most people, knew brass from gold, asked how that particular figure had been arrived at. The president replied glibly: "Oh, it's a good round number." "Well," said Buttrick, "I could tell you how to make it a good deal rounder."

An even more vivid figure was Wickliffe Rose, with his bold, fresh mind and his daring imagination. He had no interest in immediate utilitarian objectives; he believed passionately that the proper place for a foundation was on the frontiers of knowledge; and whether it was in the development of mathematics, or atomic physics, or a 200-inch telescope on Mount Palomar, he shared the spirit of Goethe's last words: "More light." The meetings of the International Education Board * were always intellectually exciting, for Rose with his quiet persuasiveness and his amazing lucidity would project the minds of his trustees into areas whose boundaries had not been explored, and we used to come away from these sessions with the feeling that we had been in the presence of one of the prophets. He died many years ago, but he left behind him a record of intellectual adventure and achievement which, although his name today has been largely forgotten, has had a profound, if immeasurable, effect on the scientific thinking of our times.

Scarcely less impressive were the trustees of these various foundations with whom I was thrown into intimate contact— Frederick T. Gates, for example, with his fire and drive and a mind that galloped to wide horizons; and Dr. William H. Welch of Johns Hopkins whose amazing erudition was balanced by modesty and simplicity. And there were others, equally unforgettable—Alderman of the University of Virginia, Wilbur of Stanford, Angell of Yale, Hopkins of Dartmouth, William Allen White, Douglas Freeman, Owen D. Young, John W. Davis—all of them positive characters who brought great intellectual gifts

---

* From 1913 to 1923 Dr. Rose was director of the International Health Division of the Rockefeller Foundation. From 1923 to 1928 he was president of the General Education Board and the International Education Board.

to their deliberations. The molding power of such men is incalculable, and their influence on their associates was an imperishable asset. Nobody could be exposed to this kind of association and escape its profoundly enriching influences.

*

During these early years, however, my preoccupation was with the League of Nations as it tried to struggle to its feet in its new home at Geneva; and the gist of my philosophy I find in a letter I wrote to Abraham Flexner with whom, for half a decade, I carried on a friendly feud on the subject.

Wilson's temperament, judgment, failures, second marriage, blindness, shortsightedness, autocracy, etc., are absolutely irrelevant to the single issue which confronts us, i.e., can the League of Nations be made an effective machine to stop war? If the answer is in the negative have you something better to suggest?

That was the point I tried to hammer home in every conceivable way and at every opportunity during the next fifteen years. It isn't enough, I said in speech after speech before all types of audiences, merely to oppose the League of Nations; the moral responsibility rests with the opposition to come up with a better idea. In the early part of this period, the proponents of the League believed that the adherence of the United States to the Covenant was just a matter of time. While I did not share with Wilson his conviction that the election of 1920 would decide the issue in our favor, I did believe that the growth of the League in Europe and the campaign of education in this country would eventually bring the two parties together. To this campaign, therefore, I devoted long and arduous hours.

In the fall of 1920, shortly after Harding's election, I started in my law office what I called "The League of Nations News

Bureau." The League had begun its work at Geneva and there was a growing need in this country for a center where its documents could be obtained, and where an interpretation of its work could be available to the press and to schools, colleges, and civic organizations. I started with an experienced newspaper man and a secretary, but the demand was so great that I soon had to add to the staff. The problem of financing this activity proved unbelievably difficult, and more than once I was close to the point of shutting it down. My partners used to say that I resorted to every expedient except standing with a tambourine in Broadway, and certainly if it had not been for the generosity of some of Woodrow Wilson's old friends like Cleveland Dodge, the enterprise would have suffered an early demise. As it was it lasted for nearly three years, and thousands of documents and releases were distributed during this period.

Those were fighting years. I was involved in controversy on a dozen fronts—with newspapers, with Senators, with numerous anti-League organizations, and with the Republican National Committee. I was trying not only to interpret the League to its friends and its foes here at home, but to defend it against misrepresentation and distortion. When Senator George H. Moses of New Hampshire charged that almost all the personnel of the League's secretariat was British, and that "the League would soon outrank the army, the navy and the church in offering careers to younger sons," I demonstrated— in words which I fear were less than urbane—the complete cosmopolitan character of the secretariat. When a newspaper syndicate loudly complained about the "extravagance" of the League I pointed out that the $140,000,000 which Congress had just voted for ten new cruisers in the navy would run the Court of International Justice for 368 years, and would cover the entire costs of the League, including the Court, for twenty-nine years—long after the cruisers had been given to the junkman.

The New York Tribune in an editorial called me a "Blue Wilsonite"—"one who falls on the floor and vainly raves"— and said my trouble was that I couldn't recover from the election of 1920.* In my rejoinder I called attention to the petition of the thirty-one Republicans, signed by such leaders as Taft, Root, Hughes, Hoover, Wickersham, Stimson and A. Lawrence Lowell, urging the American people to vote for Harding on the ground that the Republican party and its candidate "were bound by every consideration of good faith" to have the United States enter the existing League of Nations, with such modifications as necessity might require. "When the *Tribune* is able to report to its readers," I said, "that this pledge of the Republican leaders has been redeemed and is no longer a scrap of paper, the Blue Wilsonites will quickly recover from their mania." **

During this period, too, I maintained a running fire, generally through the newspapers, with the State Department and particularly with the Secretary of State, Charles Evans Hughes. The friends of the League were deeply disturbed by the attitude of the Harding administration—its failure to answer the League's letters, its attempt to thwart the newly developed International Health Section, the devious devices by which the League's activities in matters relating to the traffic in arms, the problem of mandates, the Court of International Justice, and the control of opium, were frustrated and retarded. "I believe that the League can get on and go on," Drummond wrote me early in the twenties, "but I am very doubtful whether it can survive active American hostility."

A short time later, therefore, I fired a broadside at Mr. Hughes

---

* *The New York Tribune*, September 22, 1921.
** *The New York Tribune*, September 25, 1921.

which was carried in newspapers across the country.* Armed with information which I knew was beyond challenge, I spelled out chapter and verse of the State Department's dealings with the League.

It is all very well for Mr. Hughes to say that we are not a member of the League of Nations [I remarked in conclusion], and that he has no authority to act as if we were. The point is whether in spite of our non-membership . . . we have to treat the League with cavalier contempt just to prove that we do not belong to it. Do expediency and party loyalty justify a Secretary of State in playing hide-and-seek with an agency which is working for the world's peace? . . .

The facts speak for themselves. Instead of participating with other nations in an honest endeavor to find a road out of the overwhelming peril of future wars . . . we have allowed partisan politics to place us in an obstructive role. We have no alternative to propose, no other route to suggest. . . . With new dangers all about us, with new weapons of war constantly in the making, we have played a small and unworthy part in an undertaking designed to end a system of international chaos which only recently sent five million of our men into army camps and ten billion of our dollars into the scrap heap.

Hughes answered me in a caustic speech in Baltimore,** and during the remainder of his term as Secretary of State he and I had a number of bitter exchanges. In an excellent biography of Mr. Hughes, published a few years ago, the author called me a "disgruntled pro-Leaguer," and hinted that I was a fanatic. I have no quarrel with these characterizations. Certainly no cause ever stirred me so profoundly.

After his retirement as Secretary of State, Hughes was elected a trustee of The Rockefeller Foundation. At his first

* *The New York Times,* October 19, 1924.
** *The New York Times,* October 24, 1924.

meeting he shook hands with me warmly and with a broad
smile asked: "Friends or enemies?" I must record that I never
served with an abler trustee.

*

What the friends of the League were working for in these
early years was some kind of a League of Nations Union,
similar to the organizations which had been established in
Great Britain and France; but with us the party cleavages were
still so marked and the recriminations on both sides so bitter
that we were unable at first to accomplish our aim. I remember
that one attempt under the chairmanship of President Lowell
of Harvard was defeated when former President Taft expressed
the opinion that it would embarrass Mr. Harding. Another
attempt almost foundered because Woodrow Wilson opposed
the idea of a non-partisan movement, insisting that the matter
was a Democratic issue and must remain a Democratic issue.
And there was a hint that if created he might publicly repudi-
ate it. "Mr. Wilson is tragically wrong in his point of view," I
wrote Newton Baker. "To put this thing on a partisan basis will
be to eliminate some of the League's warmest supporters in the
United States." Baker replied: "I have never been in such a
quandary in my life. . . . I have seen that lightning strike stur-
dier trees." Fortunately, as a result of a combined approach,
Wilson withdrew his objection, although I doubt whether with
the acidulous mood which his illness occasionally induced he
really changed his mind.

Finally in 1923, after many difficult meetings we formed the
League of Nations Non-Partisan Association (subsequently
shortened for convenience sake to the League of Nations Association) with Mr. Justice John H. Clarke, who resigned from
the Supreme Court Bench to work for the cause, as president,
and George W. Wickersham, president of the council. This

organization, with which we merged the League of Nations News Bureau, became the center of pro-League activities in the United States, and for nearly fifteen years I served almost continuously on its executive committee, and later as its president. During this period I spent many of my vacations in or near Geneva, generally accompanied by my family—we had acquired a son in addition to our daughter—and whenever on business trips in Europe I would take the opportunity of renewing my contacts with old friends at the League. In this way and through continuous correspondence I was able to keep in intimate touch with developments on the international front.

Moreover I was in a position where I could help interpret to Geneva the change in public opinion as I saw it in the United States. "Meetings on the League of Nations are of constant occurrence all over the country," I said in a letter to Sir Eric Drummond in 1925, "and in the last four months I have spoken before more than sixty audiences ranging in number from five hundred to five thousand, and I am just one speaker out of many. . . . I should hate to prophesy that the United States will join the League within a definite period of years, but the whole pressure of events is pushing us in that direction, and while we shall come with reluctant feet, I do not see how we can escape the irresistible logic of this new interdependent age."

To my old friend Felix Frankfurter who had written me in criticism of what he thought was my tendency to be too optimistic about the League—and his criticism, certainly at this period, was valid—I tried to explain the fundamental philosophy behind my multifarious activities.

Like you I see many flaws in the League. But all the time I am conscious of something else. Modern science has put us in a position where with another outburst of passion, similar to that which engulfed us from 1914 to 1918, we can destroy all the values that have been painfully built up in the last thousand years. The race never had such weapons before, and our situation is entirely new in history . . .

I confess I am frightened about all this. I am more than ever frightened when I see the lethargy with which the spectacle is regarded, and the ridicule that is heaped upon any new approach to the problem of international relationship. . . . The only organization that promises such an approach is the League of Nations. I am fully conscious of its imperfections, but I am persuaded that its general aim is right. . . . If we are going to save the world by some more perfect solution which we can take our time in working out, there will be no world left to save.

This theme of the race between science and social control which I touched on in my letter to Frankfurter became for me an absorbing interest. There was nothing original about the idea, but the weapons developed in the war—tanks, airplanes and poison gas—had given it fresh impetus. During my stay in London with the League of Nations I had met Frederick Soddy, professor of physical chemistry at Oxford, and his provocative book, *Science and Life*, published about the same time, had had a powerful effect on my thinking. Wickliffe Rose, president of the International Education Board—a warm, personal friend and a great scholar—was another man whose ideas profoundly influenced me; and my theme began to revolve around a series of questions, to which, of course, I had no answer. Is man to be the master of the civilization he has created, or is he to be its victim? Can he control the forces which he has himself let loose? Will this intricate machinery which he has built up and this vast body of knowledge which he has appropriated be the servant of the race, or will it be a Frankenstein monster that will slay its own maker?

With the advent of the atomic bomb these questions today are, of course, commonplace, but in the early twenties they received relatively little emphasis. I began exploring them in commencement addresses which I gave at Wellesley College, the University of Iowa, Colgate University, and Vanderbilt University, and later elaborated at the University of Virginia and before the Institute of Arts and Sciences of Columbia University. The result was a book which I published in 1928— *The Old Savage in the New Civilization.* I derived the title from J. A. Hobson's description of modern man: "A naked Polynesian parading in top hat and spats." The book is today out of print, and, with another World War in between, is definitely dated. (I wrote of military airplanes reaching a speed of 150 miles an hour!) But there are parts of the book that still seem to me valid and pertinent, although I think my chief satisfaction at the time of its publication sprang from the fact that it received the hearty endorsement of H. G. Wells, and became the means of my making the acquaintance of that amazing genius.

Of course my thesis was related to the League of Nations. With my predilections so definitely set in that direction it could not have been otherwise, and I argued for "a planetary consciousness," "a collective intelligence." "If the nations of the world are to live on each other's doorsteps," I said, "if they must rely on each other for the sheer means of existence, if they must face the same perils, then we must have some centralized mechanism, some established procedure, by which we can determine the understandings and rules of the common life. . . . The assertion of the absolute sovereignty of the state has become in our time the supreme anarchy."

Candid friends have occasionally reminded me that I spent nearly twenty years of my life in support of a lost cause. But I have no apologies. I am rather proud of the lost causes I have championed. Moreover I am not at all convinced that this cause was lost. That the League came to an inglorious end and proved to be a feeble bulwark against the outbreak of a war far more catastrophic than the one which had left so deep an impression on me—this is obvious. But in a deeper sense the League did not fail. It was people that failed. It was not the idea or the machinery that broke down at the end; the breakdown was in governments and foreign offices, in public opinion and leadership, in courage and vision. It was not a failure of the Covenant that brought about the collapse in 1939, for the Covenant as it stood was entirely adequate to see us through those difficult days. It was a failure of the human spirit.

In one respect the League can be called an unqualified success. It broke ground that had never been broken before and that did not have to be broken again. It marked out a trail in an unknown wilderness; it helped to sift the possible from the impracticable. In 1945 when the world was once more summoned to the task of creating an organization for collective security it already had had twenty years of concrete experience—an experience sharpened both by encouraging success and chastening failure. To this experience it turned instinctively, and the differences between the League and the United Nations are small indeed compared to the resemblances. In its purposes and principles, its sub-divisions and its techniques, the United Nations bears at every point the hallmark of its predecessor—the League. Whatever future awaits the United Nations, the fact that in 1945 it was eagerly created by the society of civilized people, and supported by a world-wide public opinion, is a crowning vindication not only of the founders of the League, but of the thousands of men and women who worked for it, and of the millions who believed that it represented humanity's best hope. Through all the mists of uncertainty which enshroud our time, the figure of Woodrow Wilson still beckons, calling men to a life of cooperation and concerted effort for the common safety and the common good.

When Wilson retired from the White House in 1921 and moved to his new home on S Street in Washington, I undertook, at his request, to answer the letters which people wrote him asking for information about various phases of the League's activities. These letters would be forwarded to me by the President's secretary, John Randolph Bolling, and I answered them through the League of Nations News Bureau. I also undertook to keep Mr. Wilson himself in touch with the developments at Geneva, sometimes writing to him about an interesting bit of information, and occasionally, but not often, visiting him in his home. One letter from him, received during this period, I particularly cherish. It was couched in warm and affectionate words and was more personal than was his general wont—at least with me.

The League has indeed become a vital and commanding force and will more and more dominate international relationships. I am thankful that I had something to do with its institution and I am also thankful, my dear fellow, that it has drawn to its service men like yourself in whose ideals and purposes I have perfect confidence.

In my occasional visits with him during this period I noticed that the crippling illness from which he suffered had brought with it a kind of acerbity in his comment on men and events of which I had never before been aware. It was not exactly a bitterness, because there was nothing grim about it and he often chuckled when his sallies hit squarely in the middle of the target. Perhaps it had nothing to do with his illness, but was rather a release from the long years of office holding when his natural exuberance and stormy spirit had had to be restrained and repressed. Now with his friends he could say whatever came into his mind, no matter how vitriolic the characterization might be. I remember the time when the names of Will Hays and Colonel George Harvey were being discussed in the newspapers as possible candidates for the position of Chairman of the Republican National Committee in the campaign of 1924. "Both men are eminently qualified to lead a Republican cause," Wilson said to me, "Hays is the silliest man I ever met and Harvey is just plain vicious." The President had never liked Poincaré, and when the latter as Prime Minister of France followed the disastrous course of ordering the French armies into the Ruhr in 1923, Wilson remarked to me: "I always say Poincaré as far up my nose as I can so as to get as much snarl into it as possible."

Shortly before he died in February, 1924, Wilson wrote me asking if I would come in to see him at his house on S Street. "I want to discuss with you," he said, "not a matter concerning the League of Nations, but an educational matter." I immediately went to Washington, and found him in a reminiscent mood about his days as president of Princeton. "It was the best period of my life," he said, "and I begin to realize that my contribution to my generation, if I have made any, was in connection not so much with my political work as with my activities as a teacher and college administrator." I remember he told me a story about the Master of Balliol who was asked whether it was not a dreary business to spend twenty years doing the sort of work that the head of any college has to do; to which the Master of Balliol replied: "Is it dreary business to run the British Empire?"

Wilson at this moment was dreaming of the possibility of another chance in educational work, another opportunity, as he expressed it, to help American universities to attain the high standards of scholarship which had been reached by Oxford and Cambridge.

It was, of course, the nostalgic dream of an old and crippled warrior as he thinks over the battles of his younger days—a knight with his armor laid aside, sitting by the fire in the autumn of his life and remembering the blows he had struck for causes that had inspired his youth. Wilson's desire to talk with me about it was due to my connection with the General Education Board and the fact that as a result I had some knowledge of the developments in American colleges. Wilson told me of the philosophy behind the preceptorial system which he had initiated at Princeton, and the projected division of the university into small units or colleges—ideas which he said were capable of wide elaboration and application. His body was crippled but his mind flashed with the old fire. In high spirits he reviewed the events of earlier days, and his characterizations of some of his contemporaries—particularly those of whom he was not very fond—were couched in vivid, unforgettable words.

I went down to Washington to see him once again, ostensibly on this same errand. It was less than a month before he died, and it was obvious that his strength was failing, although his mind was keen and alert. When I said to him: "How are you, Mr. President," he quoted a remark by John Quincy Adams to a similar query: "John Quincy Adams is all right, but the house he lives in is dilapidated, and it looks as if he would soon have to move out." On this occasion Wilson talked little about education. His whole thought centered on the League of Nations, and I had never heard him speak with deeper or more moving earnestness. In his weakness the tears came easily to his eyes and sometimes rolled down his cheek, but he brushed them impatiently away. I think he had a premonition that his days were numbered—"the sands are running fast," he told me—and perhaps he wanted to make his last testament clear and unmistakable. The League of Nations was a promise for a better future, he said, as well as an escape from an evil past. Constantly his mind ran back to 1914. The utter unintelligence

of it all, the sheer waste of war as a method of settling anything, oppressed him. "It must never happen again," he said.
"There is a way out if only men will use it." His voice rose as
he recalled the charge of idealism so often used against the
League. "The world is *run* by its ideals," he exclaimed. "Only
the fool thinks otherwise." The League was the answer. It
was the next logical step in man's widening conception of order
and law. The machinery might be changed by experience, but
the core of the idea was essential. It was in line with human
evolution. It was the will of God.

That was my last glimpse of him. With his gray, lined face,
his white hair, his grim, determined jaw, he seemed like the
reincarnation of one of the prophets—an Isaiah, perhaps—
crying to his country in the words which he had so often
read to us in the chapel at Princeton years before: "Awake,
awake, put on thy strength, O Zion; put on thy beautiful garments, O Jerusalem!"

Harsh allegations were made against Woodrow Wilson by
his enemies, and some of these still survive in the folklore of
today. It was said, for example, that he wanted only flattery
from his associates, and that he did not take kindly to frankness
or dissent. It was said that he was a cold, distant and arrogant
man who reached his decisions, not by rational processes, but
by intuition, and formed his conclusions in isolation.

To me these allegations seem preposterous. They do not
fit in with any experience I ever had with him, although ad-
mittedly my contacts were limited. That he was a man of
steely determination who allowed no compromise on what
he regarded as a matter of principle is true. No one could meet
him without sensing the driving power of his mind and the
flame of his spirit. Equally true is the fact that he had too little
appreciation of what Ray Stannard Baker called "human lubri-
cants": the need of explanation, conference and team play,

the ability to keep differences of opinion on an impersonal level. He did not suffer fools gladly—neither fools nor people with untidy minds. There was an element of intellectual impatience in his make-up, and more than a dash of volatile temper. It was not easy for him to forget or forgive. In other words, he was a human being, and like all of us he had his temperamental and physical limitations.

But all the world's heroes and prophets have had their limitations, too. The great leaders and idealists who in strange bursts of power have lifted the spirits of men from age to age have been made of human stuff. In retrospect we do not focus on their inadequacies. History has its own methods of achieving perspective, of sifting the gold from the dross. The last word does not belong to the cynics or the scoffers.

So with Wilson. From his grave his ideals have ruled the future. The hope of the world today, tenuous as it may seem, is a hope which more than any other man he helped to shape. And *we* are the future over which he brooded. We are his clients—the children of the next generation. It is *our* world he sought to serve and tried to save.

*

Carlyle somewhere remarks that he is interested not so much in what a man speaks up for as what he speaks out against. My generation in the twenties and thirties had plenty of occasions for opposition; and as I look back on that period now, I seem to have taken ample advantage of the opportunity. For one thing I was against prohibition. My police studies in American cities had shown me the futility of laws which interfere with customs or habits widely practiced and widely regarded as innocent. Of all the cities I visited, there was scarcely one which did not bear the marks of demoralization arising from attempts to enforce laws which instead of repre-

senting the will of the community represented hardly anybody's will. The amount of our sumptuary legislation at that
time was, and I believe still is, incredible. There were laws
against playing cards, golf or tennis on Sunday, as well as
against selling tobacco or ice cream soda. It suits the judgment
of some and the temper of others to convert into crimes practices which they deem mischievous or unethical. They attempt
to govern by means of law things which in their nature do
not admit of objective treatment or external coercion. These
people labor under the delusion that law can be used as a
short cut to a desired end, and that a few words written on a
statute book can by some alchemy alter the tastes and prefer-
ences of men.

So it was with prohibition. The 18th Amendment had been
passed when I was with the army in France, but it did not go
into effect until 1920. While the method of enforcement was
being debated I made a number of addresses before church
and civic groups in New York and Philadelphia urging that
municipal police departments be divorced from responsibility
in the matter, and that the task be committed to another body
of officers representing either the federal or the state government, or both. "It will mean the inevitable corruption and demoralization of our police," I said, "and they have enough
temptation as it is. Of course many of the members of the
new corps of enforcement officers, recruited by the national
government or by the state, will in time be corrupted in their
attempt to make people conform to a standard which a substantial part of the community does not approve; but their
demoralization will not jeopardize any other duty which they
are handling, whereas the chief business of our police is to
protect the lives and property of the citizens."

Of course my advice was drowned out by the maledictions
of the Anti-Saloon League and the Protestant churches which

constituted the core of the movement, and for a number of years I was under the suspicion of being a "secret wet." As a matter of fact, with the law written into the Constitution, I believed that an effort should be made to enforce it, although I had little hope that it could be done. It had been my observation that a rigorous attempt to enforce a law which was fundamentally unenforceable was sometimes the best way to bring about a repeal.

Thirteen years later when after a period of appalling corruption and moral collapse Prohibition was at last rescinded, Mr. Rockefeller, who had been profoundly anxious to have it succeed, asked Albert L. Scott and myself to organize on a world-wide basis of research a study of rational methods of liquor control. Our book, *Toward Liquor Control*, published in 1934, summed up the case against Prohibition as we saw it. "Permanent advance in human society," we said, "cannot be brought about by night sticks and patrol wagons. Men cannot be made good by force. . . . Law in America is what the people will back up. Victorious upon paper it is powerless elsewhere. The test of its validity is the strength of the social reaction which supports it."

The same philosophy lay behind my objection to the Outlawing of War campaign and the Kellogg-Briand Pact—an objection which startled some of my friends in the League of Nations movement. "It's the old Yankee get-rich-quick scheme applied to peace," I said at Yale in a sharp attack. "The type of thinking that makes illegal the sale of cigarettes within the boundaries of Tennessee, or places card-playing under the ban on trains in Texas, or fixes the maximum length of hat pins in Kansas, requires no stimulus to pass a law against war. It's so simple a child can understand it: we slay the dragon with words. We get the result immediately—on paper. . . . We do not have to bother with the details of enforcement or worry over such questions as sanctions and penalties. This is America's patented contribution to the solution of international difficulties."

And in a speech in New Jersey I spoke out even more vigorously—so vigorously, in fact, that it brought from Newton Baker this gentle reproof: "Conceivably a somewhat more irenic approach would be equally effective."

> That the United States which has repudiated the League of Nations [I said] and played politics with the World Court, should now promulgate the Kellogg Pact, and that some good people should think that the Pact is an alternative for the League and the Court, is enough to make the angels weep. . . . It has no enforcing machinery behind it, and it will die the death of hundreds of other statutes passed in moments of uncritical enthusiasm and sloppy emotion.

Another item of opposition which perhaps fulfills Carlyle's requirement had to do with the general subject of intolerance, and the situation which brought it to a focus in my mind was Al Smith's campaign for the presidency in 1928. I first met Smith when I was assistant corporation counsel in 1909 and he was a member of the state legislature in Albany. He was a Tammany man but he was known to be incorruptibly honest, and while he had had a minimum of formal education he was endowed with great natural ability and an instinct for leadership. Moreover there was a forthrightness about him, a refreshing spontaneity, a frank willingness to say what he thought, which distinguished him from the usual run of politicians. I never knew him intimately, but I was fond of him—as was everybody who was associated with him even in a tangential relationship. His four terms as Governor of New York marked a high point of clear-cut, unequivocal, and forward-looking public service.

When therefore he was nominated for President by the Democratic Convention in 1928, I was appalled to learn that with many thousands of people the chief argument against him seemed to be that he was a member of the Roman Catholic Church. Not only in the South but in the North as well the fiery crosses of the Ku Klux Klan were burning in the countryside. I am not a Catholic, and there are certain aspects about the Catholic faith which trouble me, as there are also aspects of Protestantism which give me concern. But these are matters of personal opinion, and they have no relationship to qualifications for public office. In my anxiety and indignation I took the stump for Al Smith in northern New Jersey. I could not give the assignment much time and I do not now recall all the places where I spoke or the burden of my message. The only thing I find in my files is a newspaper release of part of an address I gave in Montclair:

Do we learn nothing from experience? Here is an issue that after three hundred years of bloody warfare was finally given a decent burial by our forefathers. And now like ghouls we drag it from its grave. The generation that framed the Constitution was wiser than we. It built this government on the basis of religious toleration and laid down the broad principle that throughout the United States no religious test should ever be required as a qualification for public office. And here we are back again in the old days, using the same old arguments and playing with the same old ideas —as if Hamilton and Jefferson and Madison had never existed, as if the Virginia Bill of Rights had never been written, and as if Paragraph 3 of Article VI had never been added to the Constitution.

What a pity it is that in 1928 voices should have to be raised to remind us that in every crisis of this country's history, our Catholic fellow citizens have given a full measure of sacrifice and devotion! Catholics signed the Declaration of Independence; there were

Catholics on Washington's staff; Catholic soldiers were at Valley
Forge; there were Catholics in the Constitutional Convention of
1787. . . . Two chief justices of the U.S. Supreme Court were
Catholics. There have been Catholic Governors and Catholic
Senators and Congressmen. In the last war Pershing's Assistant
Chief of Staff was a Catholic; the Commanding Officer of the
Second Army of the A.E.F. was a Catholic; the Chief of Naval
Operations was a Catholic. The records show that in that great
struggle 800,000 Catholic soldiers and sailors were in our mili-
tary and naval forces, and 22,000 of them died in the service.
How can we who have profited by the sacrifices of all these men
now claim that there is something anti-American and unpatriotic
about the Catholic Church which bars one of her distinguished
communicants from occupying the Presidency!

My speaking, of course, was without result; it was another
lost cause. But the recollection of my small part in it has always
given me considerable satisfaction.

*

Newton Baker shared my belief in the justice of Al Smith's
candidacy, and worked vigorously in his support. "I felt especially grateful to him," he wrote me after the election, "for
the courage and the clearness with which he allied himself to
the principles of President Wilson when a lot of other people
in our party were mentioning no names more recent than
Thomas Jefferson."

In the years following my service with the army my relations
with Baker had become increasingly intimate. When he left
the War Department he had resumed his law practice in
Cleveland, and within a few years he was recognized as one
of the leading lawyers at the American bar. His work frequently
brought him to New York, and he often made my office his
headquarters while in the city. In between times we exchanged

letters on all kinds of common interests—books, the political scene, the League of Nations. He had a genius for letter writing, and nothing seemed to give him greater satisfaction than to sit down and write a letter in longhand to a friend—a gay, sparkling letter about some personal incident that had come to his attention, or a letter which showed a flash of his brilliant capacity for characterization. Letter writing among busy men is a lost art, but with Baker human contacts meant so much and were so essential to his outgoing spirit, that although he was one of the hardest working men I ever knew, he refused to sacrifice to busy interests the gracious art of friendship.

My files contain dozens of his letters, many of them handwritten. Thus in 1922 he wrote:

I wish I could get up some of Woodrow Wilson's partisan enthusiasm. If I were on the witness stand I should be obliged to say under oath that our partisans in Washington, when I was there, were not a damn bit better than the partisans on the other side. Always excepting Lodge, who is possessed by a special devil, I could pick out fellows on our side to exchange for fellows on their side in a way which would satisfy all the equivalence of rank requirements of the Articles of War in the exchange of prisoners. So I find my only refuge to be for or against *things* or ideas, getting help from any party that will help.

Discussing the anti-evolution trial in Tennesse in 1925 he wrote:

Except for the possible severity of the consequences, I am quite sure the trial of Galileo was more respectable than that of Scopes; for after all, Galileo had ten Cardinals as his judges, while poor Scopes had eleven semi-literates and one illiterate, and the evidence seems to consist largely in the atmosphere created by an agitated and ignorant populace.

In 1928 Secretary of War Dwight Davis in the Coolidge administration awarded to Baker the Distinguished Service Medal in recognition of his leadership in the World War. It was the same medal that Baker had pinned on me ten years before. When I wrote to congratulate him I had this light-hearted reply:

> I cordially disapprove of Republicans but I am obliged to admit that every now and then they cut the ground from under my feet, and this last generous action of the Secretary of War is as neat a piece of disarming an adversary as the War Department has been able to do in a long time.

> I still smile with amusement as I recall that General March once gravely presented to me a formal order which, if I had signed it, would have conferred this medal on me by my own act. Wouldn't that have been meat and drink to the paragraphers! And yet military men are so made that that suggestion was possible to the General Staff and the Chief of Staff!

Finally, as an example of his spontaneous letters, there is this paragraph, written early in 1924, when he was thinking of attempting, against what he knew would be determined opposition, to get the Democratic National Convention to adopt a pro-League of Nations plank:

> I have the fortunate detachment which comes from having no personal interest in public affairs, no political fortunes to safeguard or further, and no political fates to avert. For once in my life I can do what I think is right without any consequence coming to anybody else but me. So I am going to stick to the ship, adhere to the course originally charted, and go down, if I have to, with colors flying.

To which I replied:

Let's nail our flag to the top of the mast and if the ship goes down we will go down with it. Only I promise you this: if I have any strength left after the submersion, I shall rise and continue to shout for the League of Nations. I shall never acquiesce, no matter what the verdict of 1924 may be. There are plenty of Presidential campaigns ahead. I have just been reading the life of William Lloyd Garrison, and it's a mighty stimulus in times like these.

Any understanding of Newton Baker would have to take into consideration the fact that he was endowed with prodigal talents; no one could meet him without recognizing at once the amazing variety and vivacity of his mental energy. Among other things, he was one of the most eloquent and effective public speakers of his generation; and he was in constant demand by universities, bar associations and public gatherings of all sorts. He may not always have given the impression of inward molten passion which Woodrow Wilson so frequently displayed in his speeches, but there was a quality of clarity and conciseness about his addresses, an unimpeded fluidity, an appeal of sincerity and intellectual integrity which held his audiences almost breathless in their seats.

His most dramatic address was the one given before the Democratic National Convention in 1924 in the old Madison Square Garden in New York. He was pleading for the inclusion of a League of Nations plank in the platform, and I never heard him speak to better advantage. Even Wilson might have had difficulty in matching his passionate appeal. I may have been prejudiced by my pro-League sympathies, but the next morning *The New York Times* ran this editorial:

Mr. Baker made one of the best and most moving speeches heard of late in any political meeting. He showed himself a disciple worthy to wear his master's mantle. He, too, has the spirit of prophecy upon him. . . . For a moment that vast audience was lifted from partisan thoughts to heights from which it could have

a glimpse of the promised land of peace. It was such oratory as
"fulmined over Greece."

Baker appealed to the conscience of the convention, not to
its precautions, and although they cheered him madly, the
delegates in the end followed the instructions of their leaders,
and voted his resolution down.

In spite of his immense activities and the stress and pace of
his life, Baker remained the serene and quiet scholar I had
known in Washington, with a tranquil outlook upon the human
scene and an inexhaustible pleasure in the processes of thought.
Although he gave the idea no direct encouragement, a promising movement was launched to nominate him for the presidency at the Democratic National Convention in Chicago in
1932. He was the leading "dark horse," and personally I
strongly favored him over Roosevelt. If Hearst had not thrown
his support to Roosevelt at the beginning of the fourth ballot,
it seems probable that Baker would have won the nomination.

A few days after the convention he wrote me a long letter
in his own hand:

> I feel only an immense sense of relief. The possibility of having
> to hold further public office is now definitely and finally behind
> me, and I am almost afraid to think how happy I am to be free.
> The fact is that I have discovered, what you have long known,
> that there are ways of being useful in civil life which satisfy far
> more than the cluttering vexations of office. So think of me as
> happy and as eager to be more a public servant than ever. . . .
> As an elder statesman I am now free to be wise—if I can!

During the middle thirties I did not always agree with
Baker on political and economic trends, nor he with me. For
one thing he did not share my mounting admiration for Franklin Roosevelt; and I felt on my side that Baker's thinking was

slowly shifting to the right, just as he doubtless believed that my ideas were veering to the left. But these differences, frankly discussed, had no effect on the intimacy of our relationship. As Baker expressed it, it was "an adventure in friendship," and as such it remained.

He died on Christmas Day, 1937. He had anticipated the end and had spoken of it as serenely and objectively as if he were discussing the passing of a mutual friend. "Hail and farewell," he had said in his last letter to me, written in a faltering hand. With Ralph Hayes, his former secretary and life-long associate, I went to Cleveland to give the memorial address. Afterward, as I looked back on the occasion, I felt about it as Baker himself had felt about an address he had made at a memorial meeting for Woodrow Wilson ten years earlier. "I did not like the address," he had written me, "but then how can anybody like what he says in twenty-five minutes about such a person and such an influence as Woodrow Wilson?"

This was Newton Baker. If even one of our universities, every four years or so, were able to turn out a man of his stamp and stature and with his genius for great citizenship, we could face the future with larger hope. But talents such as he possessed cannot be manufactured. They come from some unknown alchemy of the human spirit.

*

To the immense surprise of those of us who knew him in his younger years, the figure who dominated the thirties and the first half of the forties here in America was Franklin Roosevelt. As I have indicated I had had considerable contact with him during the war in the days when he was Assistant Secretary of the Navy. Thereafter for some time I saw little of him. The crippling poliomyelitis which struck him down in 1921 isolated him for a number of years, although I recall that by correspondence, at least, he participated in 1923 in the creation of the Woodrow Wilson Foundation. My first definite recollection of him after his illness was when, in 1926, he invited me to lunch with him at his desk at the Fidelity and Deposit Company of Maryland on Liberty Street, where he was serving as vice-president. His interest at the moment had to do with the prevalence of crime and the reliability of criminal statistics, a subject with which I had earlier had some acquaintance. In later lunches—and there were a number of them, always served at his desk—we canvassed the question of the financing of Georgia Warm Springs about which he was beginning to be enthusiastic.

His physical handicap during this period was more obvious than it was later. Only once did I see him get up and leave his desk and it was painful to watch. But he never mentioned his illness, except by indirection, and never indulged in self-pity or complaint. There seemed to be a new air of determination about him, a seriousness which showed itself in the lines of his face, a stern kind of self-discipline. His jaw looked more prominent, and there was an upthrust of his chin and a flash in his eyes that were the marks of a man whom illness had not conquered. Once, in 1927, I believe, when I was presiding at a dinner—I think it was an occasion related to the Woodrow Wilson Foundation—I introduced him as the speaker of the evening. As he started to get out of his chair I impulsively made a motion to help him. "Let me alone," he whispered, "I can do this myself." And he literally fought his way to his feet, painfully using the arms and back of the chair as supports, and finally standing erect with the perspiration running on his forehead. The fervent applause he received was a spontaneous tribute by an audience almost in tears at his gallantry and courage.

Some time after he became governor he invited me to spend

a night with him at the Executive Mansion in Albany. I had recently made an address at the Carnegie Institute of Technology in Pittsburgh on the international implications of the depression, and F.D.R. wanted to talk with me about it. We sat in front of the fire until after midnight, and his eager mind played on various aspects of the blight which had settled over the world. I remember he kept coming back to the problem of the small, rural communities in upstate New York which had been especially hard hit. Wouldn't it be possible to introduce types of local manufacturing so that the farmers could eke out their precarious living? And what types of trade were best suited to this purpose? He seemed to be obsessed with a feeling of responsibility. "Somebody's got to do something for these people," he kept saying.

The next morning when I went to his bedroom to say goodbye—for he always had breakfast in bed—I found him in a gay and teasing mood, reading the newspapers with his cigarette holder tilted at its jaunty angle. He had just been taking some exercises with a small trapeze arrangement mounted over his bed, and he invited me to feel the muscles under his pajama top. His arms and torso were those of an athlete; from his waist up he was powerfully built—the result of the grim discipline of the last few years. And his laugh was as hearty and infectious as in those relatively carefree days, a decade and a half before, when he was Assistant Secretary of the Navy.

A short time later he asked me to take the chairmanship of the emergency relief administration which had just been established in New York State, but my responsibilities were such that it was impossible for me to consider it. I always remember his remark as he tried to persuade me to change my mind. "You won't have to do too much leg-work on this job. There's a young fellow who knows a lot about this business, and he can be your Man Friday. His name is Harry Hopkins."

On the Thanksgiving following his inauguration as President, F.D.R. asked me to spend the holidays with him at Georgia Warm Springs. For me it was a memorable visit, for in this relaxing atmosphere, surrounded by groups of afflicted children, who had gone through the same kind of suffering that he had, Roosevelt seemed to acquire a new kind of buoyancy. He was a powerful swimmer, and the children coming down to the pool would discard their crutches or wheel chairs and dive head first into the water where the President romped and roughhoused with them. There were two pools at the Warm Springs in those days, connected by a short, narrow channel or canal, and I can still see F.D.R. swimming blithely through this passage, clad in an old, torn bathing suit, with his long cigarette holder at its accustomed sprightly angle. On Thanksgiving night there was a dinner for all the children at which he presided with gaiety, wit and charm. The children had a marvelous time, but nobody enjoyed it more thoroughly or with more sparkle and élan than the President himself.

I had several long talks with him as we stretched out beside the pool or sat on the porch of his cottage, the little White House. What we talked about I do not now recall, except that once it had to do with the monetary system in relation to the gold standard, and once he related in vivid phrase the story of his fight to keep Billy Sheehan from being elected senator from New York. I had known "Blue-eyed Billy" when I was Commissioner of Accounts, and we enjoyed swapping reminiscences. On another occasion F.D.R. took me for a drive through the countryside in the small car which had been rigged so that he could manipulate it with his hands—accelerator, brakes and all. As a host he was infinitely thoughtful, and Mrs. Roosevelt, with whom I went on a long walk across the hills back of the Springs, was equally charming. There was an unaffected simplicity and a deep sincerity about them both which would

have made them delightful and companionable, even had
their role in life been on a humbler scale.

The man who entered the White House in 1933 was a different man from the one I had known in Washington during
the first war. He was a far bigger man, with new power, a new
feeling of compassion and understanding, and a sturdy faith.
I remember meeting Norman Davis shortly after the inauguration just as he was coming out of the President's office. "Ray,"
he said, "that fellow in there is not the fellow we used to know.
There's been a miracle here." And in a sense there *had* been a
miracle, an intellectual and spiritual metamorphosis induced by
adversity and triumph. Those lonely years of struggle when, as
he told me once, his sole, determined purpose was to move
his big toe, had done something to his character—something
fine and strong which brought him courage and bold confidence,
a depth of penetration and a new self-control. From now on
he feared nothing, and he faced the problems of his generation
not only with level eyes but with sympathy and imagination.
I remember watching him one night after a formal dinner at
the White House as he walked down the long hall from the
State dining room to the East Room where the guests awaited
him. He used a cane and hung heavily on the arm of an aide;
and his walk was the slow, painful, contorted shuffle of paralysis. As he approached the door the Marine Band played "Hail
to the Chief," and in a flash I realized with a lump in my
throat that this apparently broken man was indeed the chief
—with the capacity and magnetism of great leadership, and
bearing on his face and in his handsome eyes the mark of confidence and power.

I was not in any sense a member of the inner circle at the
White House. It would be closer to the truth to say that I was
a casual visitor. The President offered me a position in his administration in the early days but although it attracted me

enormously I did not feel free to accept it. I used to see him, however, on special occasions, social and otherwise. When Albert Scott and I published our book on liquor control, F.D.R. asked me to come to Washington to discuss it with him. At the moment he seemed to be specifically interested in the shattered economy of the Virgin Islands, and he was playing with the idea that perhaps some variant of rum manufacture could be introduced there as a subsistence measure. In the middle thirties he asked me to serve as a member of the President's Birthday Ball Commission for Infantile Paralysis Research. We used to meet at the White House for lunch—I remember that Edsel Ford and Felix Warburg were among the group—and F.D.R., joining us after a busy and doubtless wearing morning in his office, always seemed to turn to a mood of gaiety and enthusiasm as he plunged into this subject which interested him so deeply. During the war years I seldom saw him, except, perhaps, at some hasty conference about refugees or the morale of the armed forces. Shortly after his last election in 1944, because I had seen a picture of him that seemed to indicate growing fatigue and age, I wrote him a rather personal, affectionate letter wishing him Godspeed and good health "in the cruel years ahead." Back came his reply, written with characteristic verve. "Dear Ray," it began, "It was mighty fine of you to send me that letter. . . . I thank you with a feeling of real gratitude." * It was my last contact with F.D.R.

As I look back on the imprint which this amazing man made on the thinking of our time, I am proud to remember that I voted for him on the four occasions on which he ran for the presidency. I did not always agree with him by any means. I thought his plan to pack the Supreme Court was unfortunate, and his torpedoing of the London Monetary Conference in 1934 disastrous. I was not always happy about his easy evasions or his improvisations of policy. But with all allowances for

* November 20, 1944.

defects, mistakes and misjudgments, he remains an unforgettable and imperishable figure, who inspired confidence and self-belief in a nation victimized by the rigidities of an outworn economic system and the lethargy and blindness of its supporters.

He would be remembered with gratitude even if his only contribution had been his stubborn belief that in the last analysis the state is responsible for the security and welfare of the individual, and his determination that never again would the vacillations of business cycles be adjusted by the automatic cruelty of hunger and the blighting effects of unemployment.

The question which confronts this generation—and upon the answer depends, perhaps, the survival of our democratic society—is whether we can make Roosevelt's determination stick.

*

Sometime in the late twenties Heywood Broun, whom I greatly admired but scarcely knew, published a review of the autobiography, *The Education of Henry Adams,* which had appeared in a new edition. In his comment he criticized rather severely Adams' failure to mention the one circumstance which more than any other had profoundly affected his life —his wife's suicide. Broun felt that in a book purporting to be a frank statement of environment and growth the omission was intellectually dishonest.

The information was new to me, and I remember reading the review with considerable interest, wondering whether the question perhaps did not involve some element of sensitivity and taste which Broun had not fully weighed. It never occurred to me, of course, that someday I would be confronted with the same question. I never dreamed that such a catastrophe could overtake me. But it happened—suddenly, abruptly, with paralyzing inexpectancy—and I lost my wife and two children in a moment of manic violence. The letters which my wife left behind her showed a mind completely out of touch with reality; she was far more ill than we realized even in the anxious years that preceded her death. I know of no greater tragedy than the slow erosion of a radiant personality, when beauty and warmth become distorted, and nature's plans for maturing gentleness and grace are wrecked by an unknown malignancy.

It takes time to recover from such a blow—if indeed one ever recovers. The numbness goes, but the ache remains; and one lives with the eternal question, unanswered and unanswerable: *Why? Why?*

Late that year I went to Turkey to spend Christmas with my beloved sister Edith who was teaching in the Women's College in Istanbul, and during the long holidays we took a leisurely trip to Greece and Egypt, surveying the unfading glories of ancient Athens under the hospitable guidance of representatives of the American School of Classical Studies, and seeing the temples of Karnak and Luxor and the tombs in the Valley of the Kings through the experienced eyes of Dr. James H. Breasted, one of the world's great Egyptologists and a long-time friend.

My recollection of the trip is streaked and blurred—a montage of unrelated impressions. I still carry in my mind the startling solemnity of the Moslem service, and the fascination of the muezzins in their singsong call to prayer. I remember the flaming sunsets across the Nile from the temple of Karnak, and the sudden purple afterglow. I remember, too, the forty-mile line of pyramids that edged the desert from Sakkara north toward Cairo, seen from a grove of palms where a gigantic statue of Rameses II lay prostrate on the ground. Two things I recall with special vividness: the breath-taking beauty of the Parthenon, and the ironic smile of the Sphinx as he broods over the vast cemetery of Gizeh.

XI

*

The Rockefeller Foundation

FREDERICK T. GATES, the picturesque genius who played
so prominent a part in establishing the senior Rockefeller's
philanthropies had Spartan ideas about the conduct of officers
of foundations. "In this business you have to live the life of a
recluse," he used to say. "Never make friends. Don't join clubs.
Avoid knowing people intimately. Never put yourself in a
position where your judgment is swayed by unconscious motives."

I doubt if this monastic formula, which developed in an era
of caution and mutual suspicion, is today practicable or de-
sirable. The sensitive antennae necessary to detect opportunity
and need and to trace the changing urgencies in human effort
are not apt to be the products of isolation. Gates himself could
initiate and create, but I am not so sure that he shared with
some of his contemporaries like Dr. Welch and Wickliffe Rose
their singular capacity to grow. Nevertheless it seems to me
that Gates was not wholly wrong; there is a certain kind of
aloofness and detachment which are essential to a successful
executive of a philanthropic foundation.

These considerations became for me a matter of concern
when, late in 1935, I was offered the presidency of The Rockefeller Foundation and the General Education Board. I had been
a trustee of these organizations for fifteen years, and it had

been a liberalizing and enriching experience. It had brought me into touch with many kinds of educational activities and many types of research. But to give my entire time to the administration of this gigantic enterprise meant the abandonment of the law where I had so thoroughly enjoyed freedom and independence in participating in the current problems of my generation. Even if Gates' monasticism was not compulsive, I knew that anybody who stood before the public as head of an institution had to subscribe, as a matter of taste as well as expediency, to certain obvious restraints and limitations.

This was the problem I faced, and my affirmative decision, made after long consideration, was due to the fact that I felt the time had come to identify myself with a single consuming interest of wide significance instead of the more or less scattered interests which necessarily make up a lawyer's life. I had had earlier opportunities for academic work, but this new enterprise involved the extension of knowledge in a world without boundary lines, and its international character was a compelling attraction. To be sure, it was something of a wrench to give up the presidency of the League of Nations Association, a devoted group of men and women across the country who had kept the faith over long years. I retired, too, from the trusteeships which I held at Princeton University and other institutions, and from every organization where a conflict of interest might conceivably develop. We had a rule at the Foundation, written into the by-laws, that any trustee, personally connected with an organization or institution which was being considered as the recipient of a grant, must leave the room during the time that the project was under discussion; and I did not want a situation ever to arise where, as president, I had to withdraw when an item on the agenda was presented by the officers.

It was a modified form of Gates' Spartan code, but I never

had occasion to regret my decision to leave the law, and the twelve years of my term as president were among the most rewarding of my life.

*

I had been preceded as president by two men of unusual stature. Dr. George E. Vincent who served from 1917 to 1929, came from the presidency of the University of Minnesota, and his entire life had been spent in the academic field. He was different from the men who had earlier been enlisted in the Rockefeller organizations. Urbane, brilliantly witty, skeptical of the absolutes and finalities which always characterized the utterances of Mr. Gates, he cared passionately for fairness, tolerance and justice. His idealism was sweeping and infectious. As a speaker he was in great demand, for better than anyone I have ever known he realized that on the public platform the first essential is animation. Incidentally he was the most rapid speaker I ever listened to, his cynical yet playful wit romping at a speed that was the despair of stenographers who tried to take down his addresses.

Never was he in better form than when he was explaining and interpreting the work and purposes of The Rockefeller Foundation, and his contribution in this respect was beyond reckoning. A man of simple tastes, he was constantly alert to the temptation of wealth to be pretentious, and he hated display and ostentation. He never would go first-class on a European train or take a luxury boat across the Atlantic; nor would he ever attend a ceremony like the dedication of a laboratory or a hospital built by Foundation funds. "It is not for us to be conspicuous on these occasions," he used to say. "The money end of the achievement is the least important part." With his earnest concern for rectitude, and with a spirit which in spite of its sophistication was strongly imbued with modesty and even humbleness, he left a lasting impression on The Rockefeller Foundation.

He was succeeded by Dr. Max Mason, president of the University of Chicago. Mason was a distinguished mathematical physicist, with a wide appreciation of the integrity of science. Inasmuch as the Foundation was just entering the field of the natural sciences, Mason's creative contribution came at an opportune moment.

When I succeeded Mason, therefore, the character of the Foundation had largely been established. Its tradition of wide horizons, of idealism tempered by a pragmatic approach, of freedom from precedent, of independence from other foundations, from universities and from governments—including the United States government—all this had become a part of the unwritten philosophy of the organization, and had given it a unique status as an international agency. Moreover the program of the Foundation had been determined—at least for the moment—and the areas where work was being carried on included the natural sciences, medical education, public health, the social sciences and the humanities.* The fundamental objective behind these activities was the advancement of knowledge, broadly interpreted to include both demonstration and application. The decision of the trustees to hew to this line was based on a growing conviction that the margin between what men know and what they use is much too thin. As one professor expressed it: "We haven't enough that we can confidently teach." Or in the final words which H. G. Wells left to his generation: "There is one thing and one thing only I know and it is this—that neither you nor I know enough, nor know the little that we do know well enough, to meet the needs of the world's occasions."

---

* The work of the General Education Board, a separate organization, was confined largely to the techniques of education and to the development of educational facilities in the Southern states.

The fact that this objective synchronized with the international character of the Foundation's work was a happy circumstance. In defining in the charter the broad purpose of the
Foundation: "the welfare of mankind *throughout the world*,"
Gates with an inspired stroke of his pen had abolished the
parochial limitations which too often attach to philanthropic
effort, and had launched the new organization into a field
which, in his words, "cannot be fenced in by the boundaries of
a merely national patriotism." Geographically, therefore, we
had the whole world to work in, and the attempt to widen the
area of human knowledge, unhampered by flags or political
creeds, was to prove a stimulating and often exciting enterprise.

*

It was the campaign against diseases like hookworm, yellow
fever and malaria which had given The Rockefeller Foundation a world-wide standing. And the credit belongs largely to
Wickliffe Rose who, although he was a Ph.D. and not an M.D.,
started his work with the Foundation as director of its public
health section. Earlier, under an organization called the Rockefeller Sanitary Commission, he had carried on a brilliant offensive against hookworm in the Southern states, but when the
Foundation was created in 1913, he joined its staff and immediately embarked on the bold plan of projecting his successful
hookworm techniques around the world. "Unless public health
is conceived in international terms," he said, "the strategic opportunity of our generation will be lost."

Rose had the mind of a general and he wanted a broad area
in which to maneuver. He thought of the world as a field of
strategy in the conquest of disease, and whatever his objective
he followed its trail across oceans and continents. "Keep your
eye on the goal," he used to say; "never mind the incidentals."
And his word "incidentals" included nationalisms, geographical
frontiers, and political differences and difficulties. With this

spirit he imbued his staff; and one of the stories which has become part of the folklore of his era relates to an incident that
occurred during a revolution in a Central American country
where the Foundation was engaged in a study of yellow fever
control measures. Dr. Emmett Vaughn, who was in charge of
the work, determined to continue his research. Every morning,
with a flag of truce, he crawled through the barricades to collect his mosquitoes on one side of the fighting line, and in the
afternoon he crawled back again to gather up his specimens on
the other side. He was molested by neither army. Both sides
thought him somewhat crazy—a man who, when great issues
of human destiny were being fought out, spent his time catch-
ing mosquitoes. Today in that Central American country the
revolution has been largely forgotten, but Dr. Vaughn is remembered as the man who helped to stamp out an age-long
pestilence.

The extensive researches which Rose made on the incidence
of hookworm showed that its range spanned the earth in a great
belt, extending from parallel 36° north to parallel 30° south, and
that practically all countries lying within these two parallels,
containing about a thousand million people, were infected. In
the years that followed, Rose's daring enterprise was extended
to fifty-two countries in six continents, and to twenty-nine islands of the seas. It followed the belt all the way from Fiji and
Samoa westward through the Antipodes and the Far East to
Africa and the Mediterranean basin and thence to the West
Indies and the Americas. With the aid of teams of technicians
recruited locally, millions of people were examined for the
disease in these various regions, and millions were successfully
treated—the treatment, developed first in Italy, consisting of
capsules of thymol and salts, taken over a period of eighteen
hours.

It cannot be said that hookworm infection around the world

has been eradicated. It can be claimed, however, that as a vast public menace it has been drastically limited and brought within reasonable compass, so that it now joins the category of diseases like smallpox and typhoid which modern public health methods can readily control. Dr. William H. Welch of Johns Hopkins summed up the verdict in these words: "The agency and the man were unique in the annals of preventive medicine, and in the light of subsequent developments and of the results achieved they were of epochal significance in the history of the public health movement."

But Rose was not content with this achievement. With hookworm under control he launched a series of campaigns against other diseases which were less simple and less tangible—notably malaria, yellow fever and tuberculosis. And here he showed his statesmanship, for he was after bigger game than any particular disease. For him the attack on hookworm or yellow fever was an entering wedge, a method by which states and nations could be induced to build up permanent machinery to take care of the whole problem of public health. This was his constant preoccupation, and he drove toward this goal with his characteristic tenacity. Unless the elimination or control of a disease served to demonstrate the necessity of adequate public health organizations, supported by taxation, the results, he believed, would be superficial and ephemeral. Underlying all efforts to protect people from malaria or tuberculosis, there must be official agencies, set up on a full-time basis, staffed with thoroughly trained men, and equipped with modern facilities.

This was what Rose was driving at. He wanted the Foundation to leave behind it, wherever it went, not only an awakened public consciousness and a growing belief in the fundamental need for preventive measures, but a determination and an ability to build the necessary machinery by which modern methods of sanitation and control could be enforced.

How well he succeeded in this ambition is attested by the striking development, in the years following his work, of public health organizations, especially in countries where they had been dormant or non-existent. The seed had been planted in fertile soil, and the result defied calculation. It influenced the formation of the International Health Organization in the League of Nations in 1919, which in turn became the World Health Organization in the United Nations of today. It helped to build one of the sturdy bridges of communication between nations; it created a rallying point of unity in a world too often poisoned by suspicion and distrust. The tribute paid Rose at his death becomes him well: "In the heroic age of public health, he was one of the giants."

*

The story of the campaign against yellow fever is an epic in itself. Begun by Rose, it was carried on for over thirty years by his successors, and it absorbed the concentrated attention of a large staff of doctors and scientists, working not only in the Foundation's laboratories in New York, but in the two great endemic areas: from Senegal in West Africa to the upper reaches of the Nile, and from the Amazon valley in South America, north to the Rio Grande and south to the Argentine. It is a story of gallantry in the face of great hazard. In the Foundation's African laboratories, on the edge of the jungle, four scientists died of yellow fever, and two others succumbed to the disease in South America. After the tragic death of the distinguished Noguchi, and particularly when four of our workers in the New York laboratories came down with the disease in the early thirties, we seriously considered the advisability of closing the work. We could not foresee that the goal of all our efforts—the development of an effective vaccine—was just within reach. Only the persuasiveness of Dr. Wilbur A. Sawyer, the head of the laboratories, speaking from his yellow fever sickbed in the accents of Jenner and Pasteur, saved the day.

Behind this final development lay long years of research, years of trial and error in which hypotheses were established only to be discarded with the discovery of new facts and of better instruments of precision. Rose took up the problem where Walter Reed and General Gorgas had left off. Reed had demonstrated that the disease was spread not by contact or contaminated objects but by a particular type of mosquito—the *Aëdes aegypti*, to give it its scientific name. On the basis of this information Gorgas had cleared Havana of the disease and had made possible the building of the Panama Canal. Using the same information Rose and his successor, Dr. Frederick F. Russell, cleaned up Guayaquil where for generations yellow fever had been rampant, and then moved into Mexico, Guatemala, Honduras, Salvador, Peru, Colombia and Brazil. It was a triumphant progress. The Gorgas formula seemed like magic: all you had to do was to eliminate the *aegypti* mosquitoes; and ingenious devices were developed to accomplish this end. Where there were no *aegypti* mosquitoes it was assumed there was no yellow fever. In 1925 only three cases of the disease were reported for the entire Western Hemisphere; in 1927 no cases were reported, and it was believed that the battle which had cost years of effort and millions of dollars was practically won. Indeed the annual report of The Rockefeller Foundation made this unqualified assertion.

Then, without warning, yellow fever erupted from its hidden and hitherto unknown home in the jungle of South America, and struck for the coastal cities. Epidemics flared up in many places which for years had been free of the disease, and the hypotheses upon which the long campaign had been based had to be completely overhauled.

From the perspective of the present it is easy to see the oversimplification of the earlier assumptions. It turned out—and the new knowledge came only after patient and far-flung research in Latin America and Africa—that the *aegypti* is not the sole carrier, but only one of the carriers of the disease. Moreover man is not the principal host of yellow fever; only indirectly is he involved. It is primarily an animal disease in which monkeys play the main role, and there exists a vast permanent reservoir of infection in the jungle which has no relationship to *aegypti* mosquitoes.

The development in our laboratories of the vaccine by which people can now be protected against yellow fever as successfully as they are protected against smallpox and typhoid was the high point of the campaign. As an ominous threat to public health, the disease has been pushed back to a position of secondary importance, and while it is still capable of violent outbreak, there are techniques at hand by which it can readily be brought under control. If the function of a privately endowed foundation in the field of health is to blaze a trail, to try out techniques, to experiment with fresh methods, to pass back to the permanent authorities of the state the new ideas that are captured, then The Rockefeller Foundation lived up to its standards in meeting the challenge of yellow fever.

This story has a footnote of symbolic interest. The virus strain on which the successful vaccine was based goes back to a blood specimen taken on the Gold Coast in West Africa from a black native named Asibi who was sick with yellow fever. This specimen was inoculated into a rhesus monkey. Asibi recovered, but the monkey died of the disease. Before it died, however, its blood in turn was inoculated into other monkeys, and most of them came down with yellow fever. Practically all the vaccine manufactured since its discovery derives from the original blood specimen obtained from this humble native, Asibi. Carried down to the present day from one laboratory animal to another through hundreds of transfers and by repeated tissue cultures, it has afforded immunity to millions of people in countries around the world. Through the creative imagination of science, the blood of one man in West Africa has been made to serve the whole human race.

Nearly twenty years later it occurred to me that we ought to find out what had happened to Asibi. The doctor who had taken the blood specimen was travelling in nearby Nigeria, and I asked him to make the trip to the little village of Kpeve where Asibi lived. It proved to be an arduous trip, but he found Asibi still in his primitive house in the compound where years before the doctor had seen him despondently supporting his aching head in his hands. He knew nothing of the part he had played in the events which had culminated in the conquest of yellow fever—a disease which had wrought havoc in his village; and he was obviously pleased—particularly when one of his friends standing by in the crowd remarked: "Asibi he famous man now." We made arrangements for the medical care which he and his family needed, and for a pension which would lighten his declining years. Whether he is still living I do not know, but he was an unsung and unwitting hero in the saga of human progress.

*

We who were connected with The Rockefeller Foundation, and were thus in contact with universities and laboratories in many lands, were in a position to see on a vast scale the interrelationship of knowledge, particularly in the field of the natural sciences. For scientific growth is almost invariably the result of cross-fertilization between laboratories and groups in widely separated parts of the world. Only rarely does one man or one group of men recite with clear, loud tones a whole important chapter, or even a whole important paragraph, in the epic of science. Much more often the start comes from some isolated and perhaps timid voice, making an inspired suggestion or raising a stimulating question. This first whisper echoes through the world of science, with the reverberation of each laboratory purifying and strengthening the message, until presently the voice of science is decisive and authoritative.

This phenomenon of growth by collaboration is well illustrated by the development of the sulfa drugs. The first hint came in Germany—oddly enough in connection with the commercial dye industry—and the substance was called prontosil. Then a German scientist used this product in some experiments on mice and discovered that it had an unforeseen effect on streptococcus. At this point the Pasteur Institute in France picked up the idea, and subjecting prontosil to organic analysis discovered that its activity was localized in one particular part of its molecular structure. The potent part was separated from the rest of the molecule and is what we now know as sulfanilamide. The ball then passed to Queen Charlotte's Hospital in London, where with a grant from The Rockefeller Foundation the drug was clinically tested on women suffering from streptococcal infection associated with childbirth fever, immediately reducing the death rate from such infections by 25 per cent. The Johns Hopkins School of Medicine was the next institution to carry forward the experiments, and in the last decades research on this drug has been developed with brilliant results in laboratories around the world.

Similarly the splitting of the atom of uranium with its consequent problems to the human race is a story of international effort. The first tentative questions came from Rome; they were eagerly heard in Copenhagen and Paris, and then were definitely answered in Berlin. At once the answer spanned the Atlantic where it was seized upon so enthusiastically that literally within hours, rather than days, the critical experiments had been checked and extended.

We are today so deafened by the noisy clamor of the cold war that we do not realize the extent to which the intellectual life of mankind has already been internationalized. There is not an area of activity in which this cannot be illustrated. We are all of us the beneficiaries of contributions to knowledge made by every nation in the world. We are guarded from diphtheria by what a Japanese and a German did; we are protected from smallpox by an Englishman's work; we are saved from rabies because of a Frenchman; we are cured of pellagra through the researches of an Austrian; we are defended from malaria because of the experiments of an Italian.

From birth to death we are surrounded by an invisible host—the spirits of men who never thought in terms of flags or boundary lines and never served a lesser loyalty than the welfare of mankind. The best that any individual or group has produced anywhere in the world is available to mankind, regardless of nation or color.

Nor is this interrelationship true of the natural and medical sciences alone; it is true of all branches of human thought and experience. Whether it is music or philosophy or literature or economics or art—every nation makes its special contribution to the total product. The Russian Dostoevski and the German Thomas Mann, the English Clerk-Maxwell and the American Willard Gibbs, the Dutch van Gogh and the Spanish Picasso, the Finnish Sibelius and the French Debussy—these are the men, from every country under the sun, who have proved that the creative human spirit cannot be hedged in behind frontiers. It is only through cross-fertilization and the free exchange of ideas that society progresses. As I said in my annual report of the Foundation's work for 1939, when we were watching the ominous spread of the Second World War: "If as a result of the present cataclysm on the other side of the Atlantic, Europe freezes into an Arctic night, we shall not easily keep the fires lit in the universities and laboratories of America."

This conception of intellectual capital as an international possession was seriously undermined by the onrush of World War II. As early as 1937 I was writing in my annual report about the social sciences (Hitler's Germany was in my mind): "In some fields it is now profitless to go where we formerly went. We find ourselves stopped at some frontiers—not because the frontiers have any greater geographical significance than they had a few years ago, but because behind them the search for truth by eager and skeptical minds has been thwarted. . . . Objective scholarship is possible only where thought is free, and freedom can exist only where there are no 'Keep Out' signs against the inquisitive and questioning mind."

A year later I was even more alarmed.

> To speak of research in the field of international relations in such an anxious and disillusioned hour as this may seem almost like a jest. Everywhere reason is on the defensive and we live in danger that mass hysteria will completely overwhelm it at a time when it is most needed as a safeguard.

By 1939, when the war actually started, the intellectual blackout was complete. "No human precaution," I said in my report for that year—and my mood was one of despair—"can protect a nation from the sacrifices which war levies upon future talent: the undiscovered scientists, the gifted minds, the intellectual and spiritual leaders upon whom each generation must build the hope and promise of the generation to come. The mortgage which war places upon the economic resources of a country is as nothing compared with the mortgage levied upon its future intellectual and cultural life."

World War II was a disaster for The Rockefeller Foundation as it was for all agencies everywhere that were dedicated to human welfare. We saw the destruction in wide stretches of Europe and Asia of the libraries, laboratories and public health institutes which Vincent and Rose had so hopefully fostered. An even greater tragedy was the disappearance or death around the world of hundreds of trained people—doctors, nurses, scientists and scholars—who represented the promise of the future, and whose creative work the Foundation had supported over long years. Indeed one of the most ambitious and perhaps frustrating programs of my administration was aimed at the rescue of displaced scholars, caught up in a mass migration of unprecedented proportions—humanists and scientists driven from their countries for no cause but their race, their religion or their intellectual integrity. The madness began in Germany with the advent of Hitler; subsequently it spread to Spain, Italy, Austria, Czechoslovakia, and then, country by country, marched with the advancing armies until nearly all the continent of Europe was affected. We set up a special office in Lisbon in an attempt to rescue, as best we could, these hunted, hounded scholars who represented the intellectual values of their era; but compared with the need, the total results of our efforts seemed pitifully inadequate.

As I look back on my years as president of the Foundation I realize how much of our energy was absorbed in attempting to shore up cultural values which were crumbling under the blows of violence and hate. The relatively well-ordered world of Gates and Rose no longer existed. Instead of the "germinal ideas" which they so frequently discussed in the early days of the Foundation, we were confronted with the necessity of patch and repair work—trying to protect the "treasures of the spirit" which every generation holds in trust from the past. Much of what we did was extemporized to meet an emergency. For example we gave funds for the preparation of detailed maps of the location of cultural monuments in Europe—libraries, museums, galleries, palaces and churches—maps which were supplied to our Army bombing headquarters in the war areas in advance of military operations. The idea was that with the aid of these maps historical monuments could be spared. "The acropolis of Athens," I wrote, "the monasteries of the Balkan countries, the churches in Rome, the paintings in Florence, the vast architectural and artistic wealth of all Italy—these treasures are an important part of our cultural heritage. They are as much a part of the present as the poetry of Shakespeare or the music of Beethoven; and if through our fault they are not also a part of the future, posterity will brush aside any explanations which this generation can make."

The maps may have helped; they probably did. But one thinks with bitterness of Monte Cassino and of Dresden, and of many other places where through inadvertence or intent our generation achieved the dubious immortality of the Caliph Omar, whose troops in 640 A.D. destroyed the great library in Alexandria.

During this period of the war a substantial proportion of the appropriations of The Rockefeller Foundation related to the emergency. We furnished the yellow-fever vaccine—34,000,000 doses—for the armed forces of the Allied Powers, building up vast laboratory resources for this purpose. We threw teams of doctors into Naples to bring the typhus epidemic under control when that city was threatened with catastrophe shortly after its capture by the Allied armies. We financed the microfilming of countless historical books and documents in the British Museum, the libraries of Oxford and Cambridge and other places in England where these priceless treasures were threatened with destruction by bombing. We spent thousands of dollars for books and scholarly journals for European libraries and research centers destroyed by the war, and millions of dollars to reactivate the laboratories of that stricken continent after the fighting was over.

The fellowships which the Foundation gave during this

period represented another type of extemporization. The war had taken the cream of human resources, not only the students but many of their teachers. The task of turning out warriors and weapons had obliterated the responsibility of producing scholars, scientists and artists. Our fellowships, therefore (and the number of them in Europe alone dropped from 141 in 1939 to four in 1943), had to be related for the most part to pledges of future, post-war aid to students of exceptional promise—measures which would take effect after the fighting had stopped, that is, if the proposed recipients had survived.

The universities both here and abroad with which the Foundation customarily worked in close cooperation were in the same unhappy situation. The necessities of military mobilization decimated faculties and student bodies alike, and an intellectual blackout spread across the world. Liberal education was largely discarded for the duration, and the universities became instrumentalities of total war. Technology was left as the one subject which must be taught. History, economics, literature, philosophy—the whole range of the social sciences and the humanistic studies—were crowded out of the picture by the pressure of higher priorities. Young men were not to be trained in liberal understanding; their education had to be an education in violence. Their participation in the cultural and social heritage of their generation was adjourned. As I said in one of my annual reports: "We need to keep soberly in mind the price we are paying for victory—not in terms of dollars, nor indeed wholly in terms of human life, but in terms of values by which the worth of a civilization is ultimately measured. . . . There must be no broken link in the chain, no flaw in the title deeds by which what we most cherish is transferred to the future."

What seemed to me at the time equally disturbing was the dislocation and abandonment of fundamental research in the basic sciences. All over America scientists, technicians and students in laboratories and postgraduate departments were being mobilized for immediate jobs—often with the armed forces. Graduate schools and laboratories were only partially occupied; the cyclotrons were for the most part shut down or greatly limited in their programs in pure research. The advance of knowledge for the sake of knowledge became a luxury which a nation at war apparently could not afford. "We need to keep in perspective the requirements of the future as well as the demands of the present," I warned in my annual report for 1942; and I continued in this vein:

> The interruption of advanced training in the basic sciences seems to cost little at the moment, and it serves an emergency by releasing manpower. But it is a policy of desperation which places a crippling mortgage on the future. It grinds up the seed corn of scientific progress in the next generation to make a day's feed for the war machine.

In 1946 I said:

> The consequences of this unintelligent policy are now upon us. There is a serious, even an alarming shortage of adequate personnel in almost every field which requires advanced thinking. . . . We have sacrificed the seed corn. We have lost a generation. Our governmental policy was dictated by considerations of immediate need and was geared to the exigencies of the moment. But this was not the case in Russia or in England. In both these countries policies were guided by the long view. In Russia, students of ability in most branches of science were kept in their laboratories, while Great Britain, with some difficulty to be sure, succeeded, not in eliminating, but in minimizing interruption in the training of her future scientific teachers and leaders.

> Trained personnel is our most valuable asset in science, and it is criminal folly to gamble with the future by policies which dissi-

pate that asset. A nation which loses so much of its technical strength that it runs the risk of being unable to meet the needs of the next generation may find that Pyrrhic victories are as disastrous as defeats.

As we contemplate today the commanding lead which Russia has gained in certain branches of science and technology, the fact becomes devastatingly clear that human erosion, like soil erosion, can jeopardize the future.

*

After the first flush of Allied victory in 1945 came the reaction of disillusionment—the inevitable climax of the insanity of modern war. The losses were irreparable, and the list was all the more formidable because much of it was blank. It was the list of unknown goals which otherwise might have been reached—the advances which might have been made in ridding the world of hunger, for example, or in a creative understanding of the complexity of human relationships, if the talent and resources and tenacity of purpose which nations and peoples put into the war had been devoted to these other goals. One thinks of what might have been done in the conquering of illiteracy, in irrigating the waste places of the earth, in finding some answer to the issues of the world's bulging population, in approaches to the vast problem of human poverty and deprivation which bestrides the planet.

Perhaps a major entry on this phantom list would be the record of what might have been accomplished if the imagination and initiative which created the atomic bomb had been aimed at the constructive possibilities of this new-found energy.

But it was not to be, and at the end of the war we saw ahead of us the dark clouds that still hang over the face of this generation. Instead of a world of open windows through which the winds of freedom could blow, we found ourselves in a new climate of isolation, covered by an intellectual fog more dense than anything our generation had ever experienced. Scientific inquiry became shrouded in a rigid kind of secrecy, and the word "security" assumed new and frightening connotations. "Laboratories surrounded by barbed wire are ugly monuments to the intellectual and moral distortion of our times," I wrote. Our occasional dreams that the war with all its stupidity and unintelligence might somehow bring about a freer world and stimulate the exchange of ideas across boundary lines proved to be wishful and meaningless thinking.

Personally I have never been too easy in my mind about the part which, unintentionally and unwittingly, The Rockefeller Foundation played in the creation of the atomic bomb. Rose had been deeply interested in atomic physics because it lay on the far frontiers of human knowledge. He never dreamed of the development of a weapon of war, and fortunately for his own peace of mind he did not live to see it. But largely as a result of his enthusiasm, twenty-three of the leaders of the atomic bomb project received part of their specialized training on fellowships provided by Rockefeller funds. In this list are such names as Oppenheimer, Lawrence, Fermi, Allison, Condon, Teller, Smyth and Arthur Compton.

Moreover, direct support had been given over extended periods to such scientists as Niels Bohr and von Hevesy in Copenhagen, and Urey at Columbia—to mention only three who were called into the wartime emergency research which produced the bomb. The 184-inch cyclotron at the University of California which contributed significantly to one of the phases of the project was financed by the Foundation. No one foresaw that this instrument would lead to an atomic bomb or any other kind of military weapon. The only motive behind our assistance was to extend the boundaries of knowledge, to stimulate the search for truth, in the belief that there is no darkness but ignorance. "It is an adventure in pure discovery," I said in 1940 when I reported our support for the cyclotron. "It is . . . an emblem of the undiscourageable search for truth which is the noblest expression of the human spirit."

But it is this same search for truth which has today brought our civilization to the edge of the abyss, and man is confronted with the tragic irony that when he has been most successful in pushing out the boundaries of knowledge, he has most endangered the possibility of human life on this planet. The pursuit of truth has at last led us to the tools by which we can ourselves become the destroyers of our own institutions and all the bright hopes of the race. What are we to do—curb our science, or cling to the pursuit of truth and run the risk of returning our society to barbarism?

The dilemma has been startlingly magnified by recent events. Even if we tried to limit our science to humane and constructive objectives, the question would still be unresolved, for the good and evil that flow from research are, more often than not, indistinguishable at the point of origin. There is no way of foretelling what particular kind of knowledge is divertible to destructive ends. There is no method of sifting the potential bad from the potential good when an Einstein or a Tsiolovsky mark out a new road for eager minds to follow.

We are driven back to a question of human motives and desires. Science merely reflects the social forces by which it is surrounded. When there is peace, science is constructive; when there is war or the threat of war science is perverted to sinister ends. The towering enemy of man is not his techniques but his irrationality, not science but war; and we in this generation are faced with a cruel question: Can tolerance and understanding and creative intelligence run fast enough to keep us abreast with our own mounting capacity to destroy?

I would not want to give the impression that the $200,000,-
000 which was appropriated by The Rockefeller Foundation
and the General Education Board during my term as president
represented an exercise in futility. Even the "patch and repair
work" which we were called upon to do during this war period
included many projects which had wide social usefulness, and
no apologies are necessary. We have to remember that like all
other institutions the Foundation was faced by the deepening
tragedy of the twentieth century, and it was shaped by the era
in which it lived.

But it was by no means a negative or even ameliorative effort
which the Foundation made during this period. I recall with
satisfaction the grants given to Dr. H. W. Florey at Oxford
which led to the clinical application of Dr. Alexander Fleming's
previous discovery of penicillin, and its development on an international scale.

I remember the stout and gallant fight, led by the Foundation's public health officers, that repulsed the invasion into
South America of the *gambiae* mosquito, the most dangerous
member of a dangerous malarial family. Striking from its home
in Equatorial Africa—probably as a passenger in an airplane—
it gained a foothold in Brazil and swept up the coast toward the
Amazon valley, leaving behind death, desolation and a wrecked
economy. "This invasion," said one of the world's leading malariologists, "threatens the Americas with a catastrophe in comparison with which ordinary pestilence, conflagration and even
war are but small and temporary calamities."

The strategy of the campaign against the *gambiae* resembled
the strategy of the Battle of the Bulge. The enemy had first to
be contained within the area he had seized, and then surrounded and annihilated. An army of over two thousand doctors, technicians, inspectors and guards, recruited from Brazil,
served under the Foundation's malariologists. And it took al-

most five years and an expenditure of some millions of dollars to bring the invasion under control.

I remember, too, the beginnings of the Foundation's great work in agriculture which has revolutionized the food resources of Mexico, and has now been extended to Colombia, Chile, and India. Its genesis was a casual remark which Henry A. Wallace, then Vice President of the United States, made to me in 1941. He had just returned from a visit to Mexico, and I was lunching with him at his office in the Capitol. "If you people," he said, "could do something that would raise the yield per acre of corn and beans in Mexico you would do more for the welfare of that country and the happiness of its people than any other plan you could devise." With that bit of advice we sent a group of agricultural experts to Mexico to spy out the land. They came back with an enthusiastic report and an inspired suggestion: "Put J. G. Harrar at the head of the work." Harrar was a young professor of plant pathology in the state of Washington, and among his other qualifications he knew Mexico well and he spoke Spanish like a native.

Under his leadership, and in cooperation with the Mexican government, research was begun with corn, wheat, beans and other basic food crops from the standpoint of genetic improvement, disease and pest control, as well as soil and fertilizer problems. The results were startling and spectacular. Hundreds of thousands of acres were planted with the newly developed hybrid variety of corn, and by 1947 Mexico for the first time in its history did not have to import corn from abroad to supplement its own production. Similarly with wheat, the utilization of rust resistant varieties made it unnecessary for Mexico to rely almost exclusively on imports for this important food product. As Dean Rusk, who is now president of the Foundation, remarked in a recent report: "The eventual target [of this program] is more food for the underfed in the villages and urban centers of countries where human dignity is not yet adequately supported by a healthful diet, and where the struggle to raise food absorbs so much time and energy that other activities cannot prosper."

Someday they will be erecting monuments to Harrar, not only in Mexico but in other countries around the world where his scientific knowledge and imagination have helped to transform the lives of men. Or will his fate be like that of Wickliffe Rose or Wallace Buttrick—geniuses who contributed enormously to the thinking of their generation, but whose names today are largely forgotten?

Another constructive project which I recall with some degree of pride was the consistent support which we gave to the development of modern medicine in China. Gates was the creator in whose mind the idea was born, but it was men like Dr. Simon Flexner, Dr. Buttrick and Roger S. Greene who brought The Peking Union Medical College into being. It became "the Johns Hopkins of China," the outpost of medical teaching and research in the Far East, a symbol of high quality and objective approach. The largest single grant of my administration—$10,-000,000—was given to this institution.

Troubled fortunes have swept over China since that gift was made, but they have not erased the impact of the influence of the college during the three decades of its existence under American auspices. The scores of highly trained doctors and nurses which it developed have been an intellectual ferment across the length and breadth of China, preaching a gospel of modern medicine and what it could do for people who had never known it. No regime—communist or otherwise—would care to stem such a tide, and the school itself lives on today, supported by the government, although apparently with greater emphasis on the quantity rather than the quality of its graduates. It is people, not governments or regimes, that count; and it is the needy people of China to whom modern medicine is bringing its healing techniques. In dark hours like these it takes perhaps a leap of faith to believe that medicine can be one of the bridges across the gulf that separates this frightened present from a saner and better balanced future. We shall, of course, need other bridges, but modern medicine, bringing us a conception of common human need that overrides our irrational and suicidal differences, can surely help.

*

Still another field which was developed by the Foundation in spite of the thwarting circumstances of war was the social sciences. Public health is of vital importance—and so are medicine and biology—and money spent in their development is devoted to a basic purpose. But unless we can find successful solutions to some of the complex and fast growing problems of human relationships, we run the risk of having a world in which public health and medicine are of little significance. The supreme obligation confronting us, so I believed, was to bring to the study of man and his problems the same objectivity and the same passion for truth which have in the past given us a measure of understanding and control of the physical world.

The difficulty, of course, lies in the fact that the obstacles to productive research in the social sciences are infinitely more real than any which the physical scientist has to encounter. The nature of the problems to be solved, the character of the data, the variables involved, the less mature development of tools and methods—all these make the broad area of the social studies the refuge for activities that are often superficial and specious, and for ideas that are not infrequently cloaked in an unintelligible jargon.

Foundations working in this field are not unaware of these weaknesses; indeed officers and trustees alike live with them so intimately that they do not always escape the feeling of frustration and impatience, and the nostalgic desire to return to areas of activity, like public health and medicine, which promise more clear-cut and measurable rewards. There is something chilling about the tortuous and glacier-like movement of the social sciences.

But this is a defeatist attitude which turns its back on the overwhelming problems of our time. Unless our generation, through stubbornness or fear, takes the position that human intelligence is powerless to plan a more rational life for mankind, and that solutions to human problems are not negotiable, it is bound to support the attempt, faltering as it may be in many of its approaches, to build depth and integrity into the study of social issues, and make scientific analysis and tested fact available for social purposes.

This was the philosophy behind our work in the social sciences, and no sector of the Foundation's program was pushed more vigorously or received a larger share of concentrated attention. In addition to the wide use of fellowships and grants-in-aid, three major areas of special interest were given intensive support: economic stability, public administration, and international relations. Unlike the fields of public health and agriculture where the Foundation itself assumed the leadership and participated in the enterprise, in the social sciences and in other areas, too, our function, by a self-imposed rule, was limited to grants to outside agencies which were organized and staffed to carry on the work—agencies like the Social Science Research Council, the Brookings Institution, the National Bureau of Economic Research, the Council on Foreign Relations, the Food Research Institute, the Spelman Fund for its program in public administration, and scores of other organizations, as well as universities, located not only in the United States, but around the world.

There is little color or drama about this kind of work. There are no short-cuts—no penicillin or sulfa drug that can be discovered to cure the ills of human society. Social maladjustments can be relieved only by the slow accumulation of knowledge and wisdom influencing policies and decisions at myriad points. These influences for the most part work silently, with low visibility. They are seldom spectacular; they are never automatic; the structure has to be built brick by brick. Disciplined minds are needed, and the high integrity of objective scholarship; and the flow of first-class talent into these fields must be continuous and uninterrupted.

And yet, if we use as a measuring rod what has happened in the social sciences over the last fifty years, or even the last twenty-five years, there is little occasion for pessimism. Those who look behind the headlines can perceive the solid progress that has been made. The basis for a better understanding of social and economic issues is being steadily shaped. Today we know far more about our own economy and the economy of other nations than we did a generation ago; investigation has brought within reach fundamental information which is influencing public policy at a dozen points. We know about our national income—its size, its distribution, and the changes that occur in its character. We know about the world's food supply and where the strains and stresses are going to come. Our population estimates rest on more adequate analysis than was ever before attempted. The improvement of governmental budgetary and personnel systems, and the reform of state and local tax structures, are built on years of thorough research.

These are only a few examples, but the progress is gathering momentum. Modesty as to its pace should involve no discouragement. Along this road, if it is persistently followed, lie the possibilities of ultimate social intelligence, and the goal can be gained by patience, tenacity, and adequate and continuing support. This was the faith that guided us in The Rockefeller Foundation during the years of my administration, and it is a faith, I believe, that is still cherished.

*

This list of some of the creative activities of the Foundation, which even the blight of World War II did not cancel out, could be indefinitely expanded. A complete list would include the program in psychiatry, broadly interpreted to embrace neurology and psychology. As I said in one of my early reports: "Our tragic lack of knowledge in this backward field may be deduced from the economic, moral, social, and spiritual losses occasioned by the feeble-minded, the delinquents, the criminal insane, the emotionally unstable, the psychopathic personalities, and—less dramatic but far more widespread—the preventable anxieties, phobias, complexes, and anomalous or unbalanced behavior of otherwise normal human beings. . . . Whether he will or no, the doctor's office is a confessional of spiritual as well as physical disability. Man's eternal cry is for release, and the physician must answer it with something more than a test tube."

The approach of the Foundation to this new field of interest was direct and clean cut. It proceeded along two lines: one, the development and endowment of good teaching in a few carefully selected medical schools, with the integration of psychiatry into the regular medical curriculum; and, two, the wide support of scientific research both here and abroad. Only with longer perspective can an adequate appraisal be made of the accomplishment of this strongly-backed program, or of the influences that were set in motion. It is significant, however— whether due in part to the Foundation's activities or otherwise —that psychiatry today occupies a position far different from that which it occupied in the early thirties. It is no longer a stepchild of the medical schools, acknowledged, but not understood and really not wanted. While it has by no means paralleled the development of other branches of medicine, it is slowly developing a body of knowledge and a trained personnel of high promise. Meanwhile research in psychiatry is being productively and in some cases brilliantly expanded.

One final item on the list of the Foundation's major activities during my administration needs more elaboration than is possible in these pages. It relates to the relatively neglected field of the humanistic studies. There is a hunger in the world today which the physical and medical scientists, together with the specialists in the social studies, cannot relieve. As they have in all ages, apart from religion, men turn for their ultimate satisfactions to humanism—to the philosophers, the teachers, the historians, the artists, the poets, the novelists, the dramatists—all those who fashion ideas and concepts which give meaning and value to life. It is they who really construct the world we live in; and it is they, too, who can speak effectively to a distracted age. Every creative contribution of the natural and social sciences to the problems of society is to be welcomed; but to expect those sciences to meet the spiritual hunger for hope and belief and beauty and permanent values is a form of superstition as withering as any which humanity has thus far outlived.

This was the thinking behind our work in the humanities, and I remember with satisfaction the imaginative and many-faceted approach we made to the problem under the specialized direction of a group of able officers. It was a truly international program, and it involved scholars and scholarship in such widely diverse fields as literature and philology, Oriental studies, history, drama, broadcasting, archeology, philosophy, art, architecture, and a dozen other studies. Probably some of the work was profitless—a piling of fact upon fact, with little relation to the values needed by our times. But who can tell in advance the scholar from the pedant? Or who can determine the kind of cultural and intellectual soil out of which creativeness, imagination, and great teaching will spring? Meanwhile it can be recorded that of the scores of scholars who received support from the Foundation at this time, not a few have become the interpreters of their generation.

*

My own life during this period brought me the peculiar kind of satisfaction which comes only when a man is harnessed to a significant and worthwhile task. I remember that one of my trustees—the distinguished head of a great university—said to me one afternoon as we walked in the gardens of Williamsburg: "I would rather have your job than any job I have ever known or heard about." I was surrounded by a devoted, loyal and extraordinarily able staff of officers, chosen over the years with scrupulous care, most of them specialists in a particular field—men like Alan Gregg, Warren Weaver, Joseph Willits, David Stevens, John Marshall, George Strode and Andrew Warren, and women like Mary Beard, Elizabeth Tennant, Sydnor Walker and Flora Rhind, and dozens of others who should be mentioned in the same breath. We were a congenial family—all of us idealists, and all of us, I hope, endowed with a stabilizing minimum of realism. They did the work, each individual handling his own field of interests and training. My part was largely that of moderator, whose chief function was to keep the whole program in reasonable balance, and, when necessary, give advice based on my long experience as a trustee of the Foundation.

I served as a trustee and an officer of the Foundation for over twenty-seven years. As I look back on the varied projects and undertakings which developed during that period, I think the one that claimed my greatest personal interest was the building of the giant 200-inch telescope on Mount Palomar in California. It was financed by three Rockefeller boards—the International Education Board, the General Education Board, and the Foundation; and I was closely connected with it from its inception in 1928 until its completion twenty years later. More than anything else it seemed to me to symbolize man's thirst for knowledge—the unique characteristic which gives human life its meaning and purpose and clothes it with final dignity.

I confess my attitude toward this project contained overtones of mysticism. I felt that this titanic tool of science, which would project human sight into space so much farther than it had ever gone before, might bring into fresh focus the enigma of the universe, its apparent order, its beauty, its power. It would dramatize the questions which mankind has always asked and to which no answers have been found, and perhaps can never be found. Are there other planets that have burst into consciousness like our own? Is there an answering intelligence anywhere in space? Is there purpose behind the apparent meaninglessness and incomprehensibility of the universe? What is this divine spark of awareness which we call consciousness? And finally, in the words and spirit of the Psalmist, what is man?

The evening before the dedication of the telescope a group of us motored from the fog-enshrouded valley at the foot of Mount Palomar up along the winding road to the brilliantly-clear skies at the top. The telescope, of course, is designed primarily for the photography of the heavens, but that night the astronomers had rigged up an eye-piece, and what we saw as we gazed through the lens was a universe of stars floating in majesty 125,000,000 light years away—not one universe, but several of them. The correlation of time and space was immediately apparent: we were looking out into the immense reaches of infinity, but at the same time we were looking backward into the long history of the cosmos. Whether those particular galaxies were still in their place, or whether they had vanished in some vast and ancient nuclear disaster, the astronomers could not tell us. All they knew was that the clusters had been located at this particular spot in the heavens 125,000,000 years before.

"Against this majestic background of time and space," I said in my dedicatory address the next morning, "the petty squabbling of nations on this small planet is not only irrelevant but contemptible. Adrift in a cosmos whose shores he cannot even imagine, man spends his energies in fighting with his fellowman over issues which a single look through this telescope would show to be utterly inconsequential."

Incidentally my participation in this ceremony was in violation of one of the principles of Dr. Vincent's stern code to the effect that Foundation representatives should not be conspicuous on occasions of this kind; but it was only a few days before my retirement as president, and on this perhaps flimsy basis I rationalized my acceptance of the invitation.

Three years after I left the presidency in 1948—we retire our trustees and officers at the age of sixty-five—I published a history of The Rockefeller Foundation which tells a far wider story of its genesis and activities than is possible to include here. It gave me an opportunity to see the organization, perhaps, in clearer perspective, and to form some judgment as to the place of philanthropic foundations in modern society. Shortly after I published the book Congress started an investigation of foundations, followed a year later by a second one. It was during the hysterical days of the McCarthy era, and the two investigations were motivated by the suspicion that Communist influences had insidiously infiltrated the ranks of the foundations. At any other time the charges would have been dismissed as the imaginings of a diseased mind, but in that disastrous period there were vociferous people who believed them.

In earlier years the persistent charge against foundations had been that they were in too conservative hands, and that their purposes were too closely related, certainly in terms of personnel, to the unprogressive ideas of an outmoded past. I never expected in my lifetime to have a charge coming from exactly the opposite quarter. "I do not say that foundations have a spotless record," I said in a statement I made to the first investigating committee. "Like all human instruments they make mistakes—mistakes of judgment, mistakes due to inadequate information or to lack of infallibility in foreseeing the development of men and institutions. But to claim that there is something calculated about some of these mistakes, that there is some subversive element lurking in foundations, is, as far as my knowledge goes, utterly incredible and fantastic."

The point must again be emphasized [I went on to say] that foundations at their best represent intellectual adventure. They are concerned with the advancement of human knowledge. Whether it is astronomy or biology or physics or the social studies, they are supporting work which involves new ideas and new approaches. It would be a vast disservice to America and to the whole world if these foundations, through pressure or timidity, were forced to follow more conventional patterns, or were frightened away from controversial fields.

Controversy attaches to many types of intellectual undertaking, and our foundations, if they are to be true to their unique opportunities, must help to maintain the tradition of objective scholarship—the tradition of fearless inquiry, the unintimidated search for truth, wherever the truth may lead . . .

[We] must resist the easy temptation to apply the label "communistic" to all ideas that are new or different or unconventional. The effort to equate loyalty with conformity strikes at the root of American life. A democracy cannot wisely be concerned with monolithic thinking. That is the concern of totalitarianism. With us there must be room for unorthodoxy, room for nonconformity, room for diversity of opinion. This is the tradition of America, and this is the source of its strength and spiritual growth.

This emphasis upon the necessity of intellectual adventure and of hospitality to new ideas has always seemed to me to constitute the hallmark of the work of the most effective foundations. Without such a pioneering spirit a philanthropic foundation serves no particular purpose except to relieve the general public of responsibility for supporting worthy causes. The needle grinds round and round in the same groove, and there is no attempt to keep abreast with the challenge of a rapidly changing world. A foundation conceived in such narrow terms misses its unique opportunity. Its real place is "close to the growing edge of things." It should be concerned with future possibilities rather than with present pressures. Its capital is venture capital. It can afford to take risks. It can blaze trails, find new methods, explore new techniques, pioneer in areas where public funds cannot readily or quickly go, and where other private funds are inadequate. A fresh approach to some disease like infantile paralysis or yellow fever, or ample funds placed strategically in the development of psychiatry, or the support of promising scholarship in studies of the vexing social and economic problems which threaten our generation—these are some of the types of activity which distinguish our more progressive foundations. Without such assistance social growth would undoubtedly be a somewhat slower process, and the tools of knowledge would not be so readily available.

But why should not government funds be used for this type of activity? Why should it be left to the caprice and perhaps prejudices of the trustees of private organizations? Of course government, even in our Western society, has already moved into this field, and in my time I have witnessed the complete change-over from private to public support in wide areas of administration and research, particularly in the fields of public health and the natural sciences. But I have a feeling that many types of research, notably in the biological and social sciences, and certainly in the humanistic studies, are beyond the administrative capacity of a government already overloaded with a vast complex of difficult tasks. Moreover public money, generally speaking, can be allocated only to "sure bets," to projects that have already proven themselves in demonstrations which have been successfully applied. With public money, by and large—except in the important field of armaments or satellites—there can be little element of risk or chance, no possibility that the promise may prove a failure, or that the road may come to a dead end. "Most research," said Dr. Simon Flexner, "is a discouraging process of following trails that lead nowhere."

Moreover, there is at least the possibility that public opinion, impatient for quick results, may insist that tax money be directed to immediate utilitarian ends. Again, government-supported research usually follows the tradition of government budgeting; that is, the purpose of the appropriation is first determined, then the amount to be spent is fixed, and finally the personnel is selected. Foundation-supported research, on the other hand, is apt to reverse this process by first finding the able men, and then building the research project, whatever it may be, around their special talents. First-class brains are not made to order, nor can they always be found for particularized tasks.

I would not want to minimize the value of much publicly supported research; but it is undoubtedly a fair statement that in private institutions, where liberal foundation grants have been given, originality, spontaneity of thought, variation, and freedom from tradition have a peculiarly rich soil in which to grow.

If wisely and imaginatively administered, free to interpret its own function in society and to act boldly in implementing that interpretation, a foundation can deeply affect the advancement of human welfare. But it is not an easy task. Years ago Dr. Henry S. Pritchett, head of the Carnegie Foundation, remarked that "somebody must sweat blood with gift money, if its effect is not to do more harm than good." One of the difficulties is that social agencies, like all human agencies, have a tendency to exalt the machinery of organization above the purpose for which the organization was created. Business concerns are subject to exactly the same tendencies, but, as Pritchett pointed out, in a business organization there is an ever-present test of efficiency lacking in those agencies that deal with intellectual and social products. A business enterprise is established to make money, and when earnings dwindle, search is made to determine what is wrong. No such automatic criterion exists to test the efficiency of a social organization. It is always difficult to know whether such an organization is really paying dividends or not.

Foundations face the necessity of constant self-examination to insure their adaptability to changing conditions. If the work is to be kept out of ruts, if the organization is to avoid frustration and stagnation, programs and methods must be elastic, fresh, forward-looking, and open-minded.

Another difficulty about foundations arises from a distorted perspective in relation to the effectiveness and power of money. There is a common fallacy—and even some foundation executives may not be immune from it—that money can create ideas, and that a great deal of money can create better ideas. Nothing could be wider of the mark. You cannot buy scientists or poets as you would vegetables in a cash-and-carry store. A "crash program" cannot produce genius. It may hasten the testing of new theories, but first of all you have to have the new theories.

There is no substitute for brains. The difficulty is the lack of men with fertile spirit and imagination—men with basic training or with flaming ideas demanding expression. For them there is no alternative; without them money will purchase nothing but motion and futility. Unless a foundation understands the relatively limited usefulness of money, its performance will likewise be limited. The best that it can aim to do is to put its support in the right place at the right time. The most that it accomplishes is to expedite the development of ideas, which, without help, might be retarded. "An extra engine put on to help the train over a stiff grade"—this was Dr. Buttrick's homely description of the function of his board.

It follows, therefore, that a becoming modesty is a prerequisite for a foundation. The traditional tendency of wealth to think of itself in terms of exaggerated importance is not an appropriate attitude for a foundation official. "I sometimes wish we did not have so much money," Dr. Buttrick used to say, as he contemplated the work of the General Education Board. "I think perhaps we would do a better job with less. And I am sure it would have a good effect on our officers." What he was thinking of in this last remark was the necessity of a humble spirit in agencies of this kind—a doctrine he never failed to preach. Machiavelli in *The Prince* made a comment which I always thought foundation personnel could ponder with profit: "For the spending of that which is another's takes not away thy reputation but rather addes to it; only the wasting of that which is thine owne hurts thee."

*

I do not pretend to be wholly objective about the work and accomplishments of The Rockefeller Foundation, but over long years I saw at first hand the devotion, the integrity, and the high sense of responsibility and dedication with which its affairs were administered by officers and trustees alike. I am proud of the record, and I know that the Foundation has won for itself a place in the confidence and respect of many people in many lands. This could be demonstrated by scores of illustrations, but perhaps a single incident will serve. Two victims of the Hitler persecutions, who met their deaths in concentration camps, left wills naming The Rockefeller Foundation as a principal beneficiary. As far as can be discovered neither of these men had been in contact with the Foundation. They did not know each other. One, a Frankfurt physician, died probably of malnutrition at the Theresienstadt camp. The other, a Hungarian industrialist, was executed in the gas chambers at Auschwitz. He left the Foundation nearly $100,000 in a New York bank and other lesser funds in institutions located in Geneva, London, Cairo and Johannesburg. It would seem that in both cases the donors looked upon The Rockefeller Foundation as perhaps the one stable and enduring organization worthy of their final trust.

All this on the credit side can truly and objectively be said about The Rockefeller Foundation without in any way detracting from the myriad efforts of hundreds of other agencies working toward the same ends. The age-old task of weaving an adequate pattern of human welfare is of course a vast, conjunctive effort, and the Foundation has been merely a single thread in a mighty skein.

XII

*

Epilogue

THOSE of us who have achieved a life span of seventy-five years look back upon an era of convulsive and revolutionary change. Change, of course, is the characteristic of human environment in all ages, but never before, as I remarked earlier, has the *rate* of change been so rapid and so violent as that which has accompanied the period of my generation. We began with the horse and buggy, the advent of the bicycle, and kerosene lamps; and we are ending with airplanes at supersonic speeds, the hydrogen bomb, and man-made satellites circling the earth. The first automobile I ever saw was in a circus, and I never rode in one until after I graduated from college. It has been said —perhaps with oversimplification—that Copernicus, Darwin, Freud and Einstein were responsible for changing the shape of the world of our time almost out of recognition. Darwin died the year before I was born, and in my boyhood the tides of his doctrine were lapping around the foundations of theology. Although Freud died only twenty years ago, his first important book was not translated into English until 1909, and I never heard his name mentioned until long after. Einstein I knew personally through my work with The Rockefeller Foundation.

The point is that change has been building up over the last seventy-five years until it has now reached a dizzying climax;

and the world is in the middle of a vast technological and social revolution.

The social aspects of the revolution have always interested me far more than the technological. It wasn't the fact of change that concerned me so much as it was what men were doing with their ideas and institutions to keep up with the change. It has seemed to me that the real problem which we face lies in the outmoded patterns of our social thinking, in the growing accumulation of our mental obsolescence. This, I suspect, was the philosophy behind much of my work—particularly my advocacy of the League of Nations. The League was the logical outcome of the mechanical development of preceding years, the inevitable next step in the political evolution of our time. If the catastrophe of 1914 had not brought it into existence, sooner or later it would have come by other means. "The time has passed when any one nation can live unto itself. It cannot even die unto itself, for the whole world would then be chained to a body of death from which mortal infection would flow to the rest. For better or worse the human race has been thrust into a new unity. . . . Nations today are roped like Alpine climbers crossing a glacier: they survive or perish together."

I wrote that in 1921, and I quote it to illustrate my preoccupation with the idea that the danger to our modern civilization lies in the fact that men may not be able to alter their ideas and habits fast enough to keep up with their own machines. "If only science and invention would stand still for a while," I wrote Abraham Flexner just after the first World War, "and not crowd us so, we might achieve our salvation through the slow processes of education. But science isn't standing still. . . . It's the time element that constitutes the danger."

It was this kind of thinking which made me an earnest disciple of what in my day was called "liberalism," and I use that ill-defined word now because I know of no satisfactory substitute. What I meant by it, and what it still means to me, is that generally speaking our social operations need motive power rather than brakes, imaginative action rather than an excess of caution. There is plenty of conservatism in the world to adjust the balance if it is required. When it comes to his own pattern of life, man is instinctively conservative. As Maeterlinck observed, at every crossway on the road that leads to the future each progressive spirit is opposed by a thousand men appointed to guard the past. The least that the most timid of us can do is not to add to the immense dead weight which nature drags along.

An impressive case, bolstered by the lessons of history, can be made for the thesis that conservatism is generally wrong. Certainly the record of conservatism in America over the years of my lifetime is a sorry chronicle of mistaken judgment. It is a record of determined obstruction and long continued rearguard action against ideas which were later accepted as part of our natural inheritance. When Mr. Bryan advocated a parcel post system in his platform of 1896 he was denounced for promoting "socialism." In the same way the Interstate Commerce Commission, the Federal Reserve Act, the Social Security Act, the S.E.C., the postal savings system, the Pure Food and Drug Act, and a dozen other mechanisms and ideas which have become a normal and natural part of our American life, were anathematized by the conservatives of their day as "socialistic," "anti-Christian" and "un-American." "Communistic" is the latest adjective of objurgation.

This emphasis in my thinking, I suspect, went back in part to Miss Wald and my days at the Henry Street Settlement where I had seen incredible poverty and degradation matched with public lethargy and insensibility. Perhaps it went back even further—to my boyhood days and the family life in Western New York. From the standpoint of comforts and possessions ours was a humble and often scanty existence, and over the years my sympathies have instinctively been with the have-nots, because, while we did not use that word, and would not have understood all its connotations, that was the life into which I was born.

Consequently, I have always been in rebellion against social practices which lessened the dignity of men, or denied the preeminence of the individual over all the economic and social mechanisms which oppress him. It seems incredible today, but as late as the early twenties the United States Steel Corporation maintained a twelve-hour day and a seven-day week, as did other companies across the country. The great steel strike of 1919 was aimed at this practice, and it was fought to the finish by the officers of the company who were supported not only by many of the newspapers but by the novel use of the injunction as a weapon of industrial warfare. "Whether we agree with it or not," I wrote Mr. Rockefeller from London during this unhappy period—I was still with the League of Nations—"labor in the future is going to have a great deal to say not only about working conditions and wages, but about management and the division of profits, and I am confident that your influence can help to shape the introduction of this new age so that it can be brought about normally and peacefully. The changes that are coming are going to call for radical readjustments in the attitude of many of our friends such as Judge Gary and others. The old era that existed before the war is dead . . . and can no more be revived than the feudal system of the Middle Ages."

By an odd turn of events I was soon projected into this very field of labor contacts, because much of my work with Mr. Rockefeller had to do with industrial relations in the companies in which he was interested, and I found him warmly sympathetic to new ideas and practices. "It is absurd to think that human society or human institutions can be protected against alteration," I wrote him some years later in commenting on a letter he had received from an acquaintance who was proposing a plan for maintaining the *status quo*. "Life means growth and growth means change. Social facts must constantly be reinterpreted and given their current value. . . . Of course if things didn't change, this would be an easier world to live in. It's hard to maintain loose-leaf minds from which obsolete ideas have to be taken out and thrown away as better ideas are discovered."

This, as I see it now, was the major emphasis of my thinking during the years, and in what I said and wrote I tried to keep the point clear. Recently, as I looked over some of my earlier addresses and articles, I had a feeling that the phraseology I had used was perhaps a little more vigorous and unqualified than that which I would use today; but I am not inclined to apologize. Youth and middle age speak out boldly with an assurance and a certainty which in older years is too often muted by languor or timidity or the growing uncertainties of life. I said to the Senior Class of Smith College late in the twenties (it was before the depression):

It is customary, I understand, for Commencement speakers to express some apprehension as to whether the graduating class is prepared for the responsibilities it must assume, whether its members will bring to their new tasks a sense of deportment and a standard of right and wrong which modern society approves. I have no such apprehensions to express.

My fear is that returning to the Middletowns of the United States your lives will be very respectable and very dull. My apprehension is that coming from an institution like this where criticism and analysis range over wide fields of conduct and ideas, you will allow yourselves to be adapted far too easily and too quickly to the narrow intellectual horizons, the petty standards, and the small prejudices of the communities in which you live. My concern is that you will catch the contagion of fear, that you will too gladly pay the price of living comfortably with neighbors. My apprehension is that you will walk in the middle of the road and sit in the middle of the boat, and too soon forget the duty that is laid on all those who would call themselves educated— the duty of rebellion. I am not afraid of your non-conformity; I am afraid of your conformity. I do not worry about your dissent; I worry about your acquiescence. It is not your unrest and discontent that bother me as I think of your future; it is your complacency.

If today I were to write about this general thesis of change and adaptation I think I would give greater stress to Whitehead's point that "mere change without conservation is a passage from nothing to nothing, while conservation without change cannot conserve." In other words, the secret of life consists in combining continuity with innovation, identity with progress. Nevertheless I would want to emphasize the point that history has in our time crowded us into a corner, and sharply limited our room for maneuver. Challenged by worldwide changes which he cannot stop or retard, man can survive on this dwindling planet only as he changes himself—his ideas, his tolerances, his sympathies, his relations with his fellow men.

At this point I am conscious that a lifetime of seventy-five years takes its toll. I realize that there is a tragedy about age which I had not suspected; and it lies in the fact that after a while a man tends to stop growing, change becomes painful to contemplate, and he hugs to himself his present stock of ideas in anxious fear that somebody is going to take them away from him. It is a hardening of the intellectual arteries, and two thousand years ago Horace described the symptoms in vivid hexameters.

In contrast I think of Lord Haldane's mother who at the age

of ninety took up the study of Hebrew because she wanted what she called "a fresh interest," and at ninety-two advised her distinguished seventy-year-old son to identify himself with the Labor Party because, she said, it promised so much more for the good of England than the Liberal Party under its outworn leadership.

A capacity to keep on growing, a sympathy for that which in man is forever trying to surpass itself and which lies at the source of his eternal unrest—I should hope that this would be my portion, and that I would not come to the end of the journey hugging an armful of faded ideas which once were fresh, but from which the fragrance had long since escaped.

*

When I retired from The Rockefeller Foundation in 1948 I found myself in much the same position as I had been thirty-six years earlier when I resigned as Commissioner of Accounts; that is, I was confronted with a number of opportunities for further service. One in particular which came from my old friend, Arthur Hays Sulzberger, and which would have involved a connection with *The New York Times,* I found peculiarly tempting. But at that moment the doctors stepped into the picture and decreed a quieter kind of existence, banishing me from the busy and often exhausting activities which had absorbed my life.

Earlier I had married again—Elizabeth Miner—a Smith College graduate who had studied and traveled widely, and who as comrade and collaborator was to buttress the most satisfactory period of my life. She and I are now retired—if that is the word for a still active regime—to our beloved "farm" in Connecticut, where surrounded by books and the peace of woods and fields, I have spent most of my time in writing, although I still attend board meetings of various organizations and try to keep up with the civic responsibilities which are the lot and privilege of citizens.

But even the peace of woods and fields does not in this generation protect a man from the torments of the day's news or the shock of marching events. Human history has always been a race with catastrophe, but never was the race so close or the threatening catastrophe so universal or so overwhelming. We have been undone by a technology which came too soon and which found us utterly unprepared in point of religion, ethics, law, philosophy or politics to meet the exigencies which it created. What moral or intellectual reservoirs can we now tap that will enable us to check the accelerating drift toward an end in which the hopes and monuments of men will be buried beyond recovery?

If only we had time to work this thing out, if only we could declare a moratorium on technology until we found the answers, the future would seem far less perilous. But today time is the one commodity in scarce supply. I remember vividly an incident which occurred during my student years at Princeton. A small group of us met one evening at "Prospect," Woodrow Wilson's home on the campus, to listen to Stockton Axson, his brother-in-law, as he read to us some of the poems of Browning. Wilson lay on a rug in front of the fireplace, while the rest of us sat about the room or slouched on the floor, carried away by Axson's dramatic reading and the resonant quality of his magnificent voice. Among the poems he read us that night was "A Grammarian's Funeral"—a favorite in Browning circles in those days, although I had never heard it before. It contains these lines:

> What's time? Leave *Now* for dogs and apes!
> Man has *Forever*.

That was good Victorian doctrine—the idea of the long ages

ahead in which man could reach toward perfectibility. But today it has an ironical ring. Perhaps the dogs and apes *will* have it, but to man time has suddenly been denied. Or rather, his only time is *Now;* and unless he can make "the longest stride of soul" he ever took, the civilization which he has so laboriously built up over the centuries, with its glimpses of intellectual and spiritual values as yet only partially revealed, will vanish with a clicking abruptness.

This is the grim atmosphere in which my generation is coming to the end of its allotted term. The world *could* be made a glorious place to live in—a world of order, justice and freedom in which no individual is lost and none is forgotten. That is what I have been working toward, I suspect, most of my life. Whatever the probabilities, the possibility of such a world still exists; and to that hope, dim at the moment as it may seem, I still pin my faith. "There is something of the indomitable deep within the hearts of all of us," I wrote, some years back, "some ineradicable faith, some intimation of immortality, some unsuspected reservoir of resilience and strength, on which, as our fathers did before us, we draw in critical hours."

Index